CULTURES AT THE
SUSQUEHANNA CONFLUENCE

 PIETIST, MORAVIAN, AND ANABAPTIST STUDIES

EDITOR

Craig D. Atwood
Director of the Center for Moravian Studies, Moravian Seminary

Volumes in the Pietist, Moravian, and Anabaptist Studies Series take multidisciplinary approaches to the history and theology of these groups and their religious and cultural influence around the globe. The series seeks to enrich the dynamic international study of post-Reformation Protestantism through original works of scholarship.

ADVISORY BOARD

Katherine Faull, *Bucknell University*
Bill Leonard, *Wake Forest University*
A. G. Roeber, *Penn State University*
Jonathan Strom, *Emory University*
Rachel Wheeler, *Indiana University–Purdue University Indianapolis*

EDITED AND TRANSLATED BY
KATHERINE M. FAULL
WITH AN ESSAY BY DAVID MINDERHOUT

CULTURES AT THE SUSQUEHANNA CONFLUENCE

The Diaries of the Moravian Mission to the
Iroquois Confederacy, 1745–1755

The Pennsylvania State University Press
University Park, Pennsylvania

Library of Congress Cataloging-in-Publication Data

Names: Faull, Katherine M., editor, translator.
Title: Cultures at the Susquehanna confluence : the diaries of the Moravian
   mission to the Iroquois Confederacy, 1745–1755 / edited and translated by
   Katherine M. Faull ; with an essay by David Minderhout.
Other titles: Diaries of the Moravian mission to the Iroquois Confederacy,
   1745–1755 | Pietist, Moravian, and Anabaptist studies.
Description: University Park, Pennsylvania : The Pennsylvania State
   University Press, [2024] | Series: Pietist, Moravian, and Anabaptist
   studies | Includes bibliographical references and index.
Summary: "An annotated translation of the diaries documenting the Moravian
   mission to the Indigenous peoples of Pennsylvania at Shamokin in the
   1740s and 1750s"—Provided by publisher.
Identifiers: LCCN 2023052087 | ISBN 9780271096964 (hardback)
Subjects: LCSH: Moravian Church—Missions—Pennsylvania—
   Shamokin—History—18th century—Sources. | Moravian Church—
   Pennsylvania—History—18th century—Sources. | Six Nations—
   History—18th century—Sources. | Moravians—Pennsylvania—Diaries. |
   Indians of North America—Missions—Pennsylvania—Shamokin—
   History—18th century—Sources. | Pennsylvania—Church history—
   18th century—Sources. | Shamokin (Pa.)—History—18th century—
   Sources. | LCGFT: Diaries. | Primary sources.
Classification: LCC E78.P4 C85 2024 | DDC 284/.674809033—dc23/
   eng/20231122
LC record available at https://lccn.loc.gov/2023052087

Copyright © 2024 Katherine M. Faull
All rights reserved
Printed in the United States of America
Published by The Pennsylvania State University Press,
University Park, PA 16802–1003

The Pennsylvania State University Press is a member of the Association
of University Presses.

It is the policy of The Pennsylvania State University Press to use acid-free
paper. Publications on uncoated stock satisfy the minimum requirements
of American National Standard for Information Sciences—Permanence
of Paper for Printed Library Material, ANSI Z39.48-1992.

CONTENTS

List of Illustrations vii
Maps ix
Acknowledgments xi
Preface xv
Native Americans in Shamokin, Circa 1748 xix
DAVID MINDERHOUT

Note on Translation and Editorial Principles xxvii

Introduction 1

1 September 13–November 10, 1745 17
   MARTIN MACK

2 May 26–June 28, 1747 35
   JOHANNES HAGEN

3 June 29–August 2, 1747 42
   JOHANNES HAGEN

4 September 29–December 31, 1747 48
   MARTIN MACK

5 January 4–April 18, 1748 66
   JOSEPH POWELL

6 April 18–June 28, 1748 78
   MARTIN MACK

7 November 30, 1748–January 31, 1749 90
   DAVID ZEISBERGER

8 April 3–July 26, 1749 100
   DAVID ZEISBERGER

9 January 8–March 5, 1750 114
   CHRISTIAN RAUCH

10 April 14–June 2, 1753 120
   BERNHARD GRUBE

11	June 4–July 31, 1753 125
	BERNHARD GRUBE
12	January 11–July 2, 1754 132
	DAVID KLIEST
13	December 19–25, 1754................................ 143
	HEINRICH FREY AND GOTTLIEB ROESCH
14	April 1–May 31, 1755 146
	GOTTFRIED RÖSLER
15	June 1–July 31, 1755................................157
	GOTTFRIED RÖSLER
16	August 1–September 30, 1755 166
	GOTTFRIED RÖSLER
17	September–October 1755...............................172
	GOTTFRIED RÖSLER

Appendix A: List of Missionaries and Blacksmiths
  at Shamokin 179
Appendix B: Extracts of Letters from Frederick Cammerhof 181
Glossary of Terms...................................... 187
Notes 193
Bibliography 205
Register of Individuals 213
Register of Place Names 219
Index 223

ILLUSTRATIONS

1. Travel map of southeast Pennsylvania and northern Maryland........ xviii
2. Original agreement for blacksmith's shop with seal..................... 2
3. Painting of Shikellamy and Zinzendorf at Tulpehocken 9
4. Portrait of Martin Mack... 11
5. Portrait of David Zeisberger 91
6. Indian medal used by Moravian missionaries 118
7. Letter from August Spangenberg to Shikellamy in Onondaga 182

MAPS

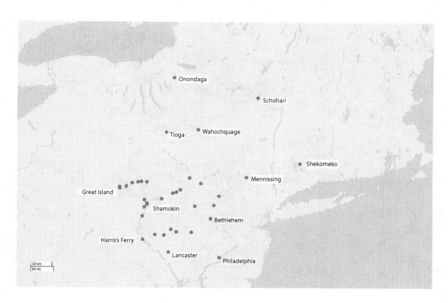

Map 1. Places mentioned in the diaries.

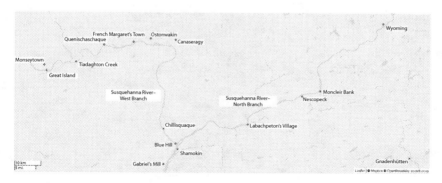

Map 2. Detail of the area around Shamokin.

Map 3. Confluence of the West and North Branches of the Susquehanna River at Shamokin.

ACKNOWLEDGMENTS

This project has been a long time in the making. Although I had worked with Moravian archival materials throughout my professional life, until 2007 I had always focused on questions of memoir, identity, gender, race, and the body. However, a welcome and intense collaboration with my colleagues—Father Paul (Alf) Siewers in the English Department, Ben Marsh in the Geography Department, and Brandn Green at the newly founded Center for Sustainability and the Environment—at Bucknell University on the environmental history of the Susquehanna River introduced me to a group of researchers, both at the university and in the wider community, who radically changed the way I thought about the cultural landscapes that have surrounded me for more than thirty years. Thus, when approached by Jennie Stevens, an undergraduate student, about the Moravian mission at nearby Sunbury, Pennsylvania, I was intrigued. What has then followed has been an incredible physical, intellectual, and metaphysical journey into areas of Native American studies and history, cultural geography, community-engaged collaborative teaching, research and scholarship, public-facing digital humanities research, and environmental and heritage advocacy.

On this journey I could not have moved forward without the encouragement and support of Father Paul, who always believed in the importance of this record and the deciphering of the sometimes almost-illegible handwriting of Moravians at the confluence of the North and West Branches of the Susquehanna River. Additionally, for his commitment to regional well-being fostered through academic engagement, I am indebted to Skip Wieder, one of the smartest and also most humble advocates of improving life in the central Susquehanna region. My understanding of place benefited deeply from the collaborative work on the *Indigenous Cultural Landscapes Study* with Ben Marsh, Brandn Green, David Minderhout, and Kristal Jones and the opportunity to work with the team from the Chesapeake Conservancy on the John Smith Connector Trail study for the National Park Service. I am forever grateful for the intellectual, moral, and financial support of President John Bravman, at Bucknell University, for the production of the WVIA documentary, *Peoples of the Susquehanna River*, which brought together so many of the voices, histories, and stories of the Native American peoples who are descendants of those who have lived in these landscapes for thousands of years before European colonialism and who have endured disease, destruction, displacement, and cultural and linguistic colonial dispossession.

One of the most important people who helped me to understand this difficult history is Sid Jamieson, member of the Haudenosaunee, Cayuga Nation, whose willingness to open up a door to the world of today's Indigenous peoples has transformed both this project and also radically changed the way in which non-Native people understand the place we both call home, Susquehanna Country. I am deeply grateful to him for his trust in me and in this work.

This project has spawned many scholarly and classroom digital projects. I thank my colleague, Diane Jakacki, who worked with me on my initial forays into text encoding, mapping, teaching, and doing digital humanities and who on occasion braved the waters of the Susquehanna with me. I also thank Janine Glathar, GIS expert, who taught me how to think spatially and how to make maps (two of which are in this volume). I thank the many Bucknell students who worked on the Stories of the Susquehanna project over the years: Emily Bitely, Steffany Meredyk, Hein Thun, Henry Stann, Alexa Gorski, Bryan Marine, Jerry Huang, and, most recently, Hannah Holmes. Many of these students have joined me on the river, usually in a kayak but also on a pontoon, on golden summer evenings, telling stories of the Susquehanna; and on multiday river sojourns with the inimitable David Buck, environmental activist, founder of the 444 Club, and erstwhile riverkeeper of the North Branch. These intrepid students were willing to brave the whitecaps of the West Branch as strong southerly winds seemed to blow the river upstream.

This project has also allowed me to witness remarkable moments of cultural restitution, tentative steps toward moving beyond land acknowledgments; when first words were spoken by Sid Hill, the Tadodaho of the Haudenosaunee, at the Susquehanna river confluence, the fish leapt out of the water, in greeting and welcome; and when the canoes of the Tuscarora youth group were retracing their own peoples' forced migration from the Carolinas to western New York, they stopped in the middle of the North Branch below the steep wooded bluffs of Indian Hill at Quicks Bend and addressed their ancestors who once lived there.

The Moravian mission diaries are fascinating but difficult documents. They are sometimes replete with details about life in Susquehanna Country in the mid-eighteenth century, describing the peoples, flora, conflicts, conferences, and climate of the confluence. We meet David Zeisberger as he grows into his life as a missionary, learns the languages and customs of the Six Nations, and negotiates the permissions to live among the Haudenosaunee in 1750. But the diaries are also frustrating, as the perspective of some of the diarists (notably Rösler) limits the lenses through which we can read this time and its events and landscape. As David Minderhout reminds us in the preface, the perspective through which we are seeing this span of ten years belongs very clearly to the Moravians and their intention to convert the Indigenous peoples of Pennsylvania and New York. To David I owe an enormous debt of gratitude for his wisdom, insights, and patience. I deeply regret that he was not able to see the book in print due to his untimely death in 2018. But his words begin this work.

I am also deeply grateful to the remarkable team at the Moravian Archives in Bethlehem, Pennsylvania, notably Dr. Paul Peucker, the head archivist; and Tom McCollough, the assistant archivist. The initial research, transcription, and translation for this volume was supported through a grant from the National Endowment for the Humanities, Collaborative Research Division (2009–11). I thank my NEH collaborators, James Merrell, Amy Schutt, Rachel Wheeler, and David Minderhout, for their initial help on this complex project. All responsibility for this final product is of course my own.

PREFACE

Beginning in the 1980s, historians such as James Merrell opened a new era of research on Native American history that challenged the binary simplicity of an oppositional way of thinking, which had for so long dominated colonial American historiography.[1] Rather than examining the identity of persons and places through a lens of only "either/or," the careful and thorough archival work of historians such as James Merrell and Jane Merritt and of textual editors such as Hermann Wellenreuther and Carola Wessel has revealed the complexities of the confluence of cultures, especially at the forks of the Susquehanna River. Those scholars, including Jane Merritt, Amy Schutt, Jon Sensbach, and Rowena McClinton, who are able to read the archaic and occasionally corrupt manuscript sources, have produced new and exciting work on the nature of Native and European interactions that challenge the traditional assumptions of earlier scholarship.

The present volume contributes to this reexamination of cultural conflict and communication among Native American peoples and diverse groups of European settlers. The Shamokin diary kept by Moravian missionaries in the 1740s and 1750s provides a wealth of information about the cultural interactions, historical events, and spiritual condition of the settlement. For example, the entry of January 1748 reports a strong earthquake during the night of January 23. Brother Joseph Powell writes, "A little past midnight was a Earth Quake, which so shook our House and Beds that sum [sic] of us awaked."[2]

The Shamokin diary, consisting of approximately 350 pages, represents a new source document for scholars and the general public. In addition to the account of the daily affairs of the community, there are approximately fifty pages of letters, documents, messages, and addresses to prominent persons such as Chief Shikellamy, Conrad Weiser, Bishop Spangenberg, and the Philadelphia Quaker Charles Brockden, in German, English, and Onondaga. All of these are of interest to scholars on the process of negotiation and agreement around the settlement of Shamokin in the crucial period prior to the outbreak of the French and Indian War in 1755. A short and vivid account by Brother Gottfried Rösler of the final days of the settlement in the summer of 1755 details the attack by the French Indians on Penn's Creek and also the flight back to Bethlehem of Brother Rösler, Brother Philip Wesa, and the blacksmith Marcus Kiefer. Of particular note is the moment when they decided to bury the blacksmith's tools in the garden of the smithy just before their departure, with the intent of returning to retrieve them and build the new smithy between Lehighton and Wyoming after the war had quieted down. However, this plan was never carried out, and excavations at the Northumberland Historical Society recently discovered those same tools in the dig, which are now displayed in the museum in Hunter House.

Therefore, as we read these diaries, written by tallow lamp in the darkness of the confluence, how might we understand and promote "a sense of the Susquehanna"? How can we teach ourselves and our students and our children the importance of "deep mapping" for both a record of ourselves and our places? The Shamokin diary provides much of the "history" of the geohistory of this area, with its record of floods, famines, cold, and disease. In it we find the flora and fauna, the plantings and harvests, the lack of seed, and the bounty of a good hunt. The landscape of the confluence provides patterns of experience, whether over water, traversing the river back and forth from one shore to the other, or into the woods, crossing the boundary from the safe world of the clearing into the unknown world of the forest. This liminal moment is marked by European and Indian alike in the Iroquois ritual ceremony "At the Edge of the Woods," in which the eyes and ears and mouth of the traveler are cleared of spider's webs, and the feet are cleared of thorns. We still have verbal vestiges of this ceremony, as we warn, perhaps in these times especially, that we are not out of the woods yet.[3] Through such sources we can ask ourselves to what extent we also witness what Cynthia Radding calls the "landscape of the divine." Perhaps it is in the uncanny profile of Chief Shikellamy in the bluff of the Blue Hill or in the petroglyphs of the Lower Susquehanna at Safe Harbor. Through such documents as the Shamokin diary we can identify what Radding terms the "plateaux of cultural theologies," overlays of differing world views that constitute our environment, the environment of the confluence of the Susquehanna River.[4]

The manuscripts that compose the diary are held in the Moravian Archives in Bethlehem, Pennsylvania, and are also included in the Fliegel Index of the Indian materials of the Moravian Church, an index compiled by the assistant archivist of the Moravian Church in the 1950s.[5] This index is invaluable in its assistance to the researcher; for many who cannot read the original text, it has become the primary source of information on which scholarship is based. Consequently, however, the categories Carl John Fliegel devised for indexing the enormous amount of manuscript materials have in some cases determined and constrained how Indian missions are described. For example, Fliegel does not index "women" other than in instances of domestic abuse. Where he indexes "visits," he does not explain that these are pastoral visits conducted frequently by European women with Native women and thus constitute a crucial locus of cultural exchange. It was during these visits that the Moravian Brothers and Sisters conducted "spiritual interviews," according to the guidelines established by Count Nicholas Zinzendorf.[6] Yet Fliegel's categories have remained the categories of inquiry more than sixty years later; through his omissions and elisions, the scholarly record displays a corresponding dearth of published research around questions to do with gender relations and female participation in these practices. In addition, Fliegel's creation of separate indices of "Indian Persons" and "White Persons" serves only to reify the separation of peoples in the mission, and thus in this volume such a separation has not been repeated. This English translation of the Shamokin diary allows us to move beyond the confines of Fliegel's categories and examine in detail the descriptions of Native American culture and cultural interchange prior to the removal of Native peoples.

Not long before his death from ALS in 2018, David Minderhout, esteemed professor of anthropology at Bloomsburg University, prepared an essay describing the culture and economy of the Native peoples closely associated with Shamokin and the Moravians. It is included in this volume to help orient the reader to the larger context of the diary, especially the vital role played in contact relations between the colonists and Haudenosaunee by the sachem (spokesperson), Swatane (Bringer of Light), also known as Shikellamy. Out of respect for Dr. Minderhout, who drew on his many years of research and reflection, the essay appears without revision. Readers are encouraged to explore more recent scholarship on Native American culture in colonial Pennsylvania as well as recent research on Moravian missions to Indigenous peoples by scholars such as Amy Schutt, Rachel Wheeler, Sarah Eyerly, and Rowena McClinton.

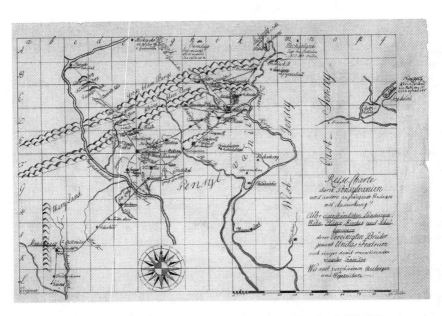

Fig. 1 Travel map of southeast Pennsylvania and northern Maryland. DP Collection of Drawings and Prints f.037.9. Courtesy of the Moravian Archives, Bethlehem, Pennsylvania.

NATIVE AMERICANS IN SHAMOKIN, CIRCA 1748

DAVID MINDERHOUT

As the Moravians settled in Shamokin in the 1740s, to carry out their mission to proselytize among the Native Americans living there, they found a bewildering variety of Native nations represented and languages spoken. Sitting at the spot where the North and West Branches of the Susquehanna River meet and then flow as a single waterway to the Chesapeake Bay, Shamokin was home to some of these Native peoples, most of whom were refugees from points east and south, and a gathering place for others using the river to travel north to Iroquois Country or south to Harrisburg, Lancaster, and the Chesapeake Bay.

Lenape/Delaware, Tutelo, Saponi, Nanticoke, Mohican, Tuscarora, Shawnee, Catawba, and all the original five members of the League of the Iroquois—Mohawk, Oneida, Onondaga, Cayuga, and Seneca—are mentioned in the diaries. Presiding over this complex mix of peoples was a man named Shikellamy, an Oneida chief who had often served as a middleman between Europeans and Natives and who had been placed in Shamokin by the league to oversee Native affairs in Pennsylvania and to protect the southern border of Iroquois territory. This complex and ever-changing array of Native peoples was not "traditional" but, as a recent text puts it, a result of "a century of upheaval and transformation that enveloped all who lived through it."[7]

Native America in 1550

As best that can be known—from Native oral histories and the earliest of European explorers' accounts—the geographic distribution of Native peoples in what would become Pennsylvania and surrounding colonies and states in the sixteenth century was far different from what the Moravians experienced in the 1740s.[8] The Lenape—subsequently called Delaware by English colonists—were to be found in a broad swath from the Hudson River Valley south along the Atlantic Coast to northern Delaware (where the Nanticoke were to be found) and west throughout southeastern Pennsylvania to the Lehigh River. The Five Nations Iroquois occupied the center of New York State. Also called the Haudenosaunee, or "People of the Longhouse," the Iroquois saw themselves as a metaphorical longhouse, with the Mohawk as the "Door to the East" and the Seneca as the "Door to the West," and then from east to west within the longhouse, the Oneida, Onondaga, and Cayuga. At the southern border of the Iroquois were another Iroquoian-language family people, the Susquehannock, after whom the river would be named; they were situated on the North Branch of the river near where present-day Athens, Pennsylvania, is located. In the northwest were the Erie or Eriechronon people, another Iroquoian family group, and in southwestern Pennsylvania there was a Native culture known today as the Monongahela, though they are known only through archaeological remains.

While the distribution of these groups was stable compared to the circumstances of the 1740s, they probably were never entirely sedentary and fixed in space. Archaeologists know that Native Americans have inhabited the Susquehanna River Valley for at least eleven thousand years, and that through most of that time they were seminomadic foragers, moving camps from place to place along the river to take advantage of seasonal resources such as anadromous fish, like shad, that migrated up the river each year to spawn, and the wild animals and plants they hunted and collected. Agriculture, in the form of Native horticulture utilizing what the Iroquois would call the "three sisters"—maize, beans, and squash—had been introduced into the river basin by 900 CE, but this new form of subsistence required the shifting of fields and villages every eight to fifteen years as old fields became played out and new ones had to be opened. Even the Iroquois League, which would play such an important part in colonial interactions, was a relatively recent innovation. Prior to the formation of the league, the various Iroquoian nations fought among themselves and with their neighbors, with the league coming into existence (estimates vary as to when) to provide unity and a common governmental structure among themselves and against their foes.[9]

Even after the formation of the league, the Iroquois traveled widely, their leaders coming together periodically at Onondaga to settle intergroup business, and their hunters traveling into northern Pennsylvania in pursuit of game. And by 1550 the Susquehannock were beginning to travel south along the river—perhaps because of conflict with the other Iroquoian peoples—where they would eventually meet Capt. John Smith at the point where the river meets the Chesapeake Bay in 1608.

However, compared to what the Moravians were experiencing in the mid-eighteenth century, the era just prior to contact with Europeans was one of relative stability. Things would quickly change after 1600. There was the already-mentioned contact between the Susquehannock and John Smith from the English Jamestown Colony in 1608. A Frenchman named Etienne Brule was living among the Susquehannock on the North Branch in 1615, as an emissary of the explorer Samuel de Champlain. A Dutch whaleboat had sailed up the Delaware River in 1633 and made contact with the Lenape; Dutch and Swedish settlements were established for trade in Delaware with the Natives soon thereafter.[10] This unleashed a sequence of events that led to tumultuous times for Native Americans.

At least four major developments in the seventeenth and early eighteenth centuries led to the complex mix of peoples at Shamokin in the 1740s. The first was the fur trade. When the Dutch met with the Lenape in 1633, the Lenape gifted the Dutch with bundles of beaver pelts, which were then transported back to Europe. This ignited a fashion craze in Europe for beaver-skin hats and other items of apparel—Europeans having devastated their own native fur-bearing animals over the centuries—and soon European ships were risking the crossing to North America to trade for more pelts. What they had to offer Native Americans was European metal and glass technology. Prior to European contact, Native American technologies were limited to stone, bone, wood, animal skins, and clay pottery—all perfectly suited to precontact cultures—which were quickly replaced by European metal implements such as cooking pots, axe heads, fish hooks, and so on, along with guns and powder. It is estimated that within a generation of contact with Europeans, Native technologies were largely replaced with European goods, and Native graves become filled with glass and metal implements and decorative items.

With iron-headed axes, more forest could be cut down for Native fields and more game, especially fur-bearing game, could be killed. To get the pelts the Europeans sought, Natives killed all the beavers they could reach: the eastern subspecies of beaver was driven into extinction, and the Erie were annihilated by the Iroquois so that the Iroquois could get access to peltry in Erie territory. The Susquehannock would travel down the river to Maryland to engage in trade for European goods; they also went overland to Manhattan Island and Delaware to trade pelts to the Dutch for guns and iron tools. In general, the fur trade set Native peoples in motion, as well as creating a dependence on European technologies. One of the continuing commentaries in the diaries is the demand for the services of the Moravians' blacksmith, once a forge had been set up, as Natives showed up to have metal pots, tools, and flintlocks repaired. Another European introduction, which resonates all through the diaries, was alcohol, another European item in high demand. Prior to contact North America above the Rio Grande was the only region of the world that had not brewed or distilled alcoholic beverages. The demand for them soon dominated trade.

The second development was the introduction of European diseases, especially smallpox, which devastated Native cultures.[11] There is still debate as to why smallpox was so contagious and deadly to Native Americans, but it is generally accepted that 90 percent of the Native population of Pennsylvania was killed off by the disease.[12] The first reported outbreak of smallpox among the Lenape occurred in 1654; among the Susquehannock it was 1661. One theory for the disappearance of the Monongahela culture in western Pennsylvania is a smallpox epidemic. Among Native peoples, generally the first people to succumb to the disease were young people, leaving communities of children and old people; reports tell of bodies being left to decay because there was no one to bury the dead. Initially smallpox spread unintentionally, but by 1763 Europeans were deliberately trading blankets from smallpox victims to Natives to undermine their resistance. One can only speculate as to what would have happened in European-Native interactions in the seventeenth and eighteenth centuries if it was not for this epidemic disease; certainly the reduction in their numbers undermined their ability to offer much resistance to colonial pressures.

The third development has to do with the policies of William Penn, the Quaker diplomat and gentleman into whose hands the colony of Pennsylvania fell in 1681. As noted, the Dutch were the first to settle in the Delaware River Valley after their initial contact with the Lenape in 1633, and the area remained in Dutch hands until their defeat in a naval battle with the English in 1664. The Dutch colony became an English colony in 1665, and in 1681 Charles II of England gave the colony (Penn's Woods) to Penn in payment for a debt owed by the Crown. In that year Penn sent a letter to the Native population of his new possession, in which he pledged that "I desire to enjoy it with your Love and Consent that we may always live together as Neighbors and Friends."[13] This was Penn's Holy Experiment, in which he was striving to build a colony in which all its citizens were treated fairly and with respect. When he arrived in Pennsylvania in 1682, he arranged a now famous meeting with two Lenape sachems, Tamamend and Metamequam, in which he pledged his peaceful intentions and then purchased land from the two. He proclaimed that Europeans could not seize Native property but must purchase it fairly and that Natives had the right to challenge European wrongdoing in court. As Dawn Marsh points out, Penn's principles were not always fulfilled, especially after his death in 1718, but compared to other English colonies in North America, Pennsylvania stood out as a well-intentioned and relatively fair-minded place for Native Americans.[14]

As a result, Pennsylvania became a sanctuary for Native Americans who were being displaced elsewhere. Thus, Nanticoke from Delaware, Conoy from

Maryland, and Tutelo, Saponi, and Tuscarora from the Carolinas all migrated into Pennsylvania in the late seventeenth and early eighteenth centuries. Shawnee from the area that is now western Kentucky also joined the mix, as did Mohican from New York; both were fleeing encroachments from other Native peoples in their own homelands. There was a Shawnee town on the North Branch of the Susquehanna by 1702 and on an island at present-day Milton, Pennsylvania, by the 1740s. Since the Susquehanna River was the conduit through which traffic flowed in central Pennsylvania, it is not surprising that so many people ended up passing through or living in Shamokin.

The fourth and final development to be discussed here is the interlinking between the rise of the Five Nations Iroquois as a power to be dealt with by Europeans and the subsequent expulsion of the Lenape/Delaware from southeastern Pennsylvania. To the colonial government in Philadelphia, the Iroquois in New York Colony were natural partners in diplomacy in the early eighteenth century. By this point the Iroquois had extinguished the Erie and defeated the Huron and Susquehannock, thus giving them a monopoly over the fur trade. They also served as middlemen between the English colonial governments and the French who controlled the upper Midwest—Michigan and the Great Lakes in particular. If an English trader wanted to do business in the Midwest, they had to work through the Iroquois. It was also possible for the Iroquois to draw on a large force of warriors, if needed, which made them potent enemies but valuable allies.

It was also the case that colonial governments were more comfortable working with the Iroquois and their centralized government than with the decentralized tribal societies like the Lenape. To an anthropologist a tribe is a social system that shares a common culture but not a common government or leadership. Each local segment of a tribe is autonomous, and no one person in any tribal segment has sovereign power over the other members. Individuals, like Tamamend, were respected and widely admired, but they exercised no control over other Lenape. William Penn seemed to understand this, as he purchased the same piece of land over and over from different Lenape, but his agents and successors did not seem to. Instead, the government in Philadelphia would declare one Lenape sachem or another a king and look to them to act on behalf of all Lenape—which they were unable to do. The Iroquois system functioned very much like the federal system adopted in the US Constitution. Each local unit, Seneca or Mohawk and so on, made their own local decisions about local matters, but each also chose chiefs who convened in Onondaga (because that group was centrally located) to discuss and decide matters that affected them all. When the chiefs' meeting in Onondaga made a decision (which had to be unanimous), it was binding on all Iroquois, a system the colonial government could understand—and with which they could negotiate.

Thus, it was the Iroquois who were the decisive factor in the action that removed the Lenape from southeastern Pennsylvania: the Walking Purchase of 1737. After William Penn's death, his sons—John, Thomas, and Richard—assumed control of Pennsylvania, and they soon proved to be far less conciliatory toward the Lenape than their father had been. And as more and more settlers poured into the Philadelphia area, the pressure on opening up more land for their use grew more intense. In 1700 there were twenty thousand European colonists in Pennsylvania, but by the 1730s that number had grown to more than one hundred thousand. In 1735 James Logan, the agent of the Penns, informed some Lenape that a treaty that had been signed in 1686 by William Penn and some Lenape "chiefs" had been discovered in London. The treaty gave the Penns the right to all the land west of Philadelphia that fell within a day and a half's walk of the current borders. The Lenape protested; they had no knowledge of the treaty or the people who had signed it; in fact, the purported treaty has never been subsequently found in English archives. The Lenape appealed to the Iroquois for support in denying the treaty but found that the Iroquois had already accepted its terms in negotiations with Logan. Shikellamy had acted as an intermediary between Onondaga and Philadelphia in confirming this "Walking Purchase." Lacking the support of the Iroquois, the Lenape agreed to the terms of the treaty, perhaps assuming that a day and a half's walk would not yield much territory. However, the Penns hired the fastest runners they could find in Philadelphia and even sent workers out in advance of the runners to clear the path on which they would run.

Instead of a leisurely stroll, the Walking Purchase became a race. One of the runners managed to cover 55 miles in thirty-six hours, which, under the terms of the treaty, brought 1,200 square miles under the control of the colonial government—an area about the size of Rhode Island. Again the Lenape protested, and again the Iroquois chose to not support them. Instead, this led to an agreement between the Iroquois and the colonial government in which the Iroquois would see to the removal of the Lenape west of the Blue Mountains, beyond modern day Allentown. In turn the Iroquois agreed to give up all land claims along the Delaware River—which had never been part of their territory to begin with. In this way many Lenape ended up as refugees in Shamokin.

As a result of these four developments, Shamokin was for a short period a place that belonged to Native Americans in Pennsylvania in the early to mid-eighteenth century. That ended in 1755, with the onset of the French and Indian

War (1755–63), called the Seven Years' War in Europe. While this war was primarily between England and France, both sides drew Native Americans into the war as fighters. This was especially true of the French, whose settlers were significantly outnumbered by English colonists. The French made use of Shawnee warriors who engaged in a war of terrorism against English settlers in the Susquehanna River Valley, killing and kidnapping them. Iroquois warriors fought on both sides, and the English recruited Cherokee from Kentucky to join the battle, thus bringing this Native nation into the Pennsylvania ethnic mixture. The Moravian diaries record the fear that was engendered among European colonists as a result of this conflict.

This war, and the subsequent Pontiac's Rebellion in 1763, fundamentally changed the relationship between Europeans and Native Americans in Pennsylvania. No longer was there any pretense of a Holy Experiment in the treatment of Native people. Instead, the Pennsylvania colonial legislature passed a Scalp Act, which offered as much as $150 for the scalp of a male Native. And in December 1763 a group of vigilantes from Dauphin County, called the Paxton Boys, massacred a community of Susquehannock in Lancaster in retaliation for Native participation in the war (even though the Susquehannock in that area had not been involved in it). The war undermined the Iroquois' position of strength, especially in the sense that the English no longer needed them to act as middlemen with the French in the Midwest because the English could now go directly into the area themselves. Subsequent treaties forced many Natives into Ohio and farther west, but others stayed in the Susquehanna River Valley and went into hiding.

Shikellamy

A prominent figure in the diaries—and in Native-colonist relations in the early eighteenth century—was Chief Shikellamy (also known as the Swatane), who was placed in Shamokin by the Five Nations to oversee Iroquois interests in the Susquehanna River Valley and to act as a mediator between Natives and colonists.[15] Shikellamy was an Oneida chief, though it has been suggested many times that he had been kidnapped as a boy from a French settlement and raised among the Oneida, a not uncommon phenomenon in seventeenth- and eighteenth-century America.[16]

Shikellamy was a close friend of many important colonial figures of his time, including the Moravian missionary David Zeisberger, Conrad Weiser—the most important intermediary between the Philadelphia government and the Five Nations—and the Penns' agent in Pennsylvania, James Logan, after whom Shikellamy named his oldest son, John Logan (also known as Tachnechdorus). Shikellamy helped negotiate the Iroquois position on the Walking Purchase and the subsequent removal of the Lenape into the Susquehanna River Valley, and he served as guide and interpreter for colonial agents who needed to go to Onondaga.

As is seen in the diaries, Shikellamy was friendly to the Moravian missionaries, intervening for them on a number of occasions when other Natives were imposing on them. He became a Moravian not long before his death in 1748. Zeisberger was present at his death, and the missionaries aided in his burial. The various diarists' accounts do not present Shikellamy as the important historical figure that he was, but as a kindly older man who liked to talk with the missionaries and who sought their help on a number of occasions, such as a request to have them build a fence around his garden to keep livestock out of it. Shikellamy had made a journey to Bethlehem, Pennsylvania—the center of the Moravian sect in America—in November 1748, and it was then that he became a member of that faith. On the way back from Bethlehem, he fell ill, and that led to his death on December 6, 1748. The diarists' accounts are the only description of these events. At his death he was succeeded in his role as leader and mediator in the Shamokin community by his son John.

NOTE ON TRANSLATION AND EDITORIAL PRINCIPLES

Most of the manuscript sources are from the holdings of the Moravian Archives in Bethlehem, Pennsylvania. All translations, unless otherwise noted, are my own. Most quotations from German have been translated and the original, if necessary, included in a note. The term "Wilde(r)" is not translated, following the example of William Starna and Corinna Starna in *Gideon's People*. As they explain, the semantic fields of the terms can include notions of wildness, savagery, and non-Christian status and therefore, to maintain the polyvalency, the German original has been retained.[17]

The reader will note the use of both "Five Nations" and "Six Nations" to refer to the peoples of the Haudenosaunee Confederacy. The Five Nations, consisting of the Mohawk, Oneida, Onondaga, Cayuga, and Seneca, formed as a confederacy around 1570, although the Haudenosaunee themselves consider the founding date immaterial. In 1722 the Tuscarora were added to the confederacy. In this text the reader will see reference to Five Nations, Six Nations, Iroquois, and Haudenosaunee, depending on the speaker's or author's perspective in the original text.

Quotations and terms from Native American languages (Delaware and Onondaga) have not been translated, but they are explained in English in a note and, for recurring terms, in the glossary. Biblical quotations are from the King James Version (KJV), unless otherwise indicated. In a few cases the text was translated from the German Luther translation.

INTRODUCTION

The Moravian presence at Shamokin on the forks of the Susquehanna River at what is today called Sunbury, Pennsylvania, represents a unique compromise between the Moravian Church's missionary impetus and the needs of the Six Nations of the Iroquois, also known as the Haudenosaunee Confederacy. Already in 1742, as he sketched out his plans for the "Colleges of the Heathen," the leader of the Moravian Church, Count Nicholas Ludwig von Zinzendorf, recognized the strategic importance of Shamokin and decided to visit, along with Conrad Weiser, the seat of Shikellamy, the vice-regent of the Iroquois.[1]

In the years that immediately followed, initial attempts to establish a mission at Shamokin, undertaken by Christian and Rachel Post in 1743 and Martin and Anna Mack in 1745, were very difficult. The near failure of the Moravian mission was averted through an agreement between Shikellamy and the Six Nations—and approved by the colonial government in Philadelphia—that the Moravians would establish a blacksmith's shop in Shamokin to service the needs of the Six Nations of the Iroquois. On May 5, 1746, a request was sent to the governor of Pennsylvania, stating that a blacksmith at Shamokin was urgently needed.[2] Eager for a response, the Quaker and friend to the Moravians Charles Brockden met with Governor Thomas about the blacksmith's shop, but there could be no assurances that the shop would be built until the outcome of the Treaty of Albany between the Six Nations and the British was known. In November a chance meeting between Single Brother John Okely, a member of the Philadelphia Moravian Church who had arrived there on the *Catherine* in May 1742 as part of the First Sea Congregation, and the governor on the street in Philadelphia provided the opportunity to ask again. Finally, the governor responded, "The Five Nations of Indians have taken up the Hatchet against our Enemies. Therefore, you may write to Mr. Spangenberg that he may send People among the Indians when he will."[3] Now that it was clear that the Iroquois were

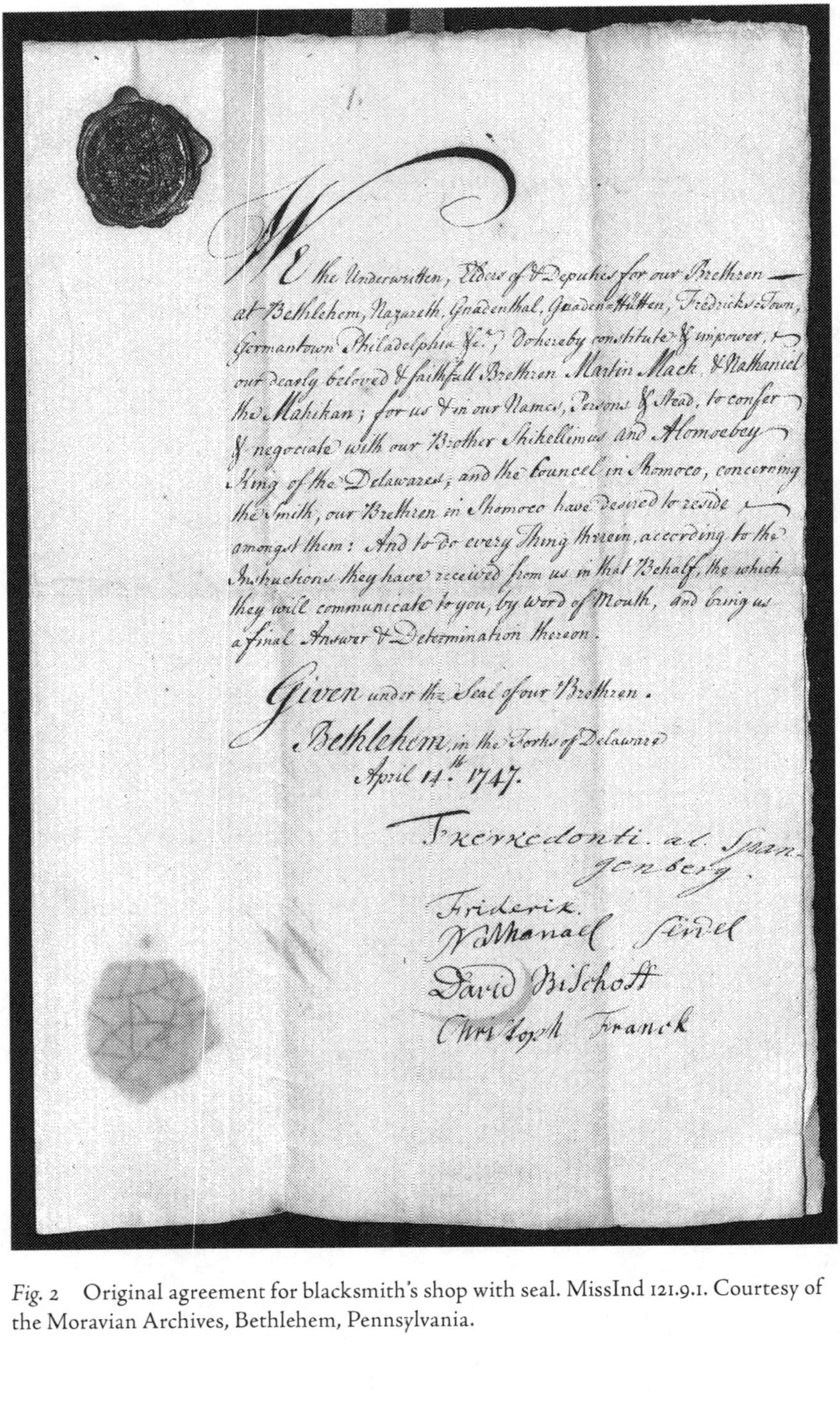

1.

We the Underwritten, Elders of & Deputies for our Brethren at Bethlehem, Nazareth, Gnadenthal, Gnaden-Hütten, Fredericks-Town, Germantown Philadelphia &c.; Do hereby constitute & impower, our dearly beloved & faithfull Brethren Martin Mack & Nathaniel the Mahikan; for us & in our Names, Persons & Stead, to confer & negociate with our Brother Shikellimus and Alomoebey King of the Delawares, and the Councel in Shomoco, concerning the Smith, our Brethren in Shomoco have desired to reside amongst them: And to do every Thing therein, according to the Instructions they have received from us in that Behalf, the which they will communicate to you, by word of Mouth, and bring us a final Answer & Determination thereon.

Given under the Seal of our Brethren.

Bethlehem, in the Forks of Delaware

April 14th. 1747.

Frerxedonti. al. Spangenberg.

Friderix.

Nathanael Seidel

David Bischoff

Christoph Franck

Fig. 2 Original agreement for blacksmith's shop with seal. MissInd 121.9.1. Courtesy of the Moravian Archives, Bethlehem, Pennsylvania.

siding with the British and not the French, approval was given to establish a blacksmith's shop at Shamokin.

In April 1747, in a conference with Brother Martin Mack, Shikellamy (also known by his Oneida name, the Swatane) explicitly outlined his expectations of how the blacksmith's shop would be run. A primary stipulation was that when members of the Six Nations were traveling downriver on their annual war parties to the Catawba, any work at the blacksmith's shop done for them should be without charge. Shikellamy says, "I desire, T'girhitondi [Spangenberg's Iroquois name], my Brother, that when something is done to their flints that it is done for free, because they have nothing with which to pay. However, when they return, and they have something done, then they would have to pay for it."[4] All other Native Americans had to pay for the blacksmith's services. They could pay in hides, primarily deer, fox, and racoon. Indians and Moravians were not permitted to trade in anything else. Furthermore, at the conference with Shikellamy, it was stipulated that the Moravians were not permitted to sell flour or milk. They were not traders; they were not to befriend traders or favor them in the blacksmith's shop. The primary purpose of the Moravian presence at Shamokin was to honor the agreement that their artisans would work for the Six Nations.

Shortly after this agreement, in the late spring of 1747, Moravian missionaries Johannes Hagen and Joseph Powell arrived in Shamokin and further discussed the blacksmith's shop in a conference with Shikellamy and his advisers. Impressed with Hagen's linguistic prowess and the good intent of the Moravians, the Iroquois chiefs agreed that work could begin. That June and July saw the erection of the forge and the mission house, and by the end of July the forge was opened, much to the joy of Shikellamy (who helped to haul lumber). The arrival on July 23 of the first blacksmith, Anton Schmidt, and his wife, Anna Catharina, was an occasion of celebration. The diary entry for that day states, "It was as though a king had arrived; even Shikellamy was very happy." He was so happy, in fact, that he gave Schmidt the Mohawk name, "Rachwistonis" (he who works with metal) and, as promised, immediately accompanied him and Hagen down the river to Harris's Ferry to collect the rest of the tools for the blacksmith's shop.

In August 1747 yet another conference was held at Shamokin to set down the conditions of the establishment of the blacksmith's shop. The Moravians were to maintain themselves there "auf Indianisch Art," as Spangenberg describes it. That meant that only the "three sisters" (corn, squash, and beans) could be planted—no wheat, rye, or oats and nothing else that would make the place seem like a European plantation. All accounts were to be held by Brother Hagen or Brother Powell, with whom the blacksmith would meet at the end of each day to review the day's transactions. The price of services would be set so that one member of the Native American nations would not get charged more than another, and the accounts had to then be sent on to the Society for the Propagation of the Gospel, which was paying for the blacksmith's supplies.

Shamokin

What kind of place was this river confluence? Why had the Moravians been so eager to agree to provide blacksmith's services for the Iroquois? The dominant view of Shamokin in the scholarly literature, promoted by historians for at least a century, paints it as a place of darkness and magic. This slice of the Pennsylvania frontier is depicted at times as a site of violence and disorder and at others as a utopian landscape of harmonious cross-cultural exchange. Historian James Merrell provides the following description of Shamokin's peculiarities: "From the 1720s to the 1760s, the Susquehanna country was a debatable land, a place marked by confusion and contention." He ascribes this uneasy quality to the desolation that preceded: "Too few 'natives' remained there to serve as a charter group that could determine the character of life in the region, the Susquehannocks having been all but destroyed by their Iroquois neighbors in the late seventeenth century."[5]

From a certain vantage, what remained in the Susquehanna Valley in the early 1700s might be optimistically called a landscape of contact. Merrell highlights the multilingualism of Shamokin, where each person seems to be speaking a different tongue, sometimes Algonquin, sometimes Iroquois, sometimes German, sometimes English. Across language barriers were moments of cross-cultural exchange: Lenni Lenape could be spotted playing European card games; European missionaries were sometimes invited to Shawnee sweat lodges. In 1742 Count Nicholas Ludwig von Zinzendorf described the Métis interpreter Andrew Montour as "decidedly European" in a "brown broadcloth coat, a scarlet damasken lappel-waistcoat, breeches, over which his shirt hung, a black Cordovan neckerchief, decked with silver bugles, shoes and stockings, and a hat." In stark contrast, his face was "encircled with a broad band of paint, applied with bear's fat" and "his ears were hung with pendants of brass and other wires plaited together."[6] According to Merrell, this cultural hybridity was not unusual for Susquehanna country: Montour, son of a French mother and an Oneida father, fit in well to a confluence of cultures at the forks of the Susquehanna at Shamokin.

Yet historians also emphasize the sinister side to this confluence. Merrell characterizes it as a "babel of voices, accents, dialects, and languages," where Europeans could not tell which language to learn when they came to visit; where an Indian warrior could tell the German children of settlers at Penn's Creek, "Seid still!" in High German as he plunged an axe into their mother's head; and where, in the early 1760s, British troops from Paxton scalped an Indian called George Allen, a name taken from one of his attackers.[7]

How might we begin to understand this site of deep ambivalence on the Pennsylvania frontier—where food, knowledge, labor, and hopes were shared during a time of such enormous political and social upheaval? The Moravian mission diary of the settlement at Shamokin from 1742 to 1755 offers a richer and more detailed insight into life on the confluence before the outbreak of the French and Indian War, inviting us to complicate accounts that would either romanticize or sensationalize these histories. This diary differs substantially from other extant published Moravian mission diaries, such as those of the older David Zeisberger from the eastern Ohio missions and those of the later Springplace Mission in Georgia.[8] Shamokin itself was not a mission settlement built by the Moravians; rather, it preexisted their advent by several centuries, first as a Susquehannock, then as a Shawnee, and then in the early eighteenth century as a primarily Lenape settlement and trading post, overseen by the Iroquois vice-regent, the Oneida chief Shikellamy.

Repeatedly, in the mission diary of those first years, are mentions of passing groups of warriors in canoes who disrupt the quieter lives of the Lenape men and women occupied with hunting for furs and meat and growing corn, squash, and beans on the large island at the confluence, today named Packer Island. However, the presence of the Moravians there was assured through the agreement with Chief Shikellamy that the Moravians would establish a blacksmith's shop in Shamokin to service the guns of the Iroquois Confederacy. This agreement also quite clearly delineates the sphere of the Moravians' activity at the confluence. They are, for example, allowed to fence in Shikellamy's garden but not permitted to plant anything other than the three sisters (corn, squash, and beans) and potatoes, for fear that any other European plantings (of fruit trees or woods) might smack too much of a "Plantage," a European plantation.

The diaries of the mission in Shamokin details life in a place of both material and cultural commerce rather than in an intentional community, as is the case with the diary of Springplace, Georgia, or Gnadenhütten, Ohio. They reveal a far more complex picture of political and cultural negotiation, confluence of cultures, and environmental knowledge.[9] They describe the missionaries' regular visits to the settlements of Delaware women on Packer Island, regular suppers with Shikellamy in their log home, trips up and down the Susquehanna River to speak with the Lenape men who were back from hunting, and visits from the envoys of the Six Nations of the Iroquois Confederacy on their way to and from important political meetings with the colonial administration in Lancaster and Philadelphia. An environmental diary of natural events includes an earthquake, floods, famine, planting, and harvesting.

Immigration

The eighteenth century saw a vast emigration of Germans to America, in search of financial wealth and religious and political freedom. By 1727 already more than twenty thousand Germans had settled in Pennsylvania. For these settlers the problem of how to interact with the Indigenous inhabitants of the area was clearly of paramount importance. To answer all questions for the future emigrant, in 1702 Daniel Falckner sat down in Halle with August Hermann Francke and answered his 103 questions on subjects as far ranging as where the other Germans lived to how the Indians might be subdued. The Pietists being persecuted in Saxony called Falckner, who had lived in central Pennsylvania, to Halle to report on the condition of the province for possible settlement. He described the Indigenous peoples of Pennsylvania as *"einfältig"* (simple) and *"argwöhnisch"* (suspicious), with a language that has *"nicht mehr Wörter als Dinge"* (no more words than things); they adhered to a Manichaeistic religion, worshipping a god of both good and evil.[10] Eight years after Falckner's report to Francke, the future leader of the Moravian Church, Count Nicholas Ludwig von Zinzendorf, entered Francke's pedagogium in Halle. During his six years there, he met his first missionaries who had returned from Tranquebar and most likely read Falckner's *Curieuse Nachricht von Pennsylvania*. In 1732, even before he sent his own missionaries out into the field, Zinzendorf outlined his mission theology in a letter sent to Johann Ernst Geister, a missionary sent to Madras by the Stollberg *Konsistorium*. In this letter Zinzendorf writes of the appropriate demeanor toward the non-Christian: "Show a happy and lively spirit and in external matters do not rule over the heathen in the slightest fashion but rather gain respect among them through the strength of your spirit, and in external matters humble yourself below them as much as possible."[11]

Zinzendorf was well aware of the problems missionaries had already encountered in their contacts with other cultures, problems he attributed to the attitude missionaries had adopted toward non-Christians. For example,

Zinzendorf claimed that the refusal of some missionaries to mix with non-Christians or to live at their level of poverty was contrary to the spirit of Christ. Missionaries and non-Christians alike should both show deference only to the invisible Savior. In another speech to the inhabitants of Saint Thomas held in Creole on February 15, 1739, Zinzendorf clearly delineated both his understanding of "the natural state of sin into which the heathen have been born" and their need for salvation from the inherently sinful characteristics of this state. To convert non-Christians was, for Zinzendorf, an extension of the kingdom of God and the creation of another instance, unique and unrepeatable, of Christ. This understanding of mission policy meant that baptisms were individual and not performed en masse, that the individual's path to salvation was charted by means of frequent "speakings" with spiritual helpers from the same national background as the candidate and the missionaries, and that each convert was a member of a small group of people who came together regularly in the evenings to discuss their spiritual growth, exchange confidences about their personal problems, encourage and forgive one another, and help one another toward Christ.

Such an individualistic approach toward conversion had both benefits and drawbacks. The benefits showed themselves in the success of the missions. The drawback was that only small numbers of converts could enter into the kingdom of God. Zinzendorf, recognizing that each human being has a personal, particular experience of religious life, became convinced that this individuality should be encouraged rather than eradicated and replaced. The individuality of each human being was balanced by the commonality of being born not only into a class, race, culture, and gender but also into humanity and, as such, being born into the world spiritually. In terms of our physiognomy, the most significant mark Zinzendorf argued that distinguishes us from all others is not skin color or gender but, as he says in his speeches to the Single Sisters Choir in Berlin in 1732, "the mark of the thorns on the brow."[12]

Zinzendorf in America

The fantasy of a universal brotherhood in Christ met with some challenges when faced with the reality of a foreign and non-Christian culture. The Moravians initiated mission activity in Pennsylvania in 1740 after a failed attempt at a settlement in Georgia. In 1741, after spending Christmas in a log cabin on a tract of land in Northampton County that had belonged to the famous itinerant preacher of the Great Revival, George Whitefield, the settlers built the first houses a few miles to the south on the banks of the Lehigh River to form the core of their Pilgrim Congregation in North America. This settlement, named Bethlehem, was to serve as the economic and spiritual base for the evangelization of the Native American peoples of Pennsylvania and New York. In 1742 Zinzendorf traveled to Pennsylvania and met with the Native American population; it was on this journey that he met with Andrew Montour; his mother, Madame Montour; and Chief Shikellamy, among others. Zinzendorf sets out in this diary his intentions to settle among the Native Americans. He does not wish to go directly to the villages and preach because the inhabitants have already acquired a great hatred for the settlers' religion. Rather, Zinzendorf tells the Six Nations of the Haudenosaunee that he is intimately acquainted with the Great Spirit and asks that he and his followers be permitted to live in their towns as friends until they have gotten to know one another better.[13]

In 1742 Zinzendorf traveled from Bethlehem west via Tulpehocken (the home of Conrad Weiser), through to Harris's Ferry (today Harrisburg) and up the Susquehanna. In his travel journal, Zinzendorf describes this journey along the river with Conrad Weiser and his companion, Anna Nitschmann. On the second day of the journey, he wrote,

> We traveled on, and soon struck the lovely Susquehanna. Riding along its bank, we came to the boundary of Shamokin, a precipitous hill, such as I scarce ever saw. This is so rugged and steep a mountain that I have hardly seen its equal; but we all got safely across. Anna went on before, for she is our greatest heroine. She wore a long riding habit, to the train of which I held fast; Conrad held on to the skirt of my coat, and Boehler had hold of Conrad's. In this way we all felt more compassed and gained additional security.

Zinzendorf goes on to describe his first meeting with Chief Shikellamy in Shamokin, his evening stroll through the village, and his chance meeting with an inhabitant with whom he exchanged his fur hat for a melon. He describes the Susquehanna River in the following passage, as the party made its way up the West Branch to meet with Madame Montour near the Great Island:

> Sept. 30. [1742] Set out on our journey. The sachem [Shikellamy] pointed out the ford over the Susquehanna. The river here is much broader than the Delaware, the water beautifully transparent, and were it not for smooth rocks in its bed, it would be easily fordable. In crossing, we had therefore to pull up our horses and keep a tight rein.

Fig. 3 Painting of Shikellamy and Nicholas Zinzendorf at Tulpehocken. GS.389. Courtesy of the Unity Archives, Herrnhut, Germany.

> The high banks of American rivers render their passage on horseback extremely difficult.[14]

As Zinzendorf passed through the forests that border the West Branch of the Susquehanna, he experienced his first Pennsylvania fall, a splendor of colors that demand a new poetic vocabulary:

The country, through which we were now riding, although a wilderness, showed indications of extreme fertility. As soon as we left the path we trod on swampy ground, over which traveling on horseback was altogether impracticable. We halted half an hour while Conrad rode along the river in search of a ford. The foliage of the forest at this season of the year, blending all conceivable shades of green, red, and yellow, was truly gorgeous, and lent a richness to the landscape that would have charmed an artist. At times, we wound through a continuous growth of diminutive oaks, reaching higher than our horses' girth, in a perfect sea of scarlet, purple, and gold, bounded along the horizon by the gigantic evergreens of the forest.[15]

Thus, through journals such as that of Zinzendorf and later of the famous missionary David Zeisberger, the banks of the Susquehanna were described to the inhabitants of communities throughout the Moravian world. These accounts would also play a central role in the development of an American aesthetic imaginary, as they provided writers such as Henry Wadsworth Longfellow and James Fennimore Cooper with primary materials for the creation of an American literature that was quite distinct from that of the European writer.[16]

The "Shamokin Diary"

Ten different missionaries, including the well-known David Zeisberger and Martin Mack, wrote the "diary" of the Shamokin settlement. It is written primarily in German script, with one section in English (chapter 5). Such regular mission reports and diaries of the communities were read to all members on Gemeintage or Congregation Days to show the workings of the Savior in the conversion of the non-Christians and also of course to hear about the activities of the Europeans in this distant land. In addition to details pertaining to the condition of the soul of both converts and missionaries, these reports contained, as we can see from the previous quotations, a wealth of information about the landscapes, people, and practices of the Indian nations where the Moravians were active.

Those sources that have been published and that pertain to the Moravian presence in Shamokin are for the most part the personal papers of the individual missionaries.[17] For example, much use has been made of the *Lebenslauf*, or memoir of Martin Mack, first published in 1857 but written in the 1790s. In his old age, as a missionary on Saint Croix, he looked back on Shamokin in 1745 as "the very seat of the Prince of Darkness" and further claimed that

Fig. 4 Portrait of Martin Mack. Artist: Valentin Haidt. 1757. PC 16. Oil on canvas. Courtesy of the Moravian Archives, Bethlehem, Pennsylvania.

he and his wife, Anna, had to spend almost every night in the woods for fear of attack by "drunken Indians." This printed source, composed much later in his life and reflecting the generic constraints of the Moravian memoir, contradicts the record found in the manuscripts written by Mack in the "Shamokin Diary." Nowhere in the diary of 1745 is the necessity for Martin and Anna Mack to sleep in the woods mentioned. Rather, the diary describes how they find lodging in the hut of the mother of Anderius, or Andrew Montour, son of Madame Montour, who was acquainted with the Moravians in Bethlehem. In the evenings they held regular services of prayer and song in English, German, and Mohican: "On the 29th [of September 1745] we helped our people to harvest their corn. In the evening we held a blessed Singstunde with one another in English, German, and Mohican. We also thanked the Lamb with prostrated hearts that He had been among us until now and that His wounds pleased us much in our hearts."[18]

Anna and Martin's contentedness with their lodging is made quite explicit, as Andrew Montour apologized for their cramped quarters as he has to leave for Philadelphia: "We thanked him greatly for this [his hospitality] and said that we were very happy with it, and it was more comfortable for us in his hut than if we lived in the most beautiful house in Philadelphia. He was very pleased that we were so happy in his hut. In the evening Martin and Anna were blessed and happy."[19] It seems, then, that Mack's later description of Shamokin as a place of darkness and the devil is a distortion of memory, one produced approximately forty years later. But it is this memory that has so colored the depiction of Shamokin in historical studies.

The diaries of September 1745 show Martin and Anna Mack retracing Zinzendorf's journey on foot as they set out from Bethlehem, through Tulpehocken (Conrad Weiser's home) to Shamokin. They arrived on September 16 and immediately looked for somewhere to sleep. They were accompanied by Andrew Montour, from whom they asked for lodging. He replied that his hut, which he shared with his mother, was very small, but it was too late in the year to build a new hut for the Moravians, as there was no bark. So, although his quarters were cramped, he took them to his hut on Packer Island, where they were greeted by his mother, Madame Montour, who immediately offered them some meat. The next day, while Andrew was away visiting his wife's family, the mother told the Moravians what she knew of Bethlehem from her son and asked what the Delaware/Lenape were doing there. Anna Mack then took over the conversation, talking to the old woman about what could almost be understood as the utopian community of Bethlehem, where the spiritual and materials needs of all were met, irrespective of gender, race, or class. Madame Montour bewailed the corrupt state of Shamokin, by contrast, a community she experienced as nothing but drunkenness and dancing. According to the diaries, the night that followed—which is the Macks' first in Shamokin for three years—acted almost as proof of the old woman's words. Mack reported that there was much drinking in the town, that revelers crashed into Anderius's hut and screamed and yelled so much that the inhabitants sought safety in the woods. The next day they crossed the water to visit with Shikellamy but again fled early from the raucous drinking they encountered there. After this less than auspicious beginning to their time in Shamokin, it took only a few days before Anna fell sick. Shaken with fever and chills, Anna was steadfast in her desire to remain in Shamokin. After a week she recovered and within two weeks was helping her neighbors on the island pick corn and was able to conduct pastoral visits with the Lenape women on the island.

From the diary one can assemble a clear picture of the movement around the confluence. As the island was inhabited by primarily Lenape—and on the shores of the North Branch on each side of the island there were also communities of Lenape and Tutelo—the river became an aquatic travelator, carrying visitors back and forth across the confluence. But when the water was too high, or the canoes were on the opposite shore, then travel became more difficult. Shikellamy welcomed the Moravians into his house, offered them bread and meat, and even took them in to stay, once Andrew had to leave. He told them, "I would not usually allow a trader or other white people to live with me, but because I know you a little and you have been living here a while, I will allow it. My cabin is for me and for you and for your Brethren, no one else."[20] Andrew was sad that the Macks were leaving and apologized for having had nothing but corn to eat for the previous seven weeks. He had never known such times of famine, but Anna and Martin assured him that was not why they were leaving.

The diary breaks off here and resumes two years later, as Brother Hagen picked up the narrative in late August 1747, after the written agreement with Shikellamy had been reached. The Moravians no longer had to worry about being long-term house guests of Shikellamy, as they were now permitted to build permanent quarters for themselves. Once their own house had been built, life became much easier; their blacksmith's shop was a place of stability, productive work, and calm in the whirlwind that Shamokin could be; Shikellamy was now their frequent dinner guest, especially after unsuccessful hunting trips. A few years later, Brother Powell wrote, "Shikellamy and his Eldest son, John, Return'd from hunting, being so Excessive cold that they could not hunt. Ware Oblig'd in about a week to Return without flesh, invited him to Dinner, had a hunter's appetite."[21] When the noise of carousing became too much for Shikellamy, he found peaceful refuge in the Moravians' house. And he went there to have the treaty signed in Philadelphia that year read to him.[22] "Shikellamy brought us to Read a Treaty held with the Indians of the Six Nations in Philadelphia this year. Had also a Letter of Recommendation wrote and given him by the Governor, which we read to him. Was much pleas'd. Breakfasted with us."[23] However, the Moravians preferred not to get involved with politics, either national or domestic. When a neighbor from down the river came to them to complain that her husband had beaten her, Brother Powell turned to Shikellamy and his eldest son to settle the domestic dispute.

In the fall of 1748, Chief Shikellamy visited Conrad Weiser in Bethlehem to meet with the leaders of the Moravian congregation. By all accounts he fell ill on his return, and, by the time David Zeisberger was writing the diary entries for November, it was clear that Shikellamy, or the Swatane, was nearing the end of his life. On December 4 Zeisberger wrote,

> Brother Anton and David visited the Swatane and found him to be so weak that he could no longer walk by himself and could no longer hear well. Otherwise, he was very friendly and watched us with love but could speak very little. We brought him some tea and bread, which he enjoyed greatly. On December 6 David visited the Swatane early in the morning and brought him something to eat and drink. He said, however, that he could eat and drink nothing, and that he could no longer hear anything, only speak a little. We saw that he would not live much longer. Around midday an Indian woman came and said to us that he was close to going home. David went to him and stayed with him. But there was a terrible wailing of lamentations, for everyone, old and young, wept incredibly about their old father. He spoke no more and looked at David with friendship and smiled and finally passed away quite contentedly. We now felt in our hearts that we should plead with the little Lamb that He should grant a place in His Side Hole for him and were able to believe that He would do the same. None of his sons were at home, only his daughter and a few women.

In contrast to the common belief among historians that Shikellamy was given a Christian burial (he was, after all, baptized at least once), from the subsequent account of his funeral it is clear that he was buried according to his people's customs. Zeisberger and Mack made his coffin as requested. Zeisberger wrote, "On December 9 they buried the Swatane. Almost everyone in Shamokin was present. In his grave they gave him two new blankets, a tobacco pipe, and three bags with tobacco and a flint as an honor, and other things too. We also went to the burial and helped to bury him. They did not fire their weapons while he was dying or at his funeral; rather, everything proceeded very quietly."[24] Shikellamy's death brought with it great uncertainty for Shamokin, as the "Light Bringer" was also clearly a "Peace Bringer." Very quickly, belts of wampum were brought from Governor Hamilton to Shikellamy's son, Thachnechtoris or John Logan, as signs that he was now to assume the mantel of leadership at the confluence. The Moravians took food to Shikellamy's wife and daughters, who were starving. But the clouds of war were gathering.

There are several gaps in the mission diary, most notably in the second half of 1749 and between 1750 and 1753. During these times there continued to be a blacksmith at Shamokin but no missionaries. However, the project at Shamokin was the subject of much diplomacy and discussion, as the presence of a white Christian mission at Shamokin was precarious, to say the least. For example, the record of all business in the Moravian community in Pennsylvania, the Bethlehem diary contains entries that describe in detail conferences in Philadelphia between the governor, the Moravians, Shikellamy's three sons, and the Six Nations on the repeated encroachment of white settlers onto Indian lands. The presence of the Moravians at Shamokin needed to be understood not as breaking the treaty that made the Blue Mountains the border between Indian and "white man's land" but rather as the fulfillment of the promise made in 1747, when the Six Nations had agreed to allow the Moravians to travel and live on their lands in return for the blacksmith's shop at Shamokin.[25] After agreements were reached in Philadelphia as to the scope of the missionaries in Shamokin, they returned. The writings in the "Shamokin Diary" from 1753 to 1755 reveal a far greater presence of white settlers on the proprietary lands along the eastern shore of the river and also illegal settlements in Indian hunting lands along the western shore of the main stem of the river.

However, even as political tensions were building between the settler colonists and the Six Nations, moments of peaceful cultural contact were still recorded. For example, in 1754 Moravian missionaries Grube and Martin Mack described their journey along the North Branch of the Susquehanna and depicted the banks of the river as a place of cultivation, plenty, and great natural beauty rather than one of desolation, famine, and disease: they visited several "plantations along the Susquehanna, where we found the aged Moses and his wife, and several sisters hoeing corn. They came and shook hands and greeted us." This welcome was accompanied by an invitation to a sweat lodge, which the Europeans accepted and then followed with a Moravian *Singstunde*, a service that was sung in Lenape/Delaware and translated into Minisink.[26] The next day the Moravians sang and preached further, and then "the youngest son of Paxinos and another Shawnee came to us with two violins, and desired to hear our melodies. We played a little at which they and our Brethren and Sisters were well pleased."[27]

Between 1753 and 1755, toward the end of the existence of the mission at Shamokin and five years after the death of Shikellamy, the place had changed. In sharp contrast to the initial agreement with Shikellamy, the Moravians now had cows and calves and were thinking about getting a bull. A new mission house had been built farther from the river and closer to a spring. Letters between Shamokin and Bethlehem talk of the need for sugar and tea (for the Moravian Lovefeasts), wine and bread for Communion, and new trousers and shirts. The racoon and deer skins received in payment were transported back to Bethlehem through intermediaries, such as Michael Schäffer, the shoemaker who lived five miles down the Tulpehocken Path. Shikellamy's sons had grown used to having the blacksmith's shop in Shamokin and would have very much liked to keep it for themselves, even though most of the trade traffic was no longer passing through the confluence but rather had shifted direction, from a north-south route to east-west. Conrad Weiser was measuring up the land for himself, intending to lay claim to it as promised by the proprietors back in the 1730s. The missionaries watched in consternation as his line passed right in front of their house. Logan (Shikellamy's son) watched this marking out of territory also and wanted to talk to the Moravians about what to do, but they did not have the language skills.

The missionary women had gone: Anna Mack died, and Catharina Schmidt moved with Anton back to Bethlehem, as had Martha Powell with her husband. The mission had become almost exactly what Shikellamy feared: a plantation. It serviced the flints of the traders and white settlers and appeared to have lost its original purpose. Spangenberg wondered if they shouldn't just shut up shop, sell the house and its contents that were no longer needed to Conrad Weiser, slaughter the livestock, and sell the meat. In October 1755, mere days before the Penn's Creek Massacre thirteen miles downstream from Shamokin, the remaining blacksmith, Daniel Kliest, who was there without a wife, drove the livestock up the North Branch to Paxinos so that he, in exchange for three blankets from the mission, could take them to Gnadenhütten.[28] The remaining Indian corn was offered to John Shikellamy, who refused it, and given instead to the Indian Schafmann.

These last gifts at Shamokin bore a profit. As in October 1755, the Western Delaware moved up the Susquehanna River from Penn's Creek, and both Schafmann and another of Paxinos's extended family came to protect Kliest and guide him up the North Branch, away from the conflict for now, back to Bethlehem. But the artisan economy of the Moravian Sisters and Brothers that maintained the mission and blacksmith's shop in the 1740s had long gone, and now only distrust, division, and destruction were traded along the shores of the Susquehanna River.

1

SEPTEMBER 13–NOVEMBER 10, 1745

MARTIN MACK

Diary of Johann Martin Mack, from His Journey to and Stay in Shamokin

On the 13th
We readied ourselves to depart from Michael Schäffer's.[1] Our travel companions, Anderius and his wife's child, came from Conrad Weiser's. They brought me a pass and a letter in which he wished us much luck on our journey. Michael Schäffer provided us with a few necessities for our journey. We departed. We had our horses shoed at Christoph Weiser's. The people were very friendly. We traveled for a few miles, and there we stayed overnight. [Anderius had purchased 6 gallons of brandy, which he brought along.][2]

On the 14th [September]
We traveled to the second Blue Mountain[3] and stayed there overnight. We thought a great deal about our dear Bethlehem and especially about the blessed hours that we have there. We asked the Lamb with many tears that he should maintain the blessed connection between us and the dear congregation, that neither through flesh or thirst we lose our peace or be distracted from a feeling of blessedness.

On the 15th [September]
We went over the Thürnstein. This day we came quite a distance. Were happy and well. The blessed life that we have enjoyed among you once again cost us a few tears. But we went to Shamokin with our whole hearts and could lay the Indians there at the heart of the Lamb, so that He could open up the doors to his heart there also.

On the 16th [September]

We reached Shamokin. I asked Anderius whether he had thought about where my wife and I could stay. He said, he did not know himself. He had a very small hut. I asked him whether it would be alright if I built a small hut next to his. He said it would be hard to build a hut at this time of year as there was no more bark.[4] It was too late in the year. He said that Conrad Weiser had already said to him that he would prefer it if they could live more with him than with Shikellamy. We went with him to his house. He lived on the island.[5] We arrived there in the evening. The old mother[6] was very happy that we had come to visit her, and she made a little room for us immediately in her hut. Anderius asked whether we could manage with this, as his hut was so very small. We accepted it with many thanks, even though it was very small.

On the 17th [September]

We stayed at home. Anderius went to visit his in-laws. The old woman told my wife that her son had told her much about Bethlehem and that there were such good people there. She thought that if she could go there too and die there then she would die in a blessed state. She also asked what kind of Indians were in Bethlehem and whether there were any of the Delaware there who would have loved us. My wife told her much of what the Savior had already done for the Delaware who were already in Bethlehem and how they praised the Savior with many tears [and] that He had opened their eyes and had given them some of the Blood in their hearts. The old mother lamented greatly that everything here is still so dead and that they know nothing except drinking and dancing. Anna [Mack] explained to her how it is that the people still were forced to behave this way, because they did not believe in the Lord Jesus, and this was only the fruit of that. In the evening there was a great uproar because almost everyone who lived around here was drunk. Some even came into our hut who looked quite frightful and bellowed like cattle. The old mother gathered everything up and hid it in the woods. We commended ourselves to the Lamb and to his eternal angels that they might keep watch over us and protect us.

On the 18th [September]

We went visiting[7] across the water.[8] We also visited Shikellamy. He was very friendly, and also his sons welcomed us well, led us into his house,[9] but we were there for hardly a quarter of an hour when four drunken Indians came. We then left for the island again. Visited a few more huts. Anna found a goodly woman who was well suited to the ways of God. We went home again. The old mother was very concerned for us for she had not been able to cook anything the whole day because of the drunken Indians. At night there was once again a great uproar of shrieking and shooting all around. Anderius said he had to leave again, as it seemed someone would be hacked or shot to death. Martin and Anna held a Singstunde and prayed to the Lamb in many tears that he should watch over us and guide the wrath of the enemy.[10] Satan was rumbling greatly because he feared that his realm would become divided.

On the 19th [September]
We stayed at home because almost everyone was drunk. We prayed to the Lamb because our plan for the time being is this: pray, weep, think that we will be grasped by a new courage that the Lamb will show himself even here with his holy wounds that were made in him for his people. The enemy is concerned with scaring us away and to make us disbelievers. But we know that we are not doing this on our own account but rather rely on the blood of the Lamb and the prayers of the *Gemeine* (congregation). We know well who we are. Poor children who can do nothing and want to do nothing if the Lamb is not our strength. In the evening we held a blessed Singstunde. Today several kin of the old mother came. Her sister's child and the legal mother of Catharina.[11] She is a white woman who has an Indian as a husband. They had come almost 400 miles. They live more than 200 miles beyond the Allegheny.[12] They are going to Philadelphia with deer hides. They have almost 20 laden horses and are very friendly. The woman, she spoke some English and lived not far from the Cherokee—but it is in New France.

On the 20th [September]
Today Anna fell very ill. Her aches started with fever and sharp pains. It affected her greatly. She had complained for a few days that she was very tired, but she did not know what was wrong until it started this morning with her having to lie down suddenly, and sometimes she felt as though the stitch would stop her heart. We commended ourselves to the Lamb, and told Him that He should give us the great strength that we needed for this task, because we had come here for His sake and furthermore wanted to stay here as long as it pleased Him and His Community of the Cross. In the evening I had the opportunity to speak with Anderius and to tell him something of the loving heart of Jesus and how it was disposed toward such poor people as us, here in Shamokin, and how it wants to help and save whoever wants to be helped and saved because everything that reveals itself here among the Indians, like gluttony, drunkenness, whoring, stealing, murder, and lies, all this is only the fruit of not believing in Jesus Christ, who died in order that these things will be removed. And whoever does not believe in Him, he has to do these things whether he wants to or not, because sin holds sway over him.

On the 21st [September]
I went visiting and had the opportunity to speak about the reason we had come here in a hut where many were gathered together. The Lamb revealed himself so that I was able to speak joyfully about His great love. In the evening Anna started to shiver greatly and had fever until morning.

On the 22nd [September]
Her sickness continued. She became very weak. We could do nothing but commend ourselves to the Lamb, who knows our circumstances here. In the evening we prayed together. The Lamb, He heard us. We were very blessed among ourselves and thanked the Lamb with subdued heart that we are His sinners, and He has accepted us with grace. Oh, we would be so downcast if we could not speak from the bottom of our hearts in similar circumstances about the Lamb's blood, oh that would make our lives so hard. Anna tried to add that nothing was certain. "But you, Lamb, my Lamb, if I were to pass away."[13] That caused us to shed some tears, and we had blessed hours filled with tears. We thought a great deal about our blessed people in Bethlehem and what we had enjoyed there and believed with our whole hearts that they would remain in consideration of the Lamb.

On the 23rd [September]
In the morning two drunken Indians came into our hut. They had been making some noise for a couple of hours. Anna was very exhausted, had a high fever and shivering in her limbs. In the night the shivering decreased somewhat. We thanked the Lamb with many tears that he had heard the prayers of his children.

On the 24th [September]
Anna started to get better. Our hearts were knelt in prayer because the Lamb showed grace to us, and we feel that He is close to our hearts. Found many blessings in His safekeeping.

On the 25th [September]
Anna is getting better and better. Today a Presbyterian came to visit us. His name is Brauer.[14] He is very friendly. He came to visit the Indians and to preach to them. He complains much about them, that they are such bad people and that they are drunk most of the time. He said that he could never get them together to preach a few words to them about God.[15] He soon would not know how to proceed. He is staying with Shikellamy. Was already here once in the spring.

On Sunday, the 26th [September]
Our thoughts were much with our blessed congregation in Bethlehem and the real opportunities[16] that one has there. Martin and Anna[17] also celebrated a small Lovefeast together, during which our hearts were so close to melting that we hardly knew what was happening to us because we became so aware of the great love that the Lamb has toward his sinner-folk. We felt very well at this because we are also counted among those. We made a new covenant with one another to devote ourselves completely for the Lamb, to be in complete accord with Him and His heart's congregation, to sacrifice all our strength for Him who sacrificed Himself for us. In the afternoon I wrote a letter to Brother Joseph[18] and reported our circumstances. In the evening I spoke with Anderius about the matter of my living in his house, because he was considering leaving tomorrow for Philadelphia. I asked him whether I could continue living in his hut with my wife and the old mother until he returned. He said we were welcome to live in his hut as long as we wanted to. It was a very bad hut. But if we could stand having so little room in it, then it was fine with him. We thanked him greatly for this and said that we were very happy with it, and it was more comfortable for us in his hut than if we lived in the most beautiful house in Philadelphia.[19] He was very pleased that we were so happy in his hut. In the evening Martin and Anna were blessed and happy and thankful to our dear Lamb and especially for His fatherly loyalty and for His care for His poor sinners. We could thank Him from our whole hearts, also for this little place, and asked Him that He should reward this house and let the people feel that we are a blessing to them. We commended them and ourselves to the Lamb in a heartfelt prayer.

On the 27th [September]
Anderius left early with his friends to go to Philadelphia. Mr. Brainerd came to visit us again. Anna got better and better. The Lamb will soon give her enough strength that we can go visiting again.

On the 28th [September]
Today Martin went across the water to visit a few huts. He found a few people to be very friendly.

On the 29th [September]
We helped our people to harvest their corn. In the evening we held a blessed Singstunde with one another in English, German, and Mohican.[20] We also thanked the Lamb with prostrated hearts that He had been among us until now and that His wounds pleased us much in our hearts.

On the 30th [September]
We helped our people once more with their corn. Today Martin and Anna went visiting with each other for the first time again. They could do nothing but thank the Lamb that He had heard them with such grace.

On the 1st [October]
We were once again the housekeepers of our people.

On the 2nd [October]
We thought a lot about our dear Bethlehem. We were deeply contented and had a special feeling about their opportunities. The dear Lamb allowed us to enjoy them with them. Today Anna also had the opportunity to speak with an Indian woman about the great love of our Lamb toward the poor people. We were able to ask on her behalf that these words would be a blessing to her heart.

On Sunday the 3rd [October]
Once again we visited a few huts on the island and found that the people were very friendly to us.

On the 4th [October]
Once again we went visiting across the water. Many knew us there, especially the wife of the king from three years ago.[21] The king welcomed us also and had food brought to us soon. We found many Indians who received us lovingly into their huts. We told them that we loved them and that was the reason why we had come here to visit them again. They marveled that we would make such a long journey out of love. We could say nothing more than to pray for them, that the Lamb might open their eyes and show them by the power of the Holy Spirit what it was they were lacking. There were many Indians there! However, we felt in our hearts that we could say nothing more to them because we felt as though it would be pointless. We believed in our hearts, though, that the time would come when the wounds of the Lamb would be preached openly here also. In the evening we felt completely contented. Our hearts overflowed with tears at the Lamb's proximity. We could pray from our hearts and know that the Lamb would show Himself soon. In the evening we discussed what we might be lacking, that we are sometimes so fearful, that we felt as though something is pressing us down, that something heavy is on our hearts, [and] found nothing but the fact that we would like to have Brothers and Sisters from these people here in Shamokin. We need a little congregation; leaving us here alone among so many Indians is very hard for us. May the Lamb

soon hear the sighs and petitions of His congregation and give our hearts joy even among this still very wild people.[22]

On the 5th [October]
We wanted to go to the other side of the island because Indians live on both sides of the island but could not cross the water because we could not find a canoe. The canoes were all on the other side. We called for about two hours, but they did not come to fetch us. We went home and prayed for them.

On the 6th and 7th [October]
We stayed at home and helped our people harvest corn. The Indians had a big feast all together. It was all quite merry according to their customs.

On the 8th [October]
In the morning we went on to the other side because we had the opportunity. We prayed to the Lamb that He should also allow this visit to be blessed so that we can invite the souls that are inclined to Him. We visited everyone. The Delaware welcomed us into almost all the huts in a friendly fashion, but in all the huts asked us when we were thinking of going away again. In one hut, where there was a man and a woman, we had the opportunity to testify about our Lamb, about the great love that He has for us poor people. He loved us so much that He gave up his life for us. We were very happy with these two people. They listened carefully. People like them we have not found here yet. Oh how happy were our hearts, and [we] thought perhaps these are the first ones. They are smiling to the Lamb in His heart. They show much love. We told them also about our Indians in Shekomeko, and how they thanked the Savior with tears that He had transformed their hearts and opened their eyes and that they no longer thought the way they had before but now could be blessed through the belief in Jesus and could be happy in their hearts that they knew God, who also died for such bad Indians as them, and through His death had wrought in us new life. We asked them whether they had understood us correctly. They both said yes. They had understood us. We said we wanted to visit them more often. The man said he would like it if we visited them more often. But tomorrow he was intending to go off hunting and would not be home for another 3 months. Our hearts wanted to pray and weep for them. We said goodbye to them, asked them not to forget what we had said to them. We went to visit the other huts before evening, and then it was evening. So we went home again and thanked the Lamb for this visit and in a childlike manner asked that His spirit might make the words that we had spoken to the Indians today clear and true in their hearts.

Saturday, the 9th [October]
We were at home and helped our people with their work. In the evening five canoes full of Indians who are going to war passed by here. They were from the Delaware who live on Moncleir Bank, near Wyoming. One came into our hut and boasted and said that tomorrow he was again going to war against the Flatheads.[23]

On the 11th [October]
We went visiting again across the water but found no one at home except the old king. He said they had all gone to the other side and had left him quite alone. He wanted to give us something to eat. But he had nothing at the moment. We thanked him greatly for his kindness. He was very friendly. Complained that he could not hear. Otherwise, he would love to listen to us. We should visit others and talk to them. He also told us that a few days ago he had been very drunk and had fallen into the fire and had burned all the flesh off his hand and was now in great pain. We pitied him greatly. In the evening we were very distressed over some circumstances in our house. Could do nothing but lay ourselves before the heart of the Lamb with many tears. We had feared for a while that the enemy would start something on the other side because he hates the fact that we should live among the Indians, and so he tries in all ways to show us how he would like to be rid of us, because we are a thorn in his eye. We notice this often. May the Lamb help us through and by means of the Holy Spirit logically let these people know that we are a blessed people and that we are among them for no other reason than for the sake of their souls.

On the 12th [October]
We went visiting again across the water. We visited the Tutelo[24] and the Delaware.[25] The former were very frivolous and acted in a very haughty fashion. We could do no more for them than to sigh to the Lamb. The Delaware—some were very friendly, and some were busy playing cards and had no time to look up at us. We also found no opportunity to teach them anything else, and even if we had the opportunity it would not have come to anything. And so we were quiet and prayed to the Lamb with heartfelt tears that He should not leave us alone for so long but rather make us joyful among these people also because they are also the reward of His pains just as much as we are.

On the 13th [October]
We went visiting again across the water but found only a few at home. We visited on the island and found an opportunity to speak with a Delaware man

about the love of God and how He so loved us that He gave up His life for us, that we were no longer permitted to be slaves to sin if we believed in Him, and that we could be blessed already here, and that when we died, so we should not be afraid of death but rather feel joy in our hearts because we knew that we were going to our dear Lord, where we could be blessed in eternity because He had accepted us as His children. I asked him whether he would not consider it good fortune if a great king were to accept him as a child. He said yes. He would be very happy about this. Thereupon I said that the great God who made Heaven and earth and who is Lord over all the kings of the world and over all people, He loved us so much that He came down to earth for us and let it be known that He wanted to free all people from the slavery of sin and the devil. Whosoever believed in Him, this person He wanted to make His child, to His inheritor and this He preached and after this He was ceremoniously slaughtered and had definitely shed his blood and thereby He had given us a power. And now it just depended on whether we believed in Him, accepted Him as our God, and then He would accept us as His children and would give us eternal happiness. And if we believed in Him, so then He would give all who sought Him a clear and revealed heart, and then we would rejoice that He is our God, and we are His children, and then we thanked Him that He had opened our eyes and hearts so that we could see what we have in Him. The Indian was very attentive. He understands English well. We then returned home and commended him to the Lamb and prayed for him to the Lamb. He was surprised that we stayed among them for so long. I told him that there was no other reason than to teach them about the love of God.

On the 14th [October]
We stayed at home. We helped our people shell beans. We were both very happy and content because we know who we are—sinners who live from His bounty. If that were not the case, then we would become scared and afraid. But thank the Lord that we have a Lamb with a quiet ear who always hears us.

On the 15th [October]
We visited a sick woman. She was very kind. We told her something about our dear God, who bled to death on the Cross.

On the 16th [October]
I went visiting across the water but could do nothing more because everyone was drunk. Several I was visiting wanted to force me to drink, but I thanked them and got away. Several looked quite fierce and bloody. I went home again. In the evening we had a Singstunde and with many tears laid all our concerns

before the Lamb and His heart, especially about our house and the conditions here that for a while have been weighing on us. Anderius's wife left today also. Was not in a good mood. We don't actually know the cause.

On the 17th [October], Sunday
We thought a great deal about our dear Bethlehem and about the blessed hours that are enjoyed there. The Lamb shared some of this with us. We felt how closely we are joined to You and how our hearts partake in Your blessings and Your love that the Lamb shares with us. Anna visited a sick woman today again and had a good opportunity to talk with her about the Savior. She listened to her closely. I have spoken to her several times. We asked the Lamb to let this woman see for herself this week through His spirit. The old woman in the house in which we are living was very worried today that Anderius has been absent for so long. She said that most of them must have starved because they have not had even a little piece of meat for almost four weeks. Every day nothing but corn. She asked us if we could stand it, eating nothing but corn. We said that we were quite happy with that; we had not come here for the good food. We had not imagined anything better. We were grateful to dear God, who allows the corn to flourish. We had actually come here for the sake of the souls, to tell them about how our dear Lord and God wants to free people from slavery to sin in which they lie by virtue of nature and do not know it because Satan, the God of this world, has blinded them. We told her much about our purpose for coming here.

On the 18th [October]
We visited the king's house across the water. He was friendly, immediately gave us something to eat from his bowl. Otherwise, there were very few at home.

On the 19th [October]
We crossed the water to Shikellamy's. On the way we met an Indian with his wife who knew both of us very well because we had visited them a few times. The man was going to visit his wife on the island. He had a few little loaves of bread made with corn in a little bag. His wife said to him, give the two people some of the bread. They are probably hungry. The man sat down right away and took the biggest out of his bag and gave it to us with great pleasure. We took it with great thanks. The two people love us. We have spoken with them several times.

We then continued on into the town and were there for hardly a quarter of an hour when three drunken Indians came along, who all had bloody heads. Also, soon heard that most of them were drunk and all looked very bloodthirsty.

Much evil there. We soon went back home. In the evening two canoes full of Indians came by that were going to war.[26] They came from Canadian lands.

In the night Anderius's brother arrived here.[27] He lives in Canada and wanted to see his brother for once. He is also going to war. He left early though because Anderius was not at home, and the company that he is in did not want to wait. In the afternoon Anderius returned from Philadelphia. He was very friendly. He told us that he had spoken to Brother Joseph in Philadelphia. He also had a few letters for us. But unfortunately he did not have them here, but they would arrive with his company either tomorrow or the day after. He was quite upset about conditions in his house, especially because his wife[28] had gone away and left us alone. He asked us whether we knew why she had left. We said that she had told us nothing more than she wanted to visit her mother, who lived more than 80 miles from here.[29]

On the 21st [October]
Anderius left again. He said he wanted to see if he could still catch up with his brother. He had never seen him in his life, and he was his full brother.[30] They were from the same birth mother. He went by way of Ostonwakin. There he met his wife, who told him that his brother had already left. We prayed to the dear Savior with many tears that He should protect Anderius and guide his heart that he not leave because of circumstances, and that he become a comrade to us rather [and] He should show him that we are here out of love for the poor Indians.

On the 22nd [October]
Anderius's company arrived here. We very much desired the letters, and they gave them to us quickly. The woman was very friendly and could not stop telling us how she had been welcomed in Philadelphia with such love and especially that the women there had kissed her. She said it really touched her heart. She said that no white people had ever greeted her like that before. She also brought us some provisions from our Brethren in Tulpehocken,[31] for which we thanked her in a heartfelt fashion, as we said. The care of the Savior for His children was once again great in our hearts. As the dear Savior said to His disciples, have you ever wanted for anything, we must say, no Lord, never for one thing. He always cares for us. We are happy when we see how loyal the dear Savior is to us and maintains His father's heart toward us. Even here in this place He has shown us a few things and has preserved our lives as full of grace and, mercifully, as full of loyalty, as He intends with His children. We savored the letters. [They] strengthen us anew in our plan because the Savior's heart and the heart of His children refreshes us anew, reminded us

how closely our hearts are bound to Yours and how we walk and proceed with one spirit and heart with You and how the Lamb teaches us through the spirit that reigns in the Gemeine. Oh we bow down to the ground because the Lamb is so close to us and so merciful.

On the 23rd [October]
Anna visited a sick woman today and told her how the Savior likes to help sinners and wants to make them blessed in eternity, whoever wishes to accept Him, and then He gives it all back to them, not first through baptism or good deeds, but rather He is so full of love that He gives this freely.[32] The woman listened attentively. In the evening Anderius and his wife returned home. Both were very friendly, which was a great joy to us, and we witnessed how the Savior listened mercifully to the prayers of our hearts and thanked Him tearfully.

On the 24th [October, Sunday]
We went visiting the Delaware across the water. They were celebrating.[33] Asked them if they minded if we stayed here. They said that, as far as they were concerned, we could stay here forever. There were six men and six women present. They had cooked a whole stag and two pots of pumpkin and twelve loaves. They made 12 piles of meat, then put a loaf on each pile, and then distributed the pumpkin into the pots that the guests had brought. Then all twelve sat down and ate as much as they wanted. They took the rest with them. It was mostly old people. The man who gave the feast was a young man, and he and his wife did not eat a bite. It all proceeded in a very orderly and modest way, and, as soon as they had finished with their food, so then they thanked them in their way. They smoked three times, they drew on the pipes slowly, and then they stood up. Then one of them said, leave our friends some food, and brought us a piece of meat from his portion and also some pumpkin, which we accepted gratefully. They then went home. And we visited them in their huts.

We also had the opportunity to speak to an old man in Jesus's love. Oh, how happy our hearts are when we find the opportunity to speak about our Lamb because here we still have so little chance as they are all drunk most of the time. So we like it when we find someone to whom we can speak about this. Until now, we have not seen any other opportunity to do anything else because it is not our way to force people but rather to seek them out in love and to wait for as long as the Savior takes to find an opportunity to do something further. There is still no way to preach openly. And if we were to do this now and wanted to do this now, it would be against our plan and against the feeling in our hearts. That is why we think it is good to stay with our method, and that is to pray and shed tears and until the Savior shows us another way. The example of Mr. Brainerd, a Presbyterian minister who was here this spring and who spent much effort in gathering the Indians and preaching to them, he did gather some of them, but he did not have a good effect. He was here again this fall. They avoided him however they could. May the good Savior teach us to act wisely through His Holy Spirit, so that we do not spoil anything in His affairs.

In the evening we had the opportunity to speak somewhat in our house about the reality of baptism, and what kind of notion we have of it, and that no one can take it amiss if we do not baptize immediately, because the grace that is given in baptism is great and priceless and because the person who is being baptized should also have a feeling for it and that remains with him, wakeful in the grace of baptism, that he has received, and that we do not think that it is enough when we have baptized someone. No, we bow down before the Savior, and we must justify our actions to Him in such weighty matters. We also do not want to deceive people, so that they think that they are no longer judged: no, there is something more. It depends on the fact that we believe in the Savior, because what matters is forgiveness, and the one who is baptized will become blessed.

On the 25th [October]
We stayed at home and presented to the Lamb's heart all our circumstances in Shamokin and prayed to Him fervently that He should soon grant us some Brothers and Sisters.

On the 26th [October]
We went visiting over the water. Few were at home.

On the 27th [October]
We stayed at home.

On the 28th [October]
We went across the water to Shikellamy's. He was very friendly and gave us something to eat immediately. We went into the Delaware town. Wherever there was someone home, they welcomed us in a friendly fashion. We told a woman and a man who love us about the love of Jesus and why He came into the world, that it happened for our sake, and that we should be saved from slavery to sin. He wants to take us as His children; He wants to share His heavenly treasures with us; He wants to help whosoever wants to be helped.

A good Savior, a loyal Savior, and dear Husband, when you know Him, you no longer think to be afraid; rather, you feel like a child does toward his father. He loves us; out of love He died for us and was resurrected. His heart is gladdened by nothing more than when many believe in him, when many help themselves out of sin. His blood is strong enough to liberate all Indians if they only want it.

The two people were very attentive. The dear Lamb wanted to announce this fervently to their hearts through prayer.

On the 29th [October]
We went visiting on the island. There were few at home.

On the 30th [October]
We were at home. The Lamb was close to us, and we thought a great deal of our dear Bethlehem, especially of all those dear to our hearts. We are afraid that we have not seen anyone for so long. We had hoped to see some of our Bethlehem hearts (friends) here soon. We also thought a great deal about our dear Shekomeko. We laid our thoughts down at the heart of the Lamb because it is His work that He began there.

On the 31st [October, Sunday]
We went visiting again across the water to Shikellamy's house. However, most of them had gone out, besides a few old people. The men are out on the hunt, and many will return only in two months, some only in spring. Many of the women have left for Tulpehocken with horses to fetch liquor. We also visited Shikellamy. There were two Indians there who had come from Wyoming. They are also going on the hunt. They knew us both. One was a Shawnee but could speak Mohican well; the other was a Mohican. The Shawnee asked us what we wanted here. The Five Nations does not want to have people teaching the Indians. You are like pigeons. When you come to a place, then it doesn't stop at one or two of you; rather, a whole flock lands here right away. He also told Shikellamy that we were like pigeons, where one of us settled then a whole flock soon came and settled together. Shikellamy was quiet and did not answer him a single word. They soon left. Shikellamy proves himself to be very friendly to us. We then returned home.

On the 1st [November]
We went visiting again on the island, but no one was home except for two old women and a few children.

On the 2nd [November]

We were at home. In the evening twelve Indians arrived here by water who are coming from Canada. They are going to war with the Cherokee. Anderius knows them; there was a friend of his among them. Anderius said these Indians had come from very far away. They came from more than 400 miles farther away than Onondaga. They looked very bloodthirsty. They camped near Anderius's hut. They soon prepared the place to dance. They got an empty barrel of rum, knocked the bottom out of it, and made a drum out of it. Then began to celebrate according to their custom. They shouted and danced for nearly two hours, during which time the enemy [Satan], to whom we are a thorn in his eye, was very occupied and would have loved to get rid of us. They soon got rum to drink and became so full of it that they behaved like wild animals. They were close to pulling down our hut. Just after midnight four of them came in here who looked terrifying and bloodthirsty. Anderius was afraid that they wanted to do harm to us. He took them out of the hut, but an hour later another one came and acted like a madman, picked up a large brand from the fire, and said he wanted to burn the white people. Anderius quickly stood up and grabbed the brand out of his hands. He [the Indian] went for his flintlock. Anderius, however, also took that away from him. He grabbed a piece of wood and came toward us. Anderius took that and said he should leave. He said he did not want to, so he said he should sit down by the fire. He sat down but soon left. (He was later murdered by another of the visitors.) Anderius was very worried that the drunken Indians would do us harm. We said to him that if he thought we should, then we would spend this night in the woods. But he did not think this was advisable because it is so cold. So we stayed, commended ourselves to the watchfulness of the Lamb and wished that it would become day soon. Soon they beat the one who wanted to kill us almost to death. We also prayed to the Lamb that He would soon let us see someone from the congregation because of my Anna's condition.[34] We laid her condition at the Savior's heart with many tears that she should be spared in soul and body.

On the 3rd [November]

In the morning our hut was full of drunken Indians. Martin and Anna counseled each other that they wanted to move out and into the woods for a while. At that moment, Brother Joseph, Hagen, and Joseph[35] came to the door to our surprise but could not enter because the drunken Indians were here. We went out to them immediately and could not believe our eyes. Then Brother Joseph welcomed the drunken Indians. One of them pulled his pack off his back and threw it into the woods and took his hat and put it on himself and ran off. Joseph was quite unruffled by this. We went into the woods together a bit to embrace and kiss each other. Anderius soon followed. He was a little downcast that things were so rough in his house. We then held a little conference with each other because I read in the letter about who should be concerned that we change our quarters. I soon explained our circumstances here to Brother Hagen because Anderius is thinking about moving away from here to his friends and that we could no longer live here on the island because apart from that there are many difficulties. We agreed to speak with Shikellamy. We asked Anderius if he thought that was good. He agreed. He offered to go with us to him straightaway and to be our interpreter. So we went there together.

When we arrived, we explained to Shikellamy that we, Martin and Anna, had been living with Anderius until now, and that this could not continue because he was now leaving, so we had thought to ask him whether these two Brothers [Spangenberg and Hagen] who had come to visit us could stay in his house and that we soon would go back. [We asked] whether he thought that it would be good if we asked around for another hut. He said that it was not necessary that they look for another hut. His hut was big enough, and we were welcome to live in his hut as long as we wanted, and he would like that and would welcome some of our people living with him. We thanked him greatly that he was offering his house to us. We also told him something of our plan here, why we were living among them, that it was not because of something we wanted for ourselves but rather out of love for their souls. Shikellamy said that if a trader or someone else from the white people wanted to live with him, then he would not allow it, but he would allow us, because he knew us a little bit, and we lived among them. We said that he should be quite honest with us. We did not want to be a burden to anyone if something came up. For example, if in some days many Indians were to stay in his house, and he could not take our Brothers, he could then tell them to leave his house or show them a house they could stay in for the time being. He said this would not be necessary. His house was big enough. The cabins were there for him and for our Brothers and no one else should live there. We thanked him greatly for the love and friendship he showed to us. We also thanked the dear Lamb for this public gift of great hope that the Lamb would soon glorify Himself here in Shamokin.

I went back to our house with Anderius to bring my things across the water to Shikellamy's house because Anderius's house was full of warriors who had arrived from Canada. I also asked him, because Anna and I had lived with him for seven weeks already, what we owed him. He said, however, that I should not mention it. He was very sad that things had been so rough for us in his house. He had nothing but corn for the past seven weeks. In his life he had never lived so poorly as he had for these past weeks. I said that we were heartily grateful that we had been able to live for such a long time in his house. We had not come here because we thought we were going to eat well, but rather we had imagined it to be the way it turned out. Our intention had been to be here for their souls and out of love for them. The old woman, Madame Montour, cried a lot that we were leaving so suddenly. Anderius accompanied us across the water, offered himself for any help needed, especially to his companions.

In the evening we held a conference with Brother Hagen about the work in Shamokin and told him how things had been with us until now in regard to the Indians and what we had done. Our main plan, which we had received from the congregation, and which was so intimate with our hearts and feelings, that we could believe with our whole hearts that the Lamb would be with us and would protect us through His Holy Spirit among this people who were still so wild, even if we were not able to do more than pray and weep. We had visited diligently. When the Indians had given us some opportunity to talk about why we were here, then we did so and took the opportunity to praise the love God has for them. If they gave us no opportunity, then we were quiet and prayed to the Lamb. We cannot even think of preaching, because for the moment there are troublesome things among them, until they themselves make the opportunity. In the meantime, we ask the dear Savior to preserve us in the faith of His love and in the hope for these still very wild hearts until their hour comes.

This evening, in Shikellamy's house, we held a Singstunde together, and everything around was quite still.

On the 4th [November]
In the morning we soon left. Shikellamy gave us a piece of [dried] venison to chew on the way. Brother Hagen and Joseph accompanied us to Eva Creek and spoke a great deal with each other about being a child in relation to the Savior and also between each other. Said farewell to each other, found it a little difficult to say farewell. Our hearts broke with tears. Martin and Anna climbed the Spangenberg. Hagen and Joseph watched us and climbed up safely just as Anna finally had to crawl on hands and knees. That day we came quite a distance. In the evening we met a trader with 25 loaded horses. We made it to Anna's Valley, and there we made our night quarters.

On the 5th [November]
We arrived in Tulpehocken and were welcomed with much love by Brother and Sister Loesch.

On the 6th [November]
We visited our Brother and Sister Meurer. They were heartily glad at our arrival and that we were both well and happy. Martin [Mack] and Philip [Meurer] visited Conrad Weiser that same evening. They had some news for him from Shikellamy. He was very happy with our stay in Shamokin and with what we had done there. He said that if we had told him that we had been very successful or that we had converted many Indians, then he would not have believed us. But he believed what we told him. He has the same ideas about converting the Indians.

On the 8th [November]
We traveled to Brother and Sister Wagner. In the evening some Brothers and Sisters came there to visit with us.

On the 10th [November]
We arrived in our dear Gemeine again. Our hearts wept for all the grace and love and loyalty and care that it had done for us, two poor souls for the past 9 weeks. Oh, we bow down in the very bottom of our hearts. Accept us again as Your children. We have experienced how good it is to be Your children, how blessed communion with You is. We neither desire to be nor can be without You.

Your poor fellow pilgrims
Martin and Anna Mack

2

MAY 26–JUNE 28, 1747

JOHANNES HAGEN

Diary of Brother Hagen's and Johannes Paul's Journey to Shamokin

May 1747
On May 26, Tuesday, we departed from our dear and beloved congregation of our Lamb and God with much blessing and grace. We felt the divine love of the Brothers and Sisters that held sway here from the most intimate place of His discipleship so that our hearts and spirits were as though drunk. The Daily Text was "out of Zion, the perfection of beauty, God hath shined. Put Your whole people here before us like a gentle cloud and a rainbow of grace that You still grant the world."[1] In the evening we arrived at Jakob Miller's, where we were well accepted. Brother Bruce was given us as a travel companion.

Wednesday, May 27
On the way to Heidelberg, we arrived at Brother and Sister Brückisch's. They were as pleased as children about our arrival, and we refreshed ourselves in one another's company and left them happy and content. In the evening we arrived at Michael Schäffer's house. He and his household were pleased that we had arrived. His youngest daughter, as she heard that we were traveling, asked for money from the others and gave us money for the trip. A good girl. She thought we had none. (M. Schäffer said that we would have to stay tomorrow as well, as there were no horses there.)

Thursday, May 28
In the morning we went to Conrad Weiser and told him that we were once again going to Shamokin. He gave us a letter for Shikellamy to take along,

with the news that from today he should be in his house in Shamokin for 20 days and that we two friends could build a house for the smith, whom T'girhitondi would send in a few days. We also got our provisions together that we were thinking of taking along.

Friday, May 29
We departed from Tulpehocken (we did not receive the horses that had been promised to us), and Michael Schäffer, who gladly equipped us and had provided us with provisions, gave us his two horses and delayed the trip that he was considering to Philadelphia. But as we were hardly beyond his fence, he came running after us and said that he had to travel with us; he felt it so in his heart. We asked him to reconsider; however, he did come with us. We thanked the Lamb that He continued to help us and could be found in our hearts. We then traveled across the Blue Mountain and then over the Thürnstein and made our Sabbath night camp at Ludwig's Ruh.

Sunday, May 31
We arrived in Shamokin. We made our camp under a tree. Shikellamy came running with his people straightaway and welcomed us. I gave him a gift of a roll of tobacco. He was very friendly. I said that I had words to say to him from T'girhitondi. After the midday meal Johann Paul[2] and I went to him. He sat in front of his summer house with his council and told us to come up. There they had spread out a bear skin, on which they instructed me and Brother Paul to sit. The council sat next to us on both sides. The interpreter sat straight in front of us. I took out my speech and read the first line to them. Then I stopped. Then they discussed this. After they had finished, I asked them in Maqua[3] whether they had understood this. Shikellamy said, "Gachrongi."[4] And so I continued and stopped after every sentence. And when they were finished, Shikellamy said, "Gachrongi." They were very surprised that I could speak their language so much better. When we were finished, they lit their tobacco pipes and conferred with one another. After this they went ahead and showed us the place where our house and plantation should be. He also said that he wanted to give us three horses to work. At the last point, I gave him the string of wampum. I wrote to Brother Joseph in Bethlehem because Michael Schäffer is leaving here tomorrow with the horses (and it would have been difficult for Michael Schäffer, if he had to take it with him). So we decided that Brother Bruce should go back with Michael Schäffer. The text for today was "all they that go down to the dust shall bow before him. Let everything serve the Community of the Cross; the Shepherd cradles it in His bosom."[5]

June 1747
Monday, June 1
M. Schäffer and Brother Bruce returned with the horses to Bethlehem. They were very blessed and content (and we believe that this journey will be a blessing for Michael Schäffer). We started to cut timber for our house. Shikellamy gave us a harness for the horses. I gave him a gift of a painted tobacco pipe that was an appropriately fitting thing for him. We prayed to the little Lamb, that He would be with us as we built and would help us.

Tuesday, June 2
[no entry]

Wednesday, June 3
We measured out the house, 30 feet long and 18 feet wide. The Daily Text was especially important to us today. We also started to drag the lumber here. A Delaware *Wilder*[6] was supposed to lend us his horses if we gave him 2 gallons of rum. We told him that we had none. At that he rode his horses over the Susquehanna. We were a little afraid of where we would get the lumber, as we had only two weak horses, and the other three we were supposed to have lived across the water, and no one could reach them. The Savior clearly helped us, however.

Thursday, June 4
We fetched the lumber and laid the thresholds to the house. Shikellamy himself helped us. The text for the day was especially significant (It is he who . . .).[7] We also believe in that which will allow this to truly come to pass (the Husband).

Friday, June 5
In the morning we fetched lumber again, and in the afternoon we continued to build. The Indians have the custom that when they are supposed to help someone with their work that then one must give them food, and we had very little. Therefore, we had to work alone, and that during the whole building process. But the little Lamb will help us through this. That gladdens us and gives us encouragement.

On the Sabbath,[8] June 6
In the morning we fetched lumber. In the afternoon we were building again. Shikellamy showed all the Indians the house and said, "the Spirit,"[9] and was

happy. Many of them watched us while we worked. We conversed much with the congregation in our hearts today, and it did us good. Shikellamy also gave us a rib of venison.

On Sunday, June 7
We contemplated the Gemeine a great deal and were reassured in our hearts of its prayers. We were peaceful and blessed in one another's company. (Brother Paul [Powell] had an attack of diarrhea, but the Savior helped him through it through a dose of balsam.)

Today Delaware *Wilden* came through here who were wanting to go to the war with the Catawba. Just as we had laid ourselves down to sleep, they all entered the big house, with the whole council, and the war was the main cause. In the house stood a post on which a human head had been carved, and they carried on there with music and dancing. Whoever brought a complaint against the Catawba there, could then put an axe into the idol, and thus he could express his feelings. This went on for half the night, after that they ate together. From our hearts we prayed to the Lamb for these people (the Daily Text was especially important to us).

On Monday, June 8
We laid the joists in the house. A trader came by and began to swear and curse. Why didn't we have the Wilden help us and in good time make them into our servants? We soon let him know why, so he became quiet. He wanted to make it up to us and offered us his hides in return, once we had the house finished. We refused. But he kept working on it and wanted to befriend us. He offered us rum, but we did not take it. We had another sleepless night because of the warriors.

On Tuesday, June 9
We worked hard at our building again. We were very exhausted and did not know what we lacked. We made ourselves a cornmeal soup, as we had nothing else. We were thus strengthened again. Four warriors left today. Shikellamy's son left with them. I could not answer to him. There were 17 altogether. There is remarkably little food here. They have grass, roots, and the like to eat, weeds that, when they are uncooked, are poisonous. But when you cook it with ferns it is a good meal.

On Wednesday, June 10
We were hard at work again.

On Thursday, June 11
We had visitors again but no helpers. The Savior fortified Hagen particularly today. The axe that Brother Paul had been using to cut above (on the roof) fell down to the ground next to his foot and cut him through his shoe on the side and cut his foot a little. But it did not stop him working.

On the Sabbath, June 13
We finished making the blocks. We thanked the little Lamb with all our hearts, that He had helped us this far and had kept us from harm and had given us hearts that are always happy and for His closeness and strength to work. Because otherwise it would not have worked—because we two were alone and had to drag the blocks thirty feet to the house. We can say that, with every block that we dragged, the Savior put His hand to it and the prayers of the congregation were there also. Shikellamy went out on the Susquehanna in his canoe today to go down to Harris's Ferry to fetch provisions for himself. We also started to work on our plantation to put the seeds in for the turnips.

On Monday, June 15
We ploughed again. Four canoes full of white people from Canaseragy passed who were fleeing the war. One of them was a trader, who made many of the Wilden drunk. The reason for this gave us many sleepless nights. We also cut down a tree for shingles and began to make them.

On Tuesday, June 16
We went to make shingles again. The drunken Indians on the way wanted to trade with us. Shikellamy's wife, who was also drunk, said my husband loves these people, and they left us in peace.

On Wednesday, June 17
In the morning we made shingles. In the afternoon we started to work on the land. It was heavy work with horses and plows. The little Lamb helped us though and it worked.

On Thursday, June 18
We made shingles and also cut a door into the house. It was rainy weather. We were especially happy in our hearts. We observed that we always dreamed of the Brothers and Sisters and believe therefore that the spirit of the Brethren is with us and converses with us, and we refreshed ourselves quite intimately at the thought of our Brethren in their absence. We worked in the house. It

was rainy weather. (The Savior protected Hagen especially, as it was slippery up on the joists. When Brother Paul was up there, a board fell down and hit his leg, but there was no great injury.)

On the Sabbath, June 20
We carried our shingles and also lumber on skids down to the water and made it possible for us to work in the dry. We also made a path to the water on which we could carry the lumber up. The Wilden watched. One woman said that they had been here so long in this place and had never made anything like this and was pleased about it. An unmarried Delaware man came to us and said he had wanted to come to us for a long time, but he had been far away on the hunt but had heard that we were here. He knew Jepse and Brodhead. He said that when we moved on he wanted to come with us. The Wilden here all regard our business here as better than theirs. Even if it is just what it is, then they think it is better because we have done it.

On Monday, June 22
We began to put the roof on our house. We thanked the little Lamb that we were given a day that allowed us to work in the dry. Shikellamy's family began to complain that they had nothing to eat and would like to have seen us share some of what we have. We conferred together on what we should do also because we had little thought that one of us would have to leave to fetch provisions from Tulpehocken.

On Tuesday, June 23
We were at our work again. At lunchtime, however, Shikellamy and our dear Brother Bruce arrived with our blacksmith's shop tools and also with provisions and dear letters. We were very happy about this and thanked the Lamb that He had brought him to us and that He had worried about us before we had even thought of this. But everything had become wet in the water, as both canoes had taken water on board on the big falls. We immediately laid everything out in the sun to dry out. We wondered how we would carry all the heavy crates, but the Savior helped us through it. No great damage had been done. Brother Bruce told us how the Savior had managed everything and that Shikellamy had been down there at Harris's Ferry, as he had arrived with the things. We could not thank the Savior enough for what He did to make Shikellamy arrive just then. He was watching our work that we did and the land that we were ploughing, and He was very joyful.

On Wednesday, June 24
We cut shingles. Shikellamy was with us constantly and watched. I delivered my greeting to him from T'girhitondi and his brothers. He thanked us greatly and was very pleased. We moved into our new house today because we had brought our new things and had enough of a roof over us that we could stay dry. The Daily Text was especially important to us as we moved in. We considered Brother Bruce's departure for Bethlehem. We thought that he should stay for a few days with us out of necessity and help us to be able to lock up the house while we are working outside. We also held a little *Gemeintag* for ourselves by reading the letters that Brother Bruce had brought along, and this in our new house. We were very happy and contented together.

Today a Wilder had got himself drunk and wanted to behave in an unruly fashion, so they bound him. That is their way of keeping order.

(On Friday, June 26
We cut another blade for making shingles.)

On June 27
The Sabbath we closed up one side of the house. The whole day the Wilden were with us and watched. They like being with us. So does Shikellamy.

On Sunday, June 28
We were quiet. Shikellamy came to us and asked whether today was Sunday. I said yes, for he could see that we were not working. So he left right away and put his chief's regalia on and returned to us.

3

JUNE 29–AUGUST 2, 1747

JOHANNES HAGEN

Brother Hagen's Diary of His Work at Shamokin

On June 29
Brother Bruce left here happy and content with news and a few letters to the Gemeine.[1] We accompanied him with our best prayers, and we commended him to the little Lamb.

On June 30
We finished the roof on the house. We also carried stones up from the Susquehanna for our fireplace.

On July 1
We carried stones to the house with Shikellamy's horses. He was very happy about that. We had much to carry, as it is something quite new here to take horses out when the water is high. A trader asked if we had been sent here by Conrad Weiser. We did not give him an answer. In the evening a drunken woman, a *Wilde*, tried to get into our house. Shikellamy called to her that she should leave us in peace. We were tired from the work.

On July 2
We began to build the chimney and fireplace. Indian traders were here too, also the one who had recently said that he wanted to see us run out of here. He was quite silent, however.

On July 3
Shikellamy came and said that he wanted to go to Tulpehocken in the morning. He is with us constantly. It seems that if it were not pleasing to him, then he would not be with us.

On July 4
Shikellamy and his household went to Tulpehocken. I gave them a greeting to the congregation to take with them. (We laid the mantlepiece for the fireplace.)

On July 7
We fetched stones from the water. We got as many as we needed.

On July 8
We worked hard on the fireplace. We also built a door into the upstairs room. We were constantly visited by the Wilden, especially when new ones arrive who had not lived here while we have been here.

On July 9
Once again we had many visitors from the Wilden. They watch our work far more than if we prayed and preached here. They brought us green beans as a present. Shikellamy also returned from Tulpehocken.

On July 10
We had visitations from the Wilden again. When one went away, then another would come. A Wilder came running and shouting strangely with an arrow in his arm. The others understood him as soon as they heard him. He brought news that a woman and a boy had been shot with arrows by Wilden. There were also traders there. Several others came, whom we had to bleed.[2]

On July 11
We finished our fireplace chimney and cleared up our house. We again were visited by Wilden. They were much in awe at our work. Traders came into the first floor of our house again. They looked angrily at Shikellamy, as he saw that we [text corrupt]. We also shaved his head according to the Indian fashion.

On July 12 [Sunday]
We went out for a blessing of our souls and looked at Shamokin. We sang the verse, "My God, you see them grazing."[3] May He bestow on us also a table on which we may feast.

On July 13
We went to fetch wood to put the ceiling over the living room. Hagen began to lay the boards, and Paul went to make the crossbars for the fence around the vines.

On July 14
We were hard at work. A Wilder came and wanted to eat with Paul. But we had no food. They brought us blueberries as a present.

On July 15
We were very happy in the contemplation of our Brothers and Sisters.

On July 16
We finished the ceiling over the living room.

On July 17
Hagen became very ill.

On July 18
We had no Daily Text.

On July 19
Hagen got a high fever. Otherwise, we were happy and content.

On July 21
Hagen once again had a high fever so much so that the [text corrupt]. Prior to this Brother Paul let his blood. We also used the good fever powders. The fever left him but also left him very weak.

On July 23
Hagen was very sick. He was somewhat strengthened by the arrival of his Brothers and Sisters[4] that it went through his body and soul so much that the illness nearly left him, and the kisses and greetings vaccinated him, and some were so juicy that they refreshed and strengthened our hearts unspeakably. The air of the Cross that wafted around them was very pleasant to us. The Wilder, who saw Brother Christel Rauch coming, came running, because he had come a little earlier, and they did not know the way to the house and asked if he knew the blacksmith.[5] I said yes, and then they were happy; they brought blueberries. It was as though a king had arrived; even Shikellamy was very

happy. We thanked with bowed hearts the little Lamb for His loyalty that He had brought our Brethren to us with the help of His holy angel.

On July 24
Anton started to sort out his blacksmith's tools. He had many with him. (We prayed with our Brethren especially with Brother Christel.)

On July 25
The dear little Lamb blessed us especially. [Hagen and Anton] we thought about our journey down to Harris's Ferry to fetch the things (that the dear Society had sent to us).[6]

On July 26
We were quiet and refreshed ourselves with the little Lamb. We talked with one another.

On July 27
We planted our turnip seeds. We started our journey down the Susquehanna with two canoes. Shikellamy joined us himself with one of his sons[7] and another Wilder, whose name was Philip. Christian, Anton, and the two Sisters stayed at home.

On July 28
We arrived safely at Harris's Ferry. We received everything in an orderly fashion, as they were stored in the lodge. We even traveled back a few miles. However, Brother Paul had an attack of the fever. We slept in the bush.

On July 29
We left again. When we got to the falls,[8] one of the canoes, where most of the things were, started taking on water. But everything was saved. Shikellamy lost his hat though. In the evening we came to the Indians called Nanticoke, where the two Indians who had been shot by arrows were. There Shikellamy himself made a fire away from the other huts and had the two kings come to him and held council with them about the two murdered Indians. We prepared some food, which they placed before the council. He himself ate nothing though, until the council was over. He heard for the first time what had happened a week ago and wanted to preach. They did not want to hear him though. They were in the thick of the traders. They were very friendly to us.

On July 31
In the evening we arrived in Shamokin again to our Brothers and Sisters, whom we met happy and content. We were overjoyed to be together and thanked the little Lamb that He had brought us here again, past all the cliffs and rocks, for the Susquehanna is no different to look at than a town full of houses; the rocks lie in the water, and the water flows crisscross between them (like a warp and weft).

On August 1
Hagen and Christel [Rauch] held a little conference with each other. They also invited our travel companions to eat at midday with us. Brother Paul got the fever today. A Wilder brought our Sisters a shirt to sew.

On Sunday, August 2
We had a blessed conference together about the things that occur here in Shamokin. In the evening the council was meeting, and Brother Christian brought them the greetings and words from T'girhitondi and the other Brothers who were dear to them. Shikellamy allowed T'girhitondi to speak;[9] he and his brothers want to be sure that no harm comes to the smith and Brother Hagen and their wives, not by the hand of the Indians, nor of the white people. For the white people especially have no say here, and also none are allowed to live here.[10] The other white people had built Shikellamy a house,[11] and it had taken until they came. If they, like him, had been there, it would have taken just as long to finish. We had said that they should have a blacksmith, and we would have come straightaway and would have built the house he could have lived in and that he would have liked.[12]

Afterward we had a blessed Lovefeast with one another, at which the little Lamb allowed the beautiful martyrs to speak. After that we had a blessed Pedelavium,[13] during which we sang many verses about the blood and wounds. The little Lamb showed Himself in our hearts especially, and we washed off from one another whatever may have stuck to us. Afterward Brother Christel held a very juicy and bloody speech on the Daily Text, which was "Rejoice, Zebulun, in thy going out: The first fruits of our Gemeine often make us cry for joy,"[14] and our hearts felt something of the pain of grace of our little Lamb. At the end of the speech, just as Christel wanted to take the book and sing a verse, there was an explosion and a bang as though a huge shot had been fired off. But we did not stray from our course, and Brother Christel blessed the bread and the wine and gave us the body of our dear little Lamb to eat and the blood that He spilled to drink. How we felt at this communion with our

Lord I cannot describe. It was also important to us because it is the first one here in the wilderness, perhaps as long as the forest has stood.

Now, dear Brethren, I lay myself and my Brethren down in the loving motherly heart of our Husband. Think of us for our dear little Lamb. We are your poor children and especially the blood of our dear little Lamb.

Johannes Hagen

[The text of Hagen's funeral service follows in verse.]

4

SEPTEMBER 29–DECEMBER 31, 1747

MARTIN MACK

On September 29
Martin Mack arrived yesterday evening in Shamokin. The Brothers and Sisters were wondrously overjoyed because they had so greatly desired to see someone from Bethlehem. He found them in their hearts to be quite happy but in their bodies to be exhausted and sickly. I gave them the little letters and many heartfelt greetings and kisses.

On September 30 (Wednesday)
We wrote to Bethlehem and reported the circumstances in Shamokin as they currently stand. Martin spoke with Shikellamy and conveyed a greeting from Brother Joseph [Spangenberg] and gave him a small present, which was most pleasing to him because he was sickly and weak after the long illness.[1]

On October 1 (Thursday)
Brother Post departed from here to Bethlehem. It was quite quiet here in Shamokin today. Brother Anton had many visitors in his blacksmith's shop.

On October 2 (Friday)
We were happy and blessed with one another. We held a heartfelt discourse about our little Lamb of God and his Gemeine, to which we also belong and are members of the same.

On October 3 (Saturday)
Martin visited Shikellamy. He begins to get better. He asked me when it was Sunday. I said tomorrow.

On October 4 (Sunday)
It was Sunday. It was very quiet in Shamokin. Martin read several letters to the Brothers and Sisters from Bethlehem that he had brought with him. The little Lamb was close to us. We felt very close in our hearts to the Brothers and Sisters in Bethlehem. Sister Hagen fell very ill again today. We commended her to the heart of the Lamb.

On October 6 (Tuesday)
Shikellamy asked that I make him a skid. At this I went off into the bush and looked for a tree. Shikellamy's son wanted to have an axe worked on by the blacksmith today. But he could not get it done. The Brothers and Sisters were all sick today. Martin was their sick-waiter. (The Daily Text was "and I will make of thee a great nation, and I will bless thee, and make thy name great; and thou shalt be a blessing.")[2]

On October 7
The sickness continued. We commend our condition to the little Lamb's heart, especially that of the sick ones (because he is the best doctor).

On October 8
Martin opened Anton's vein, and he quickly became better. We thanked the little Lamb. Sister Hagen had a difficult night (she felt as though she was being crushed because her chest was so heavy).

On October 9
Anton went down the Susquehanna to the ferry with a canoe to see whether he could pick up our provisions there.[3] We could not find anyone to go with him, and so he had to go alone. We prayed to the little Lamb and His holy angels. (Because Sister Hagen is so sick on the chest that she cannot breathe, Martin opened her vein and the little Lamb blessed this so that she became better from this hour on.) We thanked the Lamb greatly. Sister Schmidt has had the fever all these days. In the evening Conrad Weiser and his son[4] arrived here. Shikellamy told him that he should stay in our house. He came in our house and behaved very modestly. He said that Shikellamy had told him he should lodge here. We told him that this was fine.

On October 10
Our sick ones recovered. We thanked the little Lamb from our hearts. (Conrad gave Shikellamy [text corrupt] and two for his sons.)

On October 11
It was Sunday, and we were quiet but also quite cramped. Martin discussed much with Conrad Weiser. He showed himself to be quite friendly.

On October 12
Conrad Weiser and his son departed again. He bade us a friendly farewell. He asked that when we traveled through Tulpehocken that we not pass his house [without stopping].

Today fourteen warriors came home from the Flatheads (Catawba) and brought a blessing for their home with them. They had lost five of their people, and several were wounded. They soon visited us and behaved very well. In the evening the dear heart Brother Zeisberger and Brother Post arrived from Bethlehem. We were much overjoyed by their arrival, and they brought us much written and spoken news about our dear congregation. We had a blessed evening and a sinner-like evening meeting. Shikellamy soon came to our house and saw who had arrived. He recognized David and gave him his hand. He was very happy. David began to talk with him immediately.[5]

On October 13
Our sick ones were a great deal better. Martin and David asked Shikellamy to come to them and gave him greetings from Brother Joseph [and his Brethren] and gave him a present that Brother Joseph had sent. This pleased him greatly, and he was very happy. He began to discourse with David and said it would be good if he [David] were to live in Shamokin; then he could talk to him sometimes. We discussed several things with him and that we held him dear and reminded him that our Brother Johannes [Johannes de Watteville] over the great water, with whom he had traveled to Ostonwakin and Wyoming, also held him dear. He was pleased about this and said he remembered him well. And then it was midday. We said that he should have a midday meal with us, which pleased him greatly.

Today more warriors arrived who were going to the Flatheads (Catawba). There were several Shawnee among them who had stayed this summer in Gnadenhütten. They knew me well and were also able to visit us in our house. In the evening we had a very blessed evening service. We commended ourselves to the little Lamb's heart, just as we were, and thanked him with all our hearts that we have a little place in Shamokin, where we can live together in peace and quiet.

On [October] 14 (Wednesday)
We were visited a lot by Indians. Today a great many of them were drunk, and they made a lot of noise.

On [October] 15

We spoke with Shikellamy. He was very open with us. Our Brother Anton must once again return to us from the ferry by land because the Susquehanna is so shallow that you cannot float on it. We wrote to Bethlehem again today and reported our circumstances.

On [October] 16

In the morning Shikellamy came to David [Zeisberger] and said that he sent greetings to Brother Joseph and his Brethren and wanted to let them know that he was quite well again. Brother Post departed from here again for Bethlehem. Martin and David split boards to lay a floor in our house, as the ground is very damp and unhealthy, especially for the Sisters.

On October 17

We thought a great deal about our dear Bethlehem. We felt a Sabbath-like air in our hearts. We perceived the little Lamb of God in us and had a blessed evening Quarter of an Hour, laid our plan in Shamokin to the heart of the Lamb, asked Him that he should soon gladden our hearts with souls also from this nation.

On October 18

It was very quiet here. We were very blessed with one another and held a Lovefeast today. Martin read out something to the Brothers and Sisters from the letters he had received from Bethlehem (spoke with Anton and her again because the little Lamb was especially close today). We had a blessed evening Quarter of an Hour. We thought of our dear Bethlehem often and the blessed hours that one enjoys there.

On October 19

Shikellamy visited us a great deal. Anton worked for him the whole day in the blacksmith's shop. Martin and David looked for charcoal. In the evening we had a little house conference with one another.

On October 20

The Susquehanna had risen more than 2 feet so that Jed and Anton traveled down to the ferry by land to see whether they could bring the canoe and the provisions that are there for us up by water. We accompanied them with our love and prayer. We had a blessed evening Quarter of an Hour.

On October 21

Shikellamy's wife died.[6] They let off five shots immediately. He, Shikellamy, shot twice out of his hut. They buried her in the afternoon. It was conducted quite quietly, other than a few women who cried. He himself did not go to the burial. He also never visited her during her sickness. Many unknown Indians arrived here today from the Shawnee.

On October 22
We began to pull our turnips out because we will not get many otherwise. The Indians have visited them often up to now. In the evening we were very blessed and content with one another.

On October 23
Shikellamy visited us. He was very friendly. A Mohican woman who has love in her heart for us also visited us. Martin laid a floor in our house today. Three traders who arrived here today behaved very foolishly. But they left us in peace. In our evening Quarter of an Hour we thought a lot about our dear Brothers and Sister, especially of our Brothers David and Anton, and asked the little Lamb that He bring them back to us healthy in spirit and body.

On October 24
We were visited a great deal by Indians. We were in Bethlehem a great deal in our hearts and felt a Sabbath-like air. We also thought of our two Brothers who were supposed to arrive today. But they did not come. We commended them to the Lamb's heart, that He should protect them.

On October 25
It was Sunday. We were quiet in our house. The Indians made quite a lot of noise around us because several of them were drunk. Shikellamy fetched firewood. He is very happy that he has a skid again. Martin walked several miles down the Susquehanna, thinking that he might meet up with our Brothers. But they did not come. (We commended them to the Lamb's heart.)

On October 26
Several Delaware Indians who had been in Wyoming came down the Susquehanna. The man knew me well. He had spent two months this summer in Gnadenhütten. On the way they had heard a child crying on the shore. They went onto land with their canoe, and, as they approached the land, they found four children sitting together and crying, and the mother lay next to them dead. The smallest child was just three months old. They took the woman and children into the canoe and brought them down to Shamokin. It was a Delaware woman who had lived about 25 miles from here. They took her away again though. Two women took the children. Her husband is several days' journey

away on the hunt. We waited with longing for our two Brothers, but they did not come. We were visited a lot by Indians today. One brought a shirt to be sewed by our Sisters.

On October 27
Our two Brothers arrived here (with things). It took them three days to canoe back here. They also had a man with them whom they had paid to help. Shikellamy visited us a lot at lunchtime. We had a blessed evening Quarter of an Hour.

On October 28
In the morning, Martin and David went back down the Susquehanna to fetch Shikellamy's canoe, which Brother Anton had brought to the mill, and the people had taken it away from there and brought it to six miles this side of the mill.[7] Anton stayed at home because he has a lot of work for the Indians. Shikellamy's son brought two baskets of [char]coal today, which he had burned himself, because Anton did not have any more. He had to work for him.

On October 29
Anton was visited a great deal in his blacksmith's shop. However, he used up all the charcoal today.

On October 30
Anton worked on building up his charcoal pile. Shikellamy's son fetched the wood on the skid. Martin and David slept on an island in the middle of the Susquehanna. We were very happy among ourselves. We thought of our dear Bethlehem often. We were about 40 miles from Shamokin.

On October 31
Almost all of the Indians left for the hunt, and most are not thinking of returning until spring. Shikellamy is still at home and a few old women. Martin and David lodged on an island in the Susquehanna again about 4 miles from Shamokin. We had a very cold night, but made a big fire and the Sabbath-like air of Bethlehem kept us cheerful and content.

On November 1
We pushed off from the island early and arrived in a timely fashion at our Brothers and Sisters in Shamokin. We found them to be quite well. We thanked our little Lamb heartily that He had brought us happy and blessed back to our Brothers and Sisters. In the evening we had a blessed evening Quarter of an Hour.

On November 2
In the evening Brother Post and his Rachel and also Mrs. Mack[8] arrived here safely from Bethlehem. We were filled with incredible joy by the many heartfelt greetings and pieces of news that they brought with them. Shikellamy soon visited us and was happy to see my wife again. They immediately began a discourse with each other.[9]

On November 3
We began our Sabbath. The Watchword for the day was very significant to us. It was "and they that shall be of thee shall build the old waste places: thou shalt raise up the foundations of many generations, and thou shalt be called, 'The repairer of the breach, the restorer of paths to dwell in.'"[10] A few Indian women visited us and were very friendly. They had a sweet girl with them, and because she was smiling at my wife, Annerl, my wife kissed her, and then she was full of incredible joy. We had a blessed evening Quarter of an Hour (... and thanked the Lamb) who also had safely brought these Brothers and Sisters to us.

On November 3 [sic]
We visited Shikellamy. He was very friendly. David told him that he was planning to leave the next day. Shikellamy said, "It is not good that you are leaving again. You should stay here." We wrote today and reported our circumstances.

On November 4
Our Brothers and Sisters set off on their journey. As David [Zeisberger] and Brother Post and his Rachel and Sister Hagen [left], we commended them to the Lamb of God and His father that They might protect them on their way. We were blessed and content, discoursed in a heartfelt fashion with one another, and, in our evening Quarter of an Hour, the air of the Cross manifested itself, and we felt a joy in us at this.

On November 5
Sister Mack[11] visited Shikellamy. He was friendly. For the time being, he is quite alone among the men in Shamokin. (My Annerl also had a heartfelt bonding with Sister Schmidt, and Martin had the same with Anton.)

On November 6
We both worked on the charcoal-house roof, and toward evening we fired it. We had Shikellamy over today for lunch. It was very pleasing to him. He also

really liked the food, thanked us heartily for it, and we gave him some to take home. He lives now very poorly and has not had a bit of meat for some weeks, and no one is there to cook for him.

On November 7
We began our Sabbath. The Watchword for the day was very important to us. It was "and they that shall be of thee shall build the old waste places: thou shalt raise up the foundations of many generations, and thou shalt be called, 'The repairer of the breach, the restorer of paths to dwell in.'"[12] He bestows all the posts for the building of the church. (We had our Married Persons Quarter of an Hour for the first time together, during which the Lamb was very close to us.)[13] Oh, how often we thought of our dear Bethlehem. We felt some of the Sabbath air that was wafting around them. We also held a little Lovefeast with one another. Various Indians came home from the hunt who wanted to have something made for them by the smith. But he did not have any charcoal yet. In the evening we were much visited by the Indian women. Mrs. Mack spoke with them a little. Martin and Anton visited Shikellamy. Today an Indian brought us a piece of venison as payment because our Sister had sewed a shirt for him. In the evening we had a blessed Quarter of an Hour (thanked our little Lamb for the peace of the Sabbath).

On November 8
We were visited again by Indians. We also had a little Prayer Day among ourselves, where we read our short letters that we had recently received from Bethlehem, especially about Brother Cammerhof's and Gottlieb's travels around the land here.[14] The little Lamb was very close to us, and the air of the Cross wafted all day among us.

On November 9
Many Indians came home from the hunt to go to the blacksmith's shop and have things done to their flintlocks. Shikellamy received some venison today. He came immediately and gave us venison ribs and said, "There is also meat." He was very friendly and visited us several times. Two Shawnee visited us today also. My wife (Annerl) and Sister Schmidt pounded corn on Shikellamy's pounding block for us to eat today. This pleased Shikellamy greatly, and he was happy that our Sisters could pound corn also. We also pulled out our turnips today. (Sister Schmidt got a thorn in her foot around her ankle today, which stuck in there about an inch. It caused her much pain, and her foot swelled up much after that.)

On November 10
We received many visits from Indians. Today Martin and Anton began to build a charcoal house. In the evening we were very content and blessed with one another. We held heartfelt discourses about our little Lamb of God and His wounds and about our dear Bethlehem.

On November 11 and 12
Everything was very quiet in Shamokin. There were few Indians at home. Two Shawnee came to the blacksmith's shop from the hunt to have their flints repaired.

On November 13
We were visited by several Delaware Indians. In the evening we had a blessed Quarter of an Hour.

On November 14
We held our Sabbath. The little Lamb revealed Himself to us with a palpable blessing (especially in the Married [Persons] Quarter of an Hour). Martin and his Annerl visited Shikellamy today. We gave him some turnips. He thanked us in a friendly fashion. We also visited other huts but found few people at home. Today we also had a little Lovefeast, during which we were very content and blessed. We often thought of our dear Bethlehem during this.

On November 15
We were visited by various Indians. Martin and Anton visited Shikellamy and also ate with him at lunch. He was very cheerful. An Indian doctor visited us today also. The little Lamb blessed our evening Quarter of an Hour service.

On November 16
Everything was quite quiet here. We were blessed and content among ourselves.

On November 17
Shikellamy visited us in the early morning. He said that Anton had to shoe two horses for him. He wanted to go to Tulpehocken. Our Sisters[15] went visiting today in Shamokin and found several Delaware women at home who were friendly and pleased to receive a visit on this occasion. They had the opportunity to discourse with them.

On November 18
We were content and blessed among ourselves (we held heartfelt discourses about our little Lamb and His children). There was a great panic in Shamokin today about the canoes because the Susquehanna River had risen so much in the previous night that it had swept away almost all the canoes. Shikellamy visited us diligently today. He ate with us this evening.

On November 19
We removed our charcoal from the charcoal house. Anton shoed two horses for Shikellamy today. He looked very friendly during this.

On November 20
Shikellamy traveled today to Tulpehocken. In the afternoon two of his sons returned from the hunt. One of them had a Mohican as a wife.[16] She also returned home. She has a love in her heart for us and I believe she is open[17] in her heart. She had a little girl of about 4 years who also loves us. A sweet child that she took to the hunt fourteen days ago and a few days ago a Delaware Indian had hexed the child so that it died soon after and today she brought it to us and wanted to bury it here. The Mohican woman was crying greatly because it was the only child that she still had. This summer another child of hers died in the same way. My wife[18] visited her and was able to speak with her very sincerely.

On November 22[19]
The Mohican woman came into our house early in the day and said, "Have mercy on me, have mercy on me, make me a few nails. . . . I want to make a box for my child so then I can close the box." We promised to do this for her, and she thanked us greatly. The Mohican woman had told my wife that just before her child died she had said, "Mother I want to die. Tell the white people who live in Shamokin that I loved them and tell them that I did not steal any turnips from them; they should not think that of me but rather that if I had wanted to eat a turnip then I would have asked for one." The next day she died. The child affected us greatly because we loved her. We were also happy because we believe that she has gone to the Lamb. She looked quite joyous as she died.

On November 22 (Sunday)
We were visited by many Indians. Martin and Anna went visiting today also. Otherwise, we were much in our hearts with our Brethren in Bethlehem and the peace of the little Lamb of God lived among us. We were cheerful, blessed,

and content among ourselves. We were happy that we are sinners and blessed children through the blood of the Lamb whom he has chosen and who count among his people. Thanked him also with heartfelt tears for what He has done for us here in Shamokin. Also laid our plan for here to his heart anew so that He might make each of us follow Him with a whole heart and soon gladden us with the fruits of His bitter sweat and Blood, which He spilt also for these people as well as for us. The little Lamb blessed our evening Quarter of an Hour.

On November 23
In the morning Shikellamy's eldest son's 2-year old child died. They were very despondent and wept and let off shots. They brought our Sisters a piece of linen and said they should quickly make a shirt for the child, which they did. Martin and Anton also visited the child after it had died. They had painted it almost all over with red paint. In the evening they buried it.

Today we had many visitors from Indians of different nations. The Mohican woman made us a little present of dried cherries. She stayed with us for a long time and was friendly. We gave her a little bread. She said she would have to hide the bread, she could not let it be seen by the other Indians because they were envious of her and had accused her, "You are more loved by the white people than we are. One can see that you are one of their friends or from the nation that they love."

A Delaware Indian, who came to visit the blacksmith's shop today, and who lives not far from the Wyoming Valley, a good man, sat down this evening at our fire. There he complained to my wife Anna about his plight and said he had come a long way, and he was wet and cold and also very hungry, and he had been in Shamokin since yesterday and had still not received a single bite of food to eat, and whether she did not mind giving him a piece of bread. She gave him a piece of bread, and he thanked her greatly for it.

On November 24 and 25
It was very quiet in Shamokin. We were content and blessed in one another's company.

On November 26
A woman trader came to the house again who had been here for a while already. She had brought quite a lot of rum with her. We again had many Indian visitors today. (Catharina fell ill with a strong bout of the fever today. In the evening she became very ill.)

On the 27th Anton had a lot of work in the blacksmith's shop. Martin sewed shoes and the Sisters chopped wood and carried it here.

On the 28th November we held our Sabbath. We were blessed and content in one another's company and the little Lamb was intimately close to us, and we often thought of dear Bethlehem and the blessed air of the Cross that is there especially on the Sabbath. In Shamokin there was not much peace today because so many were drunk and made such a noise. Especially tonight they howled in an astonishing fashion around our house. But they did not disturb us. Shikellamy returned from Tulpehocken today. Martin and Anton visited him. He showed himself to be very friendly (he gave Martin a letter from Conrad Weiser and a piece of beef which Catharina's mother had sent us.) In the evening we held a blessed Quarter of an Hour service, and we blessedly and happily laid ourselves down in the arms of the little Lamb.

On November 29
Martin read the two sermons of Brother Ludwig (Zinzendorf) today that were very blessed to us. The Sisters went visiting today and found several good women at home. My wife, Annerl, had the opportunity to speak with the Mohican woman today about the love of God's little Lamb for us, during which she and her husband listened attentively. The Mohican woman also told my wife, Annerl, that last spring she had felt something in her heart like her cousin (that is Nathaniel, the Indian) and Martin had been present and since that time she had been troubled in her heart. The Mohican woman asked my wife, Annerl, what she thought about her child who had died, whether it were with (our) God and whether we all believe that it is with (our) God. My wife, Annerl, said that if she got to know our God then she would find her little girl with Him, because our God was also her God, and He loved us all equally and loved us so much that he died out of love for us. The Mohican woman also related to us further about her little girl that since her cousin (Nathaniel) and her husband, Martin, had been there that the girl had often spoken the words that she had heard from her cousin and until she had died she had been very obedient. The Mohican woman became very agitated and was happy and did not know why. Her husband was present during this discourse and paid great attention. He is Shikellamy's eldest son. Today Anton visited Shikellamy and gave him a present of turnips, for which he thanked us cordially. In our evening Quarter of an Hour service we laid all our concerns at the heart of the little Lamb, especially the Mohican woman concerned us greatly. We were able to pray for her to the little Lamb with our whole hearts that He might take mercy on her and open her heart.

On November 30
Anton had much work in the blacksmith's shop. We were visited by various Indians.

On December 1
The Mohican woman visited us. Also, Shikellamy. (My Annerl was sick again today. She had cramps in the side. Otherwise, we were contented in one another's company, held heartfelt discourse on the wounds of our God, the little Lamb.)

On December 2
Shikellamy's sons left for the hunt again. He is quite alone again at home. He visited us today. Also ate lunch with us.

On December 3
We were visited by several Delaware Indians. It snowed the whole day today and through the night. The snow was knee-deep. Shikellamy visited us diligently today.

On December 4
Shikellamy's sons returned from the hunt because they could not get away on account of the deep snow.

On December 5
We were happy and contented in one another's company. We felt something of the Bethlehem Sabbath air in our hearts and the little Lamb was tangibly close to us, and His Blood warmed our hearts and smelted us together anew. In our evening Quarter of an Hour service we thanked our little Lamb heartily for all He has revealed to us until now in Shamokin and that He has taken our part in such a loyal fashion both in internal and external things.

On December 6
(Anton, who had not been feeling well for a time now had a very bad cough today and took something in order to sweat). Martin and his wife, Annerl, visited Shikellamy and took him a present of turnips; he thanked them and was very friendly. Many Indian women visited us today, among them the Mohican woman who was very friendly.

On December 7
Shikellamy visited us diligently. He also inquired whether Martin and Annerl would stay in Shamokin this winter. The Mohican woman told him however

that she did not think we would stay here much longer. To this he replied that he would be very sad that those people always left who could speak to him. He had nothing against that we traveled now and again, if only there were always someone there with whom he could talk. He loved us very much as though we were his own children and for this reason he liked to visit us occasionally and talk with us. Shikellamy also told the Mohican woman today that we had often told him that he should fetch himself some turnips to eat. But he was too embarrassed to fetch something from us because we were poor ourselves and did not have much. Yes, if I could give them something, that would be better, he said. In the evening he sent the Mohican woman to us and had her ask us for a little piece of meat for his sick child. He desired some so much, and he did not have a single bite in his house to give him. We sent him some for which he was very thankful!

On December 8
Anton worked the whole day in his shop for Shikellamy. The Sisters went visiting again today. Two traders, who live on the other side of the Susquehanna, were here today to have some work done in the blacksmith's shop. In the evening the Mohican woman and her husband visited us. They said that we were a very different kind of people than those that she knew already of the white people. They did everything evil as much as they (the Indians) did, but about us they said that we were able to live so nicely with one another and were so friendly and loved one another so much and were so content the way the other people could not be. And they were mostly all like this, the ones they had seen of T'girhitondi's people. T'girhitondi must really have good people where he lives. At this the Mohican's husband said that he had traveled with T'girhitondi two years ago.[20] He had never in his life traveled with such good people or such a good man as with him, and then he said that in the spring they wanted to visit T'girhitondi and his people. We had the opportunity to tell these two people something about our God the little Lamb, what he can do for poor people when they believe in him and that He helps them too because he loves them astonishingly much. At this they asked after the big man[21] and all the people who had been with him four years ago, whether they were still alive, that they were good people also. We said yes, they were still alive, and they also loved them greatly and wished that they would get to know our God who had spilled his blood out of love for us so that we could be eternally happy together with him. In our evening Quarter of an Hour service we commended our plan anew to the heart of the little Lamb, we also commended the Mohican woman to his loyal and dear heart, that he would take mercy on her and reveal his dear heart to her.

On December 9 and 10

We were content and blessed with one another. We thought a great deal about our dear Bethlehem, also desired to hear something soon about their business, that the little Lamb tells them, asked the Lamb to receive their prayers that they were sending him for us and tell them that they should ask him to allow us to be part of them and that he should remain among us with his peace as he had done until now and allow us to keep his love and intimacy with us.

On December 11

The Mohican woman and her husband visited us. We were able to speak with them from the heart.

On December 12

We held the Sabbath (we had a blessed Married Persons Quarter of an Hour). Martin and his wife visited Shikellamy and also the Mohican woman and her husband. They once again told us much about T'girhitondi and that they desired greatly to visit him if their horses had not wandered so far into the bush, then they would go with us.

On December 13

We were visited by Indian women. Shikellamy's daughter visited us with a sick child. She asked for a piece of bread for the sick child. We gave it to her. She was very grateful. (Martin opened Catharina Schmidt's vein today, which she tolerated well.) The little Lamb was very close to us during the evening Quarter of an Hour.

On December 14 and 15

It was very quiet here. Shikellamy visited us diligently. He stays with Anton in the blacksmith's shop most of the time. A few days ago he had tools made for himself.

On December 16

It snowed very heavily all day, so that the snow is now more than 2 feet deep. Shikellamy ate lunch with us today. He thanked us greatly for it. Martin chopped firewood. The Mohican woman also visited us.

On December 17 and 18

There was a great frost here and such a bitter wind that the snow in many places had drifted to more than four feet deep. Shikellamy stayed with us a lot.

On December 19
The Susquehanna was frozen over. Two Delaware Indians came here to the blacksmith's shop, to have their flints mended. One was the brother of Beata. He had been in Gnadenhütten a lot this past summer. He knew us both well. (We had our Married [Persons] Choir Quarter of an Hour today. Our dear Bethlehem was much in our hearts. We desire to hear something from there.)

On December 20 (Sunday)
We were visited by several Delaware Indians. They begged for several turnips from us and behaved modestly. Another child of Shikellamy's son has died. They were very sad because five children of the one son have died this year. We were content and blessed with one another.

On December 21
Anton received a great deal of work in his blacksmith's shop. We were visited by various Indians.

On December 22
We were visited by many Indians. Shikellamy and his sons spent most of the day with us because Anton worked for them the whole day. In the evening Quarter of an Hour the little Lamb was very close to us and his blood melted our hearts in many tears.

On December 23
There were many drunken Indians around here. They made a lot of noise with dancing and drumming. It sounded quite terrifying. Otherwise, we were quite blessed and content with one another. Held heartfelt discourses about our little Lamb of God and his children in our evening Quarter of an Hour. We laid all our circumstances at the heart of the little Lamb.

On December 24
We thought countless times about our dear Bethlehem and about the blessed Christmas Eve vigil. Oh, how our hearts desired to enjoy that too and to hear something soon.

On December 25
It was quite quiet here. We were much in our hearts with our Brothers and Sisters in Bethlehem. We had a little Lovefeast at noon time, for which each of us had a little bread roll baked in the ashes. We were quite content with

this and we felt the tender meditations on our behalf of our Brothers and Sisters. In the evening my wife visited the Mohican woman. There were several people in her hut. She asked Annerl if today were Sunday. My wife answered no, it was Christmas Day. Oh, said the Mohican woman and her husband. Why are you so quiet? The white people usually have a fun time on that day. You are definitely a quite different kind of people than the white people we know. Yes, said Annerl, that we are. It is a great day, and we are quiet and gaze with our hearts on the Husband, God, who holds us so dear that he [text corrupt]. Annerl and she had the chance to talk about the little Lamb with him. We were visited today by several Delaware Indians. Our evening Quarter of an Hour was blessed by the little Lamb in our hearts. We made a present to Shikellamy and his people today of turnips, which were very welcome.

On December 26
We were visited by several Indians (today we had a blessed Married Persons Quarter of an Hour. The little Lamb dissolved our hearts into many tears and tied us to one another anew). Martin and his wife (Annerl) visited Shikellamy and the other huts also. In the evening we were blessed and content in one another's company. Held heartfelt discussions about our happiness that the little Lamb had accepted us to be among his children and had brought us to the Gemeine. We were humbled and grateful, gave ourselves to him anew, promised to live for him and with willing hearts to be cheerful stewards of his will.

On December 27 (Sunday)
A trader came to our house and brought some work for the blacksmith. We told him that today was Sunday. He was surprised that today was Sunday. He said they had observed Sunday yesterday. Martin read a sermon by Brother Ludwig.[22] In the evening we read the Litany of the Wounds.[23] We could feel the closeness of the little Lamb.

On December 28 and 29
Many Indians returned home from the hunt. Anton had much work in his blacksmith's shop. Most of the time our house was full of Indians. We were blessed and content among ourselves. We very much desire to see someone from Bethlehem here.

On December 30
My wife (Annerl) visited the Mohican woman. Various Shawnee were in her house. They told the Mohican woman that this last summer they had been in

the place where we had lived and had enjoyed much that was good.[24] And many good people lived there, and they gave one something to eat immediately when one arrived there. The Mohican woman and her husband showed a great desire to go there also. After this, my wife visited Shikellamy. He gave her a shirt that she should wash for him, which she accepted. In the afternoon the Mohican woman visited us. She complained bitterly that she had nothing left to eat and there were so many people who had come to lodge in her house. We gave her some turnips. Apart from this, we had nothing ourselves. In the night, two Delaware women arrived who complained bitterly for some flour. They said they had a sick person in their house. We gave them a little and said that we had only little ourselves and had not planted any this year. We could not spare any more.

On December 31
Several Indian families came home from the hunt. Anton had a lot of work with their flints and axes. Martin helped him with forging and hammering. Shikellamy ate with us at lunchtime. He was friendly. In the evening we held a little Lovefeast with one another and held a short Watch Night service.[25] We reminded ourselves of what the little Lamb of God had done for us this year, especially in Shamokin. We thought of our dear Bethlehem often during this and asked the little Lamb to make us part of their thoughts on this night also. We closed this year with a heartfelt prayer to the little Lamb and, with many hot tears, thanked Him heartily for His loyal and loving heart, which we have experienced this year greatly, and that He might forgive us for all that we have omitted to do and also for all that we have done wrong, that He might make it good again and wash us anew and clean us with His blood. Thanked him for our plan, which He has entrusted to us out of His grace. We laid especially at His heart the poor heathens among whom we lived, especially the Mohican woman and her husband and Shikellamy. We would like to see them saved soon. We blessed one another with a kiss of love during several Blood Verses and then laid ourselves down to sleep.[26]

Martin and Anna [Mack]
Anton and Catharina [Schmidt]

5

JANUARY 4–APRIL 18, 1748

JOSEPH POWELL

On Monday, January 4, 1748 [Sunday].[1]
Bro. Cammerhof kept with us the sacrament. Were quicken'd and much Bless'd thereby.

On January 5
Parted with our Dear Brothers and Sisters with many Tears. Powell accompani'd me to Eva Creek. Felt in our Evening little meeting Our Heart, low and Melted. Commended to our Dear Lamb our whole Circumstances, laying on his tender Heart the Condition of the poor Indians, prayed [to] him for this part of the World, which till now has been govern'd by Satan, lying under the powers of Darkness. Felt our Hearts *getrost* [comforted] and our Lord's promise True, that here in the midst, where three Meet in his Name.

On January 6
Came Mrs. Harris with three Traders, one of which asked Bro. Powell if we'd Employ him to split rales, to which he reply'd, Friend, it may be good first for us rightly to view this Matter then. You know splitting Rales is hard work, said he, but I'd rather do it, being Oblig'd by Trading to live so Wicked a life.

On January 7 and 8
Bro. Powell continu'd splitting Rales. Bro. Antone had many visits from Indians. Brought much work. Paid in skins. Have here so many languages that we find it very Difficult to learn anything, then it's rare to hear two Indians talking in one language. Prayed our Lamb to help and that his will might be done in us.

On January 9, Sabbath
Enjoyed our Love Feast with *Innig* [inner] Satisfaction, thro' many blessings we had enjoyed in the Dear Church ware us by this opportunity *erinnerlich* [reminded]. Thanked our Dear Savior for allowing us this privilege here. Visited us three Tootlers [Tutelo]; wonder'd we kept two Sundays; never said they knew why the white people keep more than one. In the evening, sang part of the Wounds Litany.

On January 10
Visited Shikellamy. Being Snow Weather could not well go further, invited him to sup with us.

On January 11 and 12 and 13
Came many from hunting, visited us. Some employed Br. Anton, were all very friendly and glad to see us.

On January 12 and 13
Bro. Powel widened our fence, made a field about two Acres.

On January 16
Were Cheerful and Happy together by our Sabbath Lovefeast. Our Neighbour, the Mohican, came with an other woman to visit Sister. She wept. Told the other woman it troubled her that she could not understand and speak with Sister Smith more.

On January 19 and 20 and 21 and 22
Were well, thought oft on the Sinners and prayed our Lord to help and bless our Dear Brothers and Sisters there and on the Road. Believed they thought on us and love us (tho' worth but little) as their Flesh and bone.

On January 23, Sabbath
Had as usually at 10 in the morning our marriage Quarter of an Hour. Felt the Peace of our Lamb thereby had a Sweet undisturbed Day. Enjoyed Our love feast. Love and understand each Other. Felt true fellowship. A little past Midnight was a Earthquake, which so shook our House and Beds that some of us awaked.

On January 24
Bro. Powell visited some families. Found all well. Invited Shikellamy to Dinner.

On January 25

Entertained and lodged a man of Mr. Magee, who came in Exceeding wet, having waded the Creek. Powell and he being of one Religion spoke freely with each other from real Christian principles and how a man Should and would act to have a clear Conscience and particular in Dealing with the Indians. At going to Sleep had our usual Quarter of an Hour.

On January 26

In the morning brought him in a Canoe over the River with Difficulty, being full of Ice. Was very thankful, behaving with great Respect. We observ'd [that] the Traders can with eagerness go through the greatest hardships and Difficulties for sake of gain.

On January 27

Heard by a Trader that Mr. Magee was Exceedingly Troubled having heard by two Indians that Bro. Cammerhof and Powell ware Drowned the Day we left his House.

On January 28

Came two Indians from the War with the Cattobats [Catawba] being all [who] are escaped from a number [who] went out last Spring. We hear [that] the Day they were killed, they two that are escap'd left the other and came behind a Towne of the Cattobats, expecting to kill some as they Came out. A little before, went on Out of the Town about 30 men verry Swift on foot and took the others and having scalped them cut their flesh all over their bodies to the bone while they were yet alive.

On January 29

Shikellamy made us a present of half a Deer. Gave it heartily.

On January 30

Had a still sweet Sabbath. Felt in particular our Lamb's peace. Offer'd him our Worthless poor hearts. Beg'd him to take and keep them as Reward of His pain. In the Evening two Delaware Desir'd Room for a Bundle of skins. We refus'd it, fearing others Should Demand them to whom they Did not belong—

On January 31 [Sunday]

Bro. and Sister Smith went a visiting, found very few at home. Shikellamy ask'd Powell if he'd Make him a long fence. Said he'd Pay in Skins. Told him Powel had Not time.

On February 1
Came two Traders down the river. Call'd of Shikellamy. But came not to us. We see that tho' we behave Friendly toward the Traders, yet when one happens to come in our house he's as a fish out of water—thank our Lord that they trouble us so little.

On February 2 and 3
Had Several visits from Indians we had not before seen. Some have no corn at all and cannot buy with Skins But are oblig'd first to change them For Brandy and with that buy corn.

On February 4
Came in the evening to James Logan's a Delaware by name Peter Cutfinger. Had two wives, heard his company in the Night ware very Drunk with Licker they brought.

On February 5
Came Early to see us two of our next Neighbours, purely that we might see they ware Sober. Logan prepar'd to go to Wyomack to buy Corn but was prevented by the Excessive Coldness of the weather.

On February 6
Sabbath was to us a Day of Rest. Sang by our love feast this verse, where three in love do live with Blood Baptis'd, a Church is seen tho' little not Despis'd.

On February 7 [Sunday]
Ware much troubl'd with a Drunken Delaware, Shikellamy being not at home.

On February 8
Sister Smith had a Could fit of fever, attended with Excessive pain in the Back.

On February 9
The Indians continu'd very Drunken; women and Children all made our House their Refuge.

On February 10
Sister had again the fever seemly hard, attended with much pain as before. Came from Wyoming a Mohican. Had a pretty Child, was by her Husband drove away, he having beside his three Wives.

On February 11
Shikellamy and his Eldest son, John, Return'd from hunting, being so Excessive cold that they could not hunt. Ware Oblig'd in about a week to Return without flesh, invited him to Dinner, had a hunter's appetite.

On February 12
Samuel Daniels, a Delaware, came for his gun [that] Bro. Antone had Mended, but Refus'd to pay. Shikellamy being by was Displeased with him, would have had us kept the gun by force till he paid. but it was not so in our hearts, being unwilling to make him our Enemy. He came afterward, paid. We supposed Shikellamy had spoke with him about it.

On February 13
Had a Netlech [*niedlich*] love feast Sister Smith gave, being her Birth Day.

On February 14 [Sunday]
In the Evening Bro. Powell had the fever, was unwilling to be sick, pray'd our Dear Lamb to keep and Restore his health and it was so.

On February 15
Came four Delaware. Bro. Antone mended their guns. They behav'd modestly and in the evening Return'd to the Trader over the water.

On February 16
Sister Smith got Cold, the which was attended with great hoarseness in the throat; suppose she got after a sweat she took for the fever.

On February 17 and 18
Were all well. Pray'd our Lord to keep our Hearts in Simplicity clos'ly Connected with Him and his people in health or Sickness.

On February 19
Indians ware most all Drunk except Shikellamy and his Eldest Son, he being tir'd with the noise he must Continually hear in his Own House, came to us Dined with us, was Displeas'd tho' knew not how to prevent the greatest Disorder they oft made in his own House.

    We hear Severall Nations will join to take a Town of the French call'd Teockhansoutehan.

On February 20
Sabbath felt our Hearts in union with our Savior's flock (without was nothing but tumult and noise). We had peace. Were Shut up secure and free as Sheep who know their Shepherd Watcheth and Slumbereth not.

On February 21
Visited us an Old Delaware, said when he Dye'd he Shou'd go to Hell, and he thought it would be soon, perhaps tomorrow, being very Old. Ask'd him how he came to believe so. Said he, I have liv'd with white People (who can read and know many things from God), and they all say so.

On February 22
Sister Smith has the fever.

On February 23
The Indians Continu'd verry Drunken. One Woman Burnt her Back exceedingly, for which reason we hear She'd continu'd Drinking that thereby of the Smart she might be Unsensible. Came a little before Midnight to our Door, swearing Bitterly. She using her best Endeavours to break it Down, but Bro Antone prevented it with a Bar of Iron, but the hinges she Beat almost off.

On February 24
Heard Neighbour Magee lay Exceeding Ill.

On February 25
Mrs. Harris Sent Desiring we'd immediately both came over, understanding by the messenger that her Man William had beat her and wanted to rob her of her Skins. We Refus'd to go, telling him to speak about it to Shikellamy. Shikellamy and two of his sons went. We wrote to her thus:

> Dr. Mrs. Harris. We are willing if Possible, to serve and help you, but in and with such a matter we cannot meddle; then we are People of Peace and love living alone for our Dear Lord in this World.
>
> *Smith and Powell*

She's a Woman we Respect and wish well. Have far less hopes of a Self-Righteous person than of her.

On February 26
Shikellamy sent his son John to visit Mr. Magee. Hear by him that he is something Better. Most of the Delaware are gone. We hear some intend to return at planting.

On February 27
Sabbath. Suppos'd the Sacrament to be in Bethlehem. Thank'd our Savior for the Sweet fellowship we felt.

On February 28, Sunday
Shikellamy brought us to Read a Treaty held with the Indians of the Six Nations in Philadelphia this year.[2] Had also a Letter of Recommendation wrote and given him by the Governor, which we read to him. Was much pleas'd. Breakfasted with us.

On March 1
Mrs. Harris send us Milk, the which [sic] we expected. Returning her thanks.

On March 2 and 3
Were all well, the Daily Expectation of hearing from Bethlehem gave us *muth* [courage].

On March 4
Had no flesh. Confer'd with one another how to get a little. In the evening a Delaware Woman brought and gave a fine fresh piece, her husband being just com[e] in from hunting.

On March 5
Sabbath—Sister had the fever seemly hard. A Mingo desired to sleep with us, told us Shikellamy had no room. We admitted him.

On March 6
An Old Shawnee brought work to Bro. Antone. Told us he came wide [far] thro' the Bush. Said he had been many Days verry Hungry, but every Day thought I can just get to the Smith I shall get Bread. We gave him some. His name is Neshanockeow. This is the man who told Shikellamy and Sister Mack, hearing the first time she was here, that we were like Pigeons. If he suffer'd a paire here to reside, they Draw to them whole Troops and take from him all his Lands.

On March 7
Shikellamy brought us flesh, his Son John being just come from hunting. Both din'd with us. Shikellamy told us that he and his three Sons would visit the T'girhitondi[3] as soon as the other two sons Return'd from Wyoming. Sister Smith had the fever. Shikellamy ask'd againe if we'd fence a long field. Told him we could hardly Grub and get this of our own ready before planting time, to which he reply'd the T'girhitondi should send here more Brothers.

On March 10
Were all well and well employ'd. Antone in his shop, Powel and Catherine Grubing and Burning Grubs. Lov'd one another, felt the peace of God in our Midsts.

On March 11
Were very still, most of the Indians, being from home.

On March 12
Enjoy our Sabbath in Stillness and inward Satisfaction.

On March 13
Shikellamy Dined with us. Inquir'd if the T'girhitondi was in Bethlehem and how wide from Tulpehocken.

On March 14 and 15
Severall Indians brought Bundles and Basketts of all what they had. Beg'd we'd give them room till they return.

On March 16
Andrew Smith, a Trader, Slept with us. Was verry Exact in behaviors and thankful, told us Conrad Weiser was on his journey to Allegheny with the intent to prosecute the Traders there that sold Liquor to the uttermost Severity of a new Act made February last.[4] Had in the Evening our little Quarter of an Hour as usual.

On March 17 and 18
Had many visits from traveling Indians who ware here Detained by the Exceeding highness of Water. Our Town at present is an Island, being encompass'd with Water about 8 foot Deep.

On March 19
Were well in Body and Spirit with our hearts resting on the Merits of our Bleeding Lover.

On March 20
The Indians that were here Detain'd got very Drunken, but ware not to us troublesome further than the noise they made the whole Night. One Woman had a Child, which we in the night heard Cry Bitterly. We Suppos'd her to have throw'd it in the fire.

On March 21 and 22
Being Snow and bad weather to work out made Some alterations in our House. Made our room Door in the South End, being before inconvenient. Having happen'd that Indians came in and upstairs without coming in our Dwelling room. Built also a large fore House on the South End, the wideness of the house.

On March 23
Mrs. Harris made us a present of Some milk.

On March 24
A young Delaware woman Desir'd to hide by us a keg of Brandy; we refus'd it, telling her she was not unsensible how the Indians abus'd and beat their poor Wives when Drunk. If She'd take our advice, She'd immediately throw it in the Susquehanna, being the justest way for her to be set free from too poor a way of Living.

On March 25
Widen'd our fence nearer Shikellamy. Planted before our House 14 pretty large Peach and apple Trees. Shikellamy Desir'd we'd write by him to the T'girhitondi. Said he intend'd in the morning with his Eldest Son to set out for Bethlehem. Was Displeas'd his other sons Stay'd so long at Wyoming, intending to have had them with him.

On March 26, Sabbath
We help'd them with their horses and to pack up. Gave them Bread to eat on the Road. Wrote to Bro Joseph, then a Direction from Tulpehocken to Bethlehem. Wrote in English and Dutch.

On March 27 [Sunday]
Came two Mingoes, brought work to Bro. Antone. Let one of them Blood, having bad Eyes and paine in armes and side.

On March 28
Was not one Indian man on this side of The River and only one woman and a few Children.

On March 29
Shikellamy's sons Return'd from Wyoming. Sister Smith had a hot fever.

On March 30 and 31
Came home. Saw families of Tutelars. We think they are worst Sort under all the Indians; are by all opportunities Stealing and begging and yet thereby Self Righteous.

On April 1
Came two Delaware. One was brother to Gottlieb's wife. Was friendly. Told us Gottlieb liv'd with them 15 miles up the River.

On April 2
Mrs. Harris visited us, brought us Milk. Told us Gottlieb's Brother-in-law was with her and Spoke many Evil things of the Brethren. Said the Indians told him in Gnadenhütten that the Brethren wanted to Make them to Slaves and that they just pull'd of Sum Indian Corn Cobbs of their own planting, and a Brother met them and took it from them and Beat them. Told us also that Zacheus's wife complain'd Exceedingly to her of her husband. Said he used her, Exceeding ill and wept Bitterly.

On April 3 [Sunday]
Shikellamy's two Sons and their Wives Went with the Tutelars down the River. A Trader not wide from the Mill Sent the Tutelar Nation Word that he had for them a Long Sack of flour and a Barrell of Brandy. We hear his intention is by this opportunity to Deal with them.

On April 4
Came Down the River in a Bark Canoe; Warriors. Bro. Antone made them What they Wanted. They behav'd Exceeding Well. In the Evening Drum'd and Danced after the Warriors' Method with Drawn Swords and other

Weapons in their hands. Each had a brown Coat trim'd with Lace which appear'd like Gold.

On April 5
In the Morning took their Leave. Intended to go to Harris's Ferry and from thence to the Catawba by land.

On April 6 and 7
Powel and Sister Smith Plow'd. It Went Much better than we Expected.

On April 8
Came home some of the Delaware. Brought us flesh. Lent Mrs. Harris an English song book, she having oft ask'd to see one.

On April 9, Sabbath
Were well. Were continually looking and Expecting to see Brothers and Sisters. This being oft our Meditation both by Day and Night, to hear from our Dear Congregation. Could with many tears thank our Lamb for the peace and unity he lets us seek and enjoy. This makes each burden as a feather light.

On April 10 [Sunday]
Had some visits from strangers we had not before seen.

On April 11
Mrs. Harris brought here several Indians who came about 50 miles down the North Branch. Had much Work for the Smith.

On April 12
Came 4 warriors, being part of an army that went last Spring; the other part return'd another road. Had one Scalp, the head or Captaine visited us several times, behav'd with greatest Civility. We find the warriors in general, men Worthy of Respect.

On April 13
The Captain, Desiring a little meal, we gave him Some. We could Speake but little with them, but to show their love, they came and made us Musick and took their leave.

On April 14 and 15
Finish'd plowing, but could make no Gardens for want of Seed. Could get none that's of any use. Bro. Antone had the fever verry strong.

On April 16, Sabbath
Were all well. Committed our whole Circumstances to the keeping and care of our Dear Lamb, looking to his loving Breast, letting him do what's Best.

On April 17
Bro. Antone had a second fit.

On April 18
Came our Dear Martin and David. Were by them unspeakably Refresh'd. Were asham'd with hearts bow'd for our Dear Lamb for all his care and faithfulness to us, his Sinners.

6

APRIL 18–JUNE 28, 1748

MARTIN MACK

*Short Report of the Heidenpaß (Valley of the Heathen)
in Shamokin*

On April 18, 1748
Martin and David arrived safely at noon among our Brothers and Sisters in Shamokin. They were heartily gladdened as they saw us, as they had greatly desired to see someone from Bethlehem for a long time. We communicated news to them both in writing and words and shared many kisses and greetings. We spent the afternoon with love, and God's little Lamb strengthened the Brothers and Sisters anew. The Mohican woman and her husband soon visited us and were very friendly, asked if my wife were still alive. I said yes, about which they were thankful. In the evening we had a blessed evening Quarter of an Hour.

On April 19
Shikellamy and his son came home from Tulpehocken. Martin welcomed him. He was very surprised that we had arrived before him. In the evening David and Paul [Brother Powell] visited him. He was very cheerful. Anton was very sick today. He had a strong fever, which made him very weak. There was also quite a lot of noise around our house with the drunken Indians. But they left us in peace.

On April 20
Shikellamy and his eldest son visited us. They brought Paul and Anton a letter from friends and also tobacco and said that this time we had beaten them home. They breakfasted with us, were cheerful. They asked if T'girhitondi

[Spangenberg] had arrived home. We said yes, soon after he had left. "Ei," said Shikellamy, "if only I had stayed another day I could have seen him."

We read him the words that his Brothers T'girhitondi, Gallop, as well as Annuntschi, Ganosseracheri, Hajinkones, and the other Brethren in Bethlehem, Nazareth, Gnadenthal, Gnadenhütten had written to him, which he received very well. They were both particularly happy that we used the names that they had given us. They were both very cheerful and open. We were much visited by many Indians today; also many drunken ones visited us. They behave so well when they visit us though, as well as they possibly can. Paul and David planted some Indian corn and many other things. Martin wrote letters and busied himself with the Brethren. In the afternoon Sister Schmidt had a strong fever with much heat. In the evening we held a blessed Quarter of an Hour service.

On April 21
Brother Martin set off again down the Susquehanna by land to Quitapahilla to order provisions and some steel and iron for Shamokin. The Brothers and Sisters were blessed and content with one another.

On April 24, Sunday
Brother Joseph Paul [Powell] and David traveled by water down the Susquehanna. Anton and the others watched them leave with sorrow in their hearts because they are now alone at home.

On April 26
Ten warriors returned from the Flatheads [Catawba]. They immediately began to drink and caroused horribly the whole night long.

On April 27
It was once again very noisy in Shamokin because of the drunken people.

On April 28
Everywhere was filled with drunken men and womenfolk apart from old Shikellamy, who visited with Anton a lot in his shop.

On April 29
Brother Martin returned safely to Shamokin in the night with the provisions. He found Anton and us cheerful and well and joyful in their hearts. We held another blessed evening Quarter of an Hour service with one another, where we thanked the little Lamb heartily that He had helped us get here

again so safely, and, as we had been in danger for our lives a few times on the Susquehanna and sometimes could hardly see how we would get through without harm, then He helped us so palpably that we are quite astonished at His love and care toward us poor children. We committed ourselves anew to live for Him and to do His will with great cheer. We blessed one another with the kiss [of peace] and laid ourselves down in the arms of the little Lamb.

On April 30
We held our Sabbath, where we did good things for ourselves both in body and spirit. We had many visits from the warriors, who were slightly more sober. Shikellamy visited us at midday. We held a little Lovefeast with one another, at which the little Lamb truly and deeply appeared to us.

On Sunday, May 1
In the morning we heard that there were several sick people on the island. Martin sent Anton and Joseph Paul [Powell] over to visit, whom the Indians there received well and with much love. Brother Powell opened the veins of some of them. Today several of the warriors left. In the evening Shikellamy came and asked us to make a fence for him around his land so that he could plant Indian corn. We said we could not do this. We had no time, and we made suggestions to him that he should get people who could do this for him sooner. He said he could find no one. Finally, he said, "Brothers, have mercy on us and help us this time. This is the reason we suffer so much hunger, because we have no fence, and the horses eat up all our Indian corn." We said that we would consider it further. But we could not promise him anything. Around midnight the dear hearts Nathaniel and Heinrich Frey arrived here unexpectedly and brought us many heartfelt kisses and short letters. We thanked our little Lamb heartily, who has brought these two Brothers to us so safely.

On May 2
Early in the morning Shikellamy visited us. He asked who had arrived in the night. We told him that Annuntschi along with another brother had come. He was happy. There were also several warriors visiting who were very friendly. We were visited a great deal by Delaware and other nations today. Nathaniel and Martin held a conference about several issues. We were very happy today among ourselves. In the evening, Brother Nathaniel held a blessed evening Quarter of an Hour service.

On May 3

Shikellamy was with us and also ate at midday with us. After this Brother Nathaniel reported the words of T'girhitondi and his Brothers to Shikellamy. Shikellamy again asked that we build him a fence. We said that we could not do this without T'girhitondi's knowledge. He first had to ask T'girhitondi and his Brothers about the matter, which he immediately did through Brother Nathaniel, who soon is traveling there. Otherwise, he was quite cheerful and content in his own manner. In the evening Nathaniel visited Shikellamy. The Mohican woman brought a pair of shoes today and gave them to Catharina Schmidt and said that she should give them to Jannische [Anna Mack] as a sign of her love.[1]

On May 4

It was quite quiet here. Shikellamy ate at midday with us. Brother Nathaniel told him that the blacksmith was going away for a short time, so he should help keep an eye on the blacksmith's shop so that the Indians did not damage anything in it, and he should indicate to the Indians that if they brought work then they would have to wait until the smith returned. He should also keep an eye on the Brothers who stay here and see that no harm comes to them. He received this all very well. In the evening Brother Nathaniel held another blessed Quarter of an Hour for us.

On May 5

Brother Nathaniel, Joseph Paul, Anton Schmidt departed from here to Bethlehem, the latter two for a visit there. Martin and David stayed here alone, watching them depart with sorrow. We had heavy rain the whole day, thought countless times about our Brethren who had left us today. (In the evening Quarter of an Hour we committed ourselves to the little Lamb's heart just as we are.) Today Shikellamy said that he was thinking of traveling tomorrow to Thomas Magee's with his son.[2]

On May 7

Shikellamy and his son traveled to Thomas Magee. Otherwise, we had a very quiet Sabbath both outwardly and inwardly. Almost nothing happened the whole day.

On May 8 Sunday

Shikellamy and his son returned home again. We were visited by many Indians. In the evening Martin and David were very blessed in one another's company.

We rejoiced in the beautiful wounds of our Lamb of God. Our dear Bethlehem was much on our minds.

On May 9
Today the Indians got almost sixteen gallons of liquor from the woman trader across the water, and then they gathered and did not stop drinking until it was all gone. They made quite a noise, especially during the night.

On May 10
We had many visits from drunken Indians. They were friendly and modest toward us. Shikellamy ate at noon with us. He told us that he had not been able to sleep the previous night because of the drunken Indians. In our evening Quarter of an Hour, we laid these poor people in the area at the heart of the little Lamb.

On May 11
Shikellamy visited us. David learned many words from him. The Mohican woman also visited us. She brought us a little bear meat.

On May 12
We hoed in order to plant some Indian corn. Various Indians visited us and watched as we worked.

On May 13
David visited Shikellamy, and he explained to him that the horses had trampled down his Indian corn. Oh, he said, if only T'girhitondi would soon send me someone to mend my fence! We also ploughed today and planted some Indian corn. In the evening Heinrich Frey and Marcus Kiefer arrived from Bethlehem, the latter in order to make a fence for Shikellamy and the former as company for him on the journey. They brought us heartfelt little letters and little kisses that quickened us both inside and outside. Throughout the night it was very quiet with the drunken Indians. The trading woman who lived across the water moved away today too.

On May 14
It was the Sabbath. Externally we had quite a great uproar, as most were once again drunk. But in our hearts we were content and happy little birds of the Cross air. We had happy hours in one another's company, thought much of our dear Bethlehem. Shikellamy ate with us today at noon. We also let him know the words that his Brother T'girhitondi had sent to him, which he

received with pleasure and thanked us that someone had come to make him a fence. His son Tachnechdorus also visited with us much and grabbed several drunken Indians by the arm and took them out of our house. In the evening, as we were wanting to go to bed, four drunken Indian women with a drunken man came and wanted to sleep in our house. Shikellamy soon found out and came and tactfully removed them from our house.

On May 15 [Sunday]
It was quite peaceful. Shikellamy visited us quite diligently and ate with us at noon. We also visited him and his family. He also showed us today the land that he wants to have fenced in.

On May 16
Shikellamy visited us in the morning and said that I should let T'girhitondi know that he greeted him and his wife and his Brother Gallichwio and his wife and Annuntschi and Ganniatarechoo and his wife and all Brothers, and he promised that T'girhitondi had sent us to make his fence. He breakfasted with us and thanked us heartily for that. Heinrich Frey set off from here. David accompanied him until his night camp. Martin had the opportunity today to speak quite reasonably with a Delaware Indian, especially about the way in which they lived. He complained that they had to suffer so much hunger. Martin said that they had no need to suffer hunger, that they could live quite well if only they wanted to work a little and not drink so much. He said, yes, that might well be true. I said, I bewailed the poor Indians as often as I looked on them, that they allowed themselves to be dragged around by the enemy with a fool's rope when they could have it so good. He was quite reasonable to this. Today Marcus Kiefer began splitting rails for Shikellamy.[3]

On May 17
Eight canoes full of Indians came up the river, about fifty of them. They made camp opposite us, over on the island. They will move to Wyoming [Valley]. Their nation is called the Nanticoke. They have otherwise lived on the Susquehanna, where it runs into the sea.[4] They say that this fall more will follow. They all speak good English, even the children, but they have otherwise a very odd way of speaking. There are several reasonable people among them. Toward evening the dear heart David returned to me. I was very joyful, and we kissed each other and hugged, and our evening Quarter of an Hour was quite blessed. We were able to plea from the heart to the little Lamb for this whole area, that the dear Mother (the Holy Spirit) might make her Son's suffering known in the hearts of the poor Indians.

On May 18
Many of the Nanticoke people visited us. They wanted the blacksmith to mend their flints and axes. Martin began to hoe the Indian corn today, and David baked bread and at the same time washed our shirts.

On May 19
David helped Marcus Kiefer to split rails for Shikellamy. He visited with us a great deal today. Martin cooked and hoed the corn.

On May 20
Thachnechtoris, Shikellamy's son, left here with two other Oneida to go up the Susquehanna about 100 miles. An Indian from the Nanticoke came to Martin and asked for a piece of bread for his children. He said that they were crying so for white people's bread. They were used to it. Martin gave him a little piece. He was a good man. He had something of the Brethren about him in his face. He really captured my and David's heart. The Mohican woman and her husband visited with us a great deal today and were very friendly.

On May 21
We had our Sabbath. We were very blessed and cheerful in one another's company. We rested in the little Side Hole,[5] really treated ourselves, also enjoyed some quiet from without, and in our hearts were in Bethlehem a great deal. The Nanticoke left today also and traveled farther up the Susquehanna. One family, however, left to go down to the white people. David visited Shikellamy today, who is alone now most of the time and sat in his storehouse and spoke.

On May 22 [Sunday]
David visited Shikellamy. He was very open. He learned many words from him.[6] We received many visits from several Delaware Indians. In the evening we had a blessed Quarter of an Hour service, thought greatly of our Brothers and Sisters. In our hearts felt that they were with us.

On May 23
It was quiet here. Martin visited Shikellamy, who was ill. He had a headache and sick eyes. Gave him a piece of bread, for which he was very grateful.

On May 28
We were visited by many. Otherwise, we had a peaceful and blessed Sabbath, both within and without. Shikellamy, who was a little better, ate lunch with us. He stayed with us a long time and had a long discourse with David.

On May 29 [Sunday]
The Mohican woman brought us some venison. She asked for a little piece of bread, which we gave her.

On May 31
Marcus Kiefer went in to the bush to chop wood. In an hour he returned and had cut himself in the foot. David carried planks for Shikellamy's fence. Martin helped him. The dear Savior had clearly protected him today because he stepped on a big rattlesnake, and it was very angry. In the evening a trader came and, without asking permission, lodged in our house. He came up the river by land. Shikellamy came right away and was pleased. Gave him his hand in a heartfelt manner. He thought it was one of T'girhitondi's people. He also asked right away who he was, but we said no, he was a trader and unknown to us. That really upset him that he had given him his hand and had been so friendly to him.

On June 1
The trader left again. We had much rain today. Planted some cabbage. Oh, how many times today did we think of our Brothers and Sisters who were gathering today from all over in our dear Bethlehem. We also thought of all the work that the laborers had done and blessed them in our prayers.[7]

On June 2
We thought of the synod and asked the little Lamb to send us all His sympathies that we were not there in person and He should make us remembered. We also felt that the little Lamb was quite palpable among us.

On June 2
Toward evening Shikellamy came and said that he was hungry. This evening he wanted to eat his night meal with us. It tasted very good to him also. It seemed that he had nothing to eat all day because most of them were all drunk, and so they did not get to cooking. In our evening Quarter of an Hour we laid ourselves at the little Lamb's heart just as we were feeling, asked Him in a childlike fashion to bless our laborers greatly in Bethlehem in their work that they had before them and that He should make them successful in everything that He wanted them to do through the power of the Holy Mother [Holy Spirit]. In particular, the plan with the heathen because they are his great prize.

On July 3
Martin carried rails for Shikellamy. He helped him a great deal. Some unknown Indians arrived here also.

On June 4
We held the Sabbath. Were blessed and content. Rested in the little Side Hole with our Brothers and Sisters in Bethlehem, which did us much good. Felt as though they were really thinking about us today. Martin and David visited the Delaware on the island but found that there was only one sober [person] there, because the others were all drunk. Also visited on the side where we live. Came to a sick woman who was very weak and had such great pains.

On June 5
Most people were drunk here. We were also visited the whole day by them who looked quite angry. We were quiet. David visited Shikellamy. But a drunken man came right away and complained to Shikellamy that an Indian had hit him, and now he wanted to be angry. Just then the other man came along who had hit him and wanted to make things good with Shikellamy. But he chased him off and said he wanted to have nothing to do with him. He was a bad man. In the evening the Mohican woman brought us some venison.

On June 6
Marcus Kiefer went back to his work. His foot was quite better again. David helped him. A Delaware man visited us from Nescopeck. Martin hoed the corn.

On June 8
We were out working hard when in the afternoon a strong thunderstorm came, and for the Quarter of an Hour it hailed so hard that the ground was quite white afterward. The hailstones were so big that our corn that otherwise was growing so nicely and was almost three feet high was so beaten down that it was no longer recognizable. It was the best in Shamokin, and the Indians were astonished that we had such beautiful corn. We wondered whether this was the reason this happened, so that they would not get envious.

On June 9
We started to set Shikellamy's fence. He helped us and several of his people. Various Delaware Indians came down from Nescopeck and wanted to visit the blacksmith's shop. They visited us. Were very friendly to us. The Delaware Indians here were mostly all drunk. For three days they had been trying to get him [Shikellamy] to drink. He always avoided them and fled to us twice.

On June 11
We held the Sabbath. Were blessed and cheerful among ourselves. Shikellamy sent five people with six horses to Tulpehocken to fetch flour, which had been

given to him by the men in Philadelphia when he had been there last. He visited us, was very sickly. He lamented greatly that the blacksmith was absent so long. In the afternoon Martin and David brought him a piece of bread. He was very grateful. David learned many words from him.

On June 12
Various Indians arrived here and wanted to come to the blacksmith's shop and had come a long way. We also visited Shikellamy today.

On June 13
Several Delaware Indians visited us and complained that the blacksmith was away for so long. Shikellamy was with us for a long time today and ate at midday with us. He was very relaxed. We were very busy today with hoeing the corn. In the evening we were blessed among ourselves, especially in our Quarter of an Hour. Asked the little Lamb to bless the Brothers and Sisters who were on the journey to us here and to protect them in soul and body and bring them to us soon.

On June 14
We were visited by many Delaware, who were drunk.

On June 15
We were busy with hoeing the corn. In the afternoon the little Lamb brought Brothers and Sisters Paul and Anton here safely. Oh how happy we were! We thanked our little Lamb with all our hearts for the Brothers and Sisters and the heartfelt little kisses and little letters. Shikellamy came running right away and several other Indians. Welcomed them with much joy. In the evening we had a blessed Quarter of an Hour. Our hearts melted in many tears.

On June 16
We were visited much by Indians. Brought much work to Anton. Martin and David visited Shikellamy and brought the words that his Brothers T'girhitondi and Gallichwio had sent to him, which he received well, and one could tell that he was happy to hear something from his Brothers. He then asked Ganachragejat [Martin Mack] whether he had heard if his wife and children were also well. Ganachragejat said yes, he had heard that they were well. After this he said he was happy. Then he asked whether Gallichwio's [Cammerhof's] wife and his small child were well. We said that we had heard that they were well. After this he said, "I am happy." He said after this that he had seen Gallichwio's and Janekeaguhontis's child. They were 2 beautiful children.[8]

After this we told him that T'girhitondi's wife had heard that his daughter was now a widow, and so she had sent his daughter a blouse, which made a special impression on the man, and a while later he gave it to his daughter. After this she appeared so happy and light as though something wonderful had happened to her. I definitely believe that this will be a reminder for her.

On June 27
Martin and David both went out to work on Shikellamy's fence because we would very much like to have it finished. Anton was busy in his blacksmith's shop. An Indian woman brought us some venison.

On June 28
We held our Sabbath. Two traders arrived here and behaved quite scandalously. In the presence of many Indians, they called each other many shameful names that they could think of and finally they both beat each other's heads bloody. Shikellamy said, "Jachte go janneri traders!"[9]

David visited Shikellamy. He was very talkative. He asked David when Brother Johannes would be returning to the land. David said he did not know. When Brother Johannes would be back—maybe in seven years. He did not know if he would come. He had much work over there.

He asked about what T'girhitondi was doing in Virginia.[10] David said he was visiting the people who lived there. There were several Indians present, as Shikellamy began to say the Genousseracheri [Zeisberger] was still single and that Annuntschi [Seidel] too, who had been here in the past, and that many Single Brethren lived together. They had their own land where they live, and now they were building a big house.[11] They had started on it when he had been there before, and he had been in the room where the Single Brethren slept, each one having his own place for a bed. It looked as though it would be very nice.

At midday, we had a very blessed Lovefeast with one another. Oh, how our dear Bethlehem occurred to us so many times, and the blessed times that one had there when a heart is really thirsty and hungry. In the afternoon our Brethren Paul and Anton went to visit the Delaware Indians, who were friendly and revealed themselves to be full of love. In the evening Quarter of an Hour we felt ourselves to be sinners and asked the dear Mother to reveal our plan to us clearly and to make Her Son's suffering known in the hearts of the poor Indians soon. We especially felt our hearts pleading for Shikellamy and his family. Thereupon we laid ourselves gladly down in the arms of our dear Husband.

On the 19th David visited Shikellamy a great deal. He also ate at midday with us. Was cheerful and alert. In the afternoon we visited on the island and found many at home.

          From your dear hearts, Martin and David

7

NOVEMBER 30, 1748–JANUARY 31, 1749

DAVID ZEISBERGER

Im Heidenpaß (In the Valley of the Heathen)

[On November 30]
Brothers Martin and David visited the Swatane, who was very ill.[1] We made him some tea,[2] for which he was very grateful. We also told him that Brother Martin and Boehler were thinking of leaving for Bethlehem tomorrow. In any case, Brother Martin and Boehler were preparing for a journey.

In the evening we had a blessed Lovefeast. Brother Martin shared much news with the Brothers and Sisters about Bethlehem, about the little Lamb there at the synod and who was then later made into an Elder at the festival,[3] and also in the whole land, which was very emotional. We were happy about this and took part in the blessing that had poured itself out over the people. Brother Martin spoke then a great deal about our little Lamb's office of Elder, and that even here in Shamokin. He had declared His news as Elder, which was for us all an astonishingly great and weighty matter, that the little Lamb, even here in this place, where it has always been so dark, wishes to be recognized as Elder, and thanked Him with many tears, that He makes room for us even here, and has given us a place where He can be worshipped. After this Brother Martin conducted a very emotional and blessed Quarter of an Hour, at which he blessed and absolved Brother and Sister Anton in the name of our Eldest. Thereupon we had a very dear meal of our little Lamb, and our Elder allowed Himself to be felt in our hearts, that He was among us and fed us with His Body and quenched us with His Blood. Our hearts melted in many tears about our Husband, and fell to His bored-through Feet and worshipped Him for His closeness and for His news, and then we went to our rest as blessed and happy Cross-air little birds in His Side Hole.

Fig. 5 Portrait of David Zeisberger. Artist: Valentin Haidt. 1761. PC 31. Oil on canvas. Courtesy of the Moravian Archives, Bethlehem, Pennsylvania.

On December 1

In the morning Brother Martin held another anointed Quarter of an Hour and recommended to the little Lamb those who were to stay here, as well as those who were to leave, and in general the whole mission here, as well as the Swatane's family. He offered them up to the little Lamb's heart and then with a tender kiss of love they took leave from one another, and when Brother Martin took his leave from the Swatane, who was still very ill but who could still speak freely, Brother Martin and Boehler, happily and blessed, set on their path into the Side Hole.

On December 3
We had a very quiet and contented Sabbath in the Side Hole.

On December 4
Brother Anton and David visited the Swatane and found him to be so weak that he could no longer walk by himself and could no longer hear well. Otherwise, he was very friendly and watched us with love but could speak very little. We brought him some tea and bread, which he enjoyed greatly.

On December 6
David visited the Swatane early in the morning and brought him something to eat and drink. He said, however, that he could eat and drink nothing, and that he could no longer hear anything, only speak a little. We saw that he would not live much longer. Around midday an Indian woman came and said to us that he was close to going home. David went to him and stayed with him. But there was a terrible wailing of lamentations, for everyone, old and young, wept incredibly about their old father. He spoke no more and looked at David with friendship and smiled and finally passed away quite contentedly. We now felt in our hearts that we should plead with the little Lamb that He should grant a place in His Side Hole for him and were able to believe that He would do the same. None of his sons were at home, only his daughter and a few women. Brother Anton was sickly and had to lie down but soon recovered.

On December 7
We went out and split shingles to improve our house.

On December 8
James Logan returned home from the hunt because they had sent for him. He soon visited us, and David told him that his father had become very ill on the way back from Tulpehocken. He looked very sad. He asked us to make him a coffin, which we did.

On December 9
They buried the Swatane. Almost everyone in Shamokin was present. In his grave they gave him two new blankets, a tobacco pipe, and three bags with tobacco and a flint as an honor, and other things too. We also went to the burial and helped to bury him. They did not fire their weapons while he was dying or at his funeral; rather, everything proceeded very quietly.

On December 10

Things were pretty unruly in Shamokin, because whiskey gained the upper hand among the Indians. But they were very peaceful with us and did not prevent us from going about our business, and we were alone with one another peacefully in the Side Hole.

On December 12

Logan came and asked David to write him a letter to Conrad Weiser to tell him that his father had died, which he also did. He did the same to Brother T'girhitondi. Otherwise we had many visits from Indians. Swatane's daughter, who is very sick and can hardly eat anything, also visited us. Sister Catherine gave her something to eat, of which she took a lot. She repeated *niàwo* many times and carried herself with great modesty and politeness.[4]

On December 14

Logan visited us with his wife and discussed many things with David. He asked all kinds of questions, among other things, why Brother Powell had gone away from Shamokin and whether another Sister could come here because it was very difficult for Catharina to take care of everything by herself. David also told him that we were soon expecting a Brother from Bethlehem, namely, Christian Rauch, whom he knew. He also said that he wanted to go on the hunt tomorrow a few miles over the river with his whole family. David should visit him there sometime, and, if he had meat, then he could bring some meat back home with him. He is very modest and carries himself toward us with great friendship and loves us.

On December 17

It became rather empty in Shamokin. Logan and his whole family went hunting again so that we were left alone. Logan gave us the key to his *Store* to take care of and is thinking of staying out on the hunt until John [Logan] returns, which he is expecting as soon as the bucks lose their horns. We were quite alone in the quiet and had a contented and blessed Sabbath and were happy to see the dear heart Christel again soon. Sometimes we looked out down the path to see if anyone was coming.

On December 23

It was quite rowdy in Shamokin because everyone was full of whiskey. They were as modest in their behavior toward us as they could be.

On December 24
We were much in Bethlehem in spirit, and the little Lamb permitted us to feel something of the communal blessing of His congregation.

On December 26
We were visited by many Indians, Maqua and Delaware. Logan and his family came home from the hunt and visited us, also cooked themselves something to eat at our fire because they did not want to go to the drunken Indians in their huts. Logan also had received a letter from Conrad Weiser that David translated for him. They soon left again though, and Logan said he wanted to visit us again soon.

On December 28 and 29
Various familiar neighbors of ours came home from the hunt and visited us soon also. One sees that they love us and are truly good people, if only they didn't occasionally indulge in their weakness and were tempted to drink, for if they resolved not to drink, then they would be required to wait a long time before they did.

On December 31
We had a blessed Sabbath, and we were much in our hearts among our Brothers and Sisters in Bethlehem.

In the year 1749 (OS)
On Sunday, January 1
We waited with longing for our dear heart Christel. But he did not come. We gave up thinking he would come.

On January 2
Our dear hearts Christian and Heinrich Frey arrived in Shamokin to our great joy and contentment and gladdened us with many juicy little letters and news from our dear Brothers and Sisters in Bethlehem, for we had waited longingly for someone for a long time.

On January 3
We spent a contented and very blessed day, and our dear and precious heart Christian gave us many happy tidings from our dear congregation, and we were quite blessed and content together in the little Side Hole.

On January 5
David and Heinrich Frey readied themselves to travel to Bethlehem to the synod. Brother Christian wrote letters to Bethlehem. A few Indian women from Logan's family came to the house and visited us, and we let Logan know that Brother Christian had arrived here and that David would soon go to Bethlehem. We also sent him many greetings from T'girhitondi, Johannes, and Gallichwio and all our brothers because we could not easily get over the river.

On Wednesday, January 6
Our two dear little hearts, David Zeisberger and Heinrich Frey, left in the morning for Bethlehem, quite blessed and content, and our dear little spirit left with them too. The few Indians who were left in Shamokin began to get into the whiskey, and the latter held such powerful sway over them that they reveled the whole night as though they had lost their minds.

On the Sabbath, January 7
We were surrounded by a great tumult, and the drunken Indians visited us much and complained to us of their sorry state that whiskey had become their master and also cried a little as well. The poor tormented hearts wailed to us greatly, and we showed them our sympathy. We, for our part, held a blessed and contented Sabbath, and we were much with our two hearts on their journey, also with our precious hearts in Bethlehem and felt among us a gentle peace.

On Sunday, January 8
We visited the Indian huts and silently sent to the little Lamb one little sigh of concern after another. Christian especially felt how his heart burned for them. In the evening Brother Christian held a blessed and anointed Quarter of an Hour with the Antons.

On Monday and Tuesday nothing much else happened.

On Wednesday, January 11
The three sons of Shikellamy came home from the hunt with their wives and various others of their extended family. They came straight to our house, visited with us, and were very friendly and neighborly to us. Brother Christian conveyed his greetings to them from his Brothers that were sent with him to them and assured them thereby that when the Brothers and Sisters heard from David that their father had died, they would be very downcast and that they believed also quite earnestly. James Logan and his younger brother asked

if they could sleep the night in our house. Brother Anton S. permitted them. Toward evening the others all began to get into the whiskey and spent the whole night drinking and carousing and around midnight came rushing into our house so that we, poor hearts, had to spend the whole night without sleep.

On Thursday, January 12
We were much visited by drunken Indians. They brought their little whiskey barrels with them and would very much have liked to have moved in with Logan and his younger brother. But Logan and his older brother held themselves like men; however, the younger one succumbed to weakness and maintained the loudest rumpus throughout the day, and Christian and Anton fetched themselves firewood today for the house. For ourselves and in ourselves we were very blessed, and our hearts tended in all blessed a burning love toward Bethlehem today, and we were in spirit present at the synod.

On Friday, January 13
Logan with his wife and several other Indians left again for the hunt. Two of his brothers with their wives and those who had not yet had their fill of whiskey stayed here. Our whole heart hung and cleaved to Bethlehem today with tender and burning feelings of love, and we noticed in our hearts some little airs of blessing that wafted from our dear hearts to us and were contented even amid all the noise that we were surrounded by.

On January 14, the Sabbath
Our dearest Husband was indescribably gracious. We felt most heavenly blessed in our hearts and rejoiced half to death over his beloved little Side Hole, from which so much blessing comes to us, three poor little things in Shamokin, and we sang it from morning to late night.

Today a few more Indians left from here to go to the hunt. In the evening Brother Christian and Brother and Sister Anton held a sweet and blessed Quarter of an Hour, and after that we went to sleep in the arms of our Husband, and our bodies enjoyed the first peaceful night for a week.

On Sunday, January 15
We had Shikellamy's eldest son, John, here for breakfast. He was friendly and modest; he told us that he would leave here today around midday to visit his wife's friends. And everyone else who was still here left today also, and so Shamokin became quite quiet and homely. We were quite content and blessed among us today. Brother Christian read the most favorite sermons from the *Homilies on the Wounds*,[5] and that was our confection today that has a taste

of strength and His body for us. Brother Anton went visiting and Christel spent the time in prayer.

On Monday, January 16
Shikellamy's daughter arrived here with four children, and soon after her arrival she came to visit us in our house, and she showed herself to be very friendly toward us.

On Wednesday, January 18
An unknown Delaware came to us by the name of Labachpeton, and he showed himself to be very friendly toward our Brother Anton and all of us.

On Thursday, January 19
Labachpeton visited us with another three Delaware Indians.

On the Sabbath, January 21
We had a blessed and quiet Sabbath. In the evening an unknown Delaware came to us from Thomas McKee. He was very hungry. We gave him something to eat. He behaved very well in our house. In the evening Brother Christian and Brother and Sister Anton held a blessed Quarter of an Hour.

On Sunday, January 22
Shikellamy's daughter visited us. She also ate at midday with us and was very friendly. We were especially blessed among ourselves and spent most of the day reading various sermons from the *Homilies on the Wounds*. In the evening we waited in great expectation for our dear heart David Zeisberger to return from Bethlehem. Three Delaware Indians came to visit us and gave us a present of a quarter of venison.

On Monday, January 23
Two Shawnee Indians had some work done for them by Brother Anton in the blacksmith's shop. In the evening two traders arrived here from Lancaster and brought with them two horses laden with goods.

On Tuesday, January 24
Thomas Ton from Shikellamy's extended family arrived here with his wife and brought another Indian along. The traders visited us today and were very modest, also wanted work done by Brother Anton. This evening our neighbors dwelled on rum and spent the night drinking and making noise, and it was impossible for us to sleep as they were raving so insanely.

On Wednesday, January 25
Our neighbors misbehaved beyond all belief. One of the traders fell into the folly of drinking for a bet with them, but because he behaved very coarsely with his company, they covered his back with blows, and that in a pretty tough Indian fashion on top of it. In the evening two warriors arrived here from the Catawba. They came first into our house and warmed themselves by our fire. They could both speak English and had dressed themselves completely in bear skins and colored their faces black so that they could look quite terrifying like the devil.

On Thursday, January 26
James Logan and his wife and John Petty with his wife arrived here with several other Indians. We were soon visited by them. They had hoped that David [Zeisberger] would be back from Bethlehem, as they very much desired to see him.

On Friday, January 27
Logan and his party departed from here again to go hunting across the Susquehanna, and his brother John Senior came home today from visiting his wife's extended family and brought several Tutelo with him. Also, an unknown Indian arrived here, who had owed Brother Anton three thalers a long time ago and paid him, and he was very friendly.

On Saturday, the Sabbath, January 28
Shikellamy's eldest son John visited us early on. Various unknown Indians arrived here today of different sorts—Maqua, Shawnee, and Tutelo. We had a blessed Sabbath among ourselves. Our dearest Husband was very close to our hearts the whole day, and our thoughts turned to Bethlehem a great deal. We also waited with great expectation [for] our dear heart David today. We hoped for his arrival until late into the evening. But we gave it up with pain.

On Sunday, January 29
We had some external disturbances. Some of the unknown Indians behaved very badly and senselessly and attempted to do burning sorrow to us. Several times we thought that they would tear our house down. Christian took this very much to heart and went away and thought about it a little in peace and felt great sympathy for them and from this feeling began to sing:

> My God, you see them grazing
> Spread out both your wings below.[6]

Suddenly everything went quiet, and they all went away from our house, and for the rest of the time we were left in peace from them. Otherwise, we were happy, blessed, and comforted little doves in the Side Wound, and the little Lamb did all things beautiful with us whenever things go crazy here. The Antons met up with David Zeisberger today, and Christian was happy down here, but especially with his little Heart [Jesus] in the little Side Wound.

On Monday, January 30
Thomas Dunn came home from the hunt and visited us several times. He was very friendly to us, and so was Schafmann, a dear Indian whose friendliness shines out of his eyes. He told us that he would go back on the hunt in the morning.

On Tuesday, January 31
Several went out on the hunt, and Shamokin became once again quite empty and quiet.

8

APRIL 3–JULY 26, 1749

DAVID ZEISBERGER

On Monday, April 3
Our dear little heart Christel Rauch departed from Shamokin to Bethlehem, and David accompanied him to his night camp. The Indian festival was concluded today with a dance, after they had made music and danced the whole night, and straight afterward whiskey had to hold sway, and then in a few minutes everything was mad and full of menfolk, and they tore about terribly that they almost killed one another.

On Tuesday, April 4
David came home again and brought many cordial little greetings and kisses to Brother and Sister Smith from Brother Christel, whom he had left at the foot of the Thürnstein Mountain, well and healthy. The Indians continued with drinking today. Some were already so ill that they could take no more. But they left us quite undisturbed.

On April 5 and 6
Everyone dispersed from here. Most of them went home, some to the hunt, and so Shamokin became quite empty again.

On April 8, Saturday
We celebrated a peaceful and contented Sabbath, and our hearts were much with our Brothers and Sisters in Bethlehem. We were also visited today by Logan and his wife, who told us that he was thinking of going up the river to Womphallepang to fetch Indian corn for his family because they had nothing more to eat, and that Blackfish, who had lived last year in Womphallepang

and who had often visited our Brothers and Sisters in Gnadenhütten and who had even stayed there for a while, was going to plant there this summer. We gave them some Indian corn for the journey because they had none. He told David all kinds of historical matters that related to the Indians of several nations.

On Sunday, April 9
Logan and Blackfish left here [deleted material], and there was no one left at home but an old woman.

On Monday, April 10
An Indian came down from up north, a Cayuga by the name of Tianoge, who claimed to still remember seeing T'girhitondi and Ganosseracheri in Onondaga four years ago. He bewailed the death of the Swatane greatly, who had been his great friend. He asked whether or not we wanted to visit them again. David told him perhaps soon. He was very pleased that David could converse with him and said that he should make the effort to learn their language, which he also promised him to do. He recounted how he had heard much about us, that we loved the Indians, and that we were their Brothers. David told him that, yes, we did love the Indians and that they were our Brothers. At that he gave David his hand and said, "Oh'oh niawo n'twatathege," "I am so happy that you are our Brothers." David asked him whether the Great Councils of the Five Nations were considering coming down here this summer. He said, yes, as soon as the bark peeled from the trees so that they could make canoes, they would probably come. They would have come down a year ago, but they had been held up for a long time in Albany; that is why they had not been able to come, because it had become too late. He himself had been present there; that is why he had received the beautiful frockcoat he was wearing, which was embroidered with golden fringes. He also recounted how he had hunted with Heinrich, of the Maqua lands, who had already lodged with David this past winter on the Ostonwakin Creek, only two days' journey from here, where Heinrich still was with his family. But he was thinking about making a journey to Conrad Weiser, whom he knew well, to speak with him, and then he would return and travel home. He needed something done to his flintlock, which Brother Anton did for him for free.

On April 11, Tuesday
He left here, and we gave him something to eat for the way. He complained that hereabouts there was such a famine, and there was nothing to eat, and that when the Five Nations finally came down, they would have nothing to eat. He gave us all his hand and bade us adieu.

Today a Tuscarora and a Shawnee came through, who were coming from a war. They had brought two scalps with them. The first one had come from Wahochquage, a large city (as one says) of the Tuscaroras, two days' journey from Tioga, near Schohari.

There also arrived Swatane's grandson down from Ohio and visited us, also brought work for the smith.

On Wednesday, April 12
A Delaware woman, our neighbor, who visits us diligently, visited Sister Catherine today, and told her that Philip's house was haunted at night and that she was afraid to be there alone because her people had all gone to Tulpehocken. Catherine asked her what she thought it might be. She said she did not know. Doubtless it is Philip's brother, who had drunk himself to death.

On Wednesday, April 19
John Shikellamy came home again. He told us that he had met Conrad Weiser on the way to Shamokin to bring them gifts from the government. David asked him whether he had told Conrad that they were undertaking a journey to the Five Nations, and he said yes. [David asked] whether he had also asked him that we would go along, he said yes, whereupon David asked him what he had to say to that. He had nothing more to say to that, other than he had considered it a good thing that Ganosseracheri was going along because he understood the language. He also told us that Ostonwakin was going to be inhabited again by the Maqua and the Cayuga, who were coming down from up north. The one called Tianoge was going to plant there this summer, but only after a trip to Onondaga. He also said that there were many Delaware on the West River [Branch], who would plant seed this summer.

On Thursday, April 20
John Shikellamy left again to go to Tgochari to his wife's people. He complained that there was nothing here to eat, and, when he came home, he would be hungry. That is why he could not stay home a great deal and that he had had nothing to eat since he had been here. We gave him something for the journey. He was very friendly and cheerful.

On April 22
It was very quiet here, and we were almost completely alone, but we were quite happy and content in the Side Hole, and the Lamb was among us with His most beloved Side Hole, so that we could feel it. Today one of our neighbors, Schafmann, visited us, a well-mannered Indian. He told us that

the government had placed John Shikellamy in the Swatane's place, because his father had died, and that Conrad Weiser had sent a fathom of wampum to the Five Nations with Tianoge, the Cayuga, who was traveling up to Onondaga.

He complained greatly that the Indians here drank so much and drank away all they had. David said to him, yes, that was true, but the poor Indians could do nothing else because they were under the influence of the Evil Spirit, and that the Evil Spirit ruled over them. However, if one of them would come to know the Savior and love Him, he would not think about doing evil anymore, and that is why we had great sympathy with the poor Indians, because they did not know God, who loved them so remarkably and had died for them and had spilled His blood for them so that they could be blessed, if they only chose to be, which they could not do; that is why they had to sin and do evil. He said to all this, *"tegerge,"* "that is true," and was very friendly.

On April 24, Monday
Logan came home again, and with him came an Indian from Meniolagomeka, who visited us immediately and was very friendly to us. He told us that he had been in Bethlehem nine days ago and had seen nine Indians from Meniolagomeka being baptized, whom Brother Cammerhof and another Brother had baptized.[1] He also told us that he had spoken with Brother Christel in Bethlehem, who had comforted him with the news that in a week someone would be leaving Bethlehem for Shamokin.

There also came another, Armstrong, a Delaware Indian, who had lived for a winter in Gnadenhütten and now lived some forty miles above Wyoming on the Susquehanna. He was very friendly and modest with us. We took them in with friendship and gave them something to eat.

On April 25
John Shikellamy came back home again, visited us diligently. He is very friendly to us and carries himself with dignity. He is diligently teaching David to speak Cayuga. He has a good talent for teaching. There was also much dancing today, but the Indian from Meniolagomeka sat among them and did not dance; he is different from the others.

On April 26
Logan visited us and had a long discourse with David. He pointed out a great enmity with the Delaware because he believes that they have the power of evil witchcraft, and they bewitched his child and also his wife, and that is why they are never well. For he thinks that they had forgiven them, and that is

why the Delaware all moved away from here and dispersed themselves like others because they were killing one another.

On Saturday, April 29
We looked carefully for our Brothers and Sisters from Bethlehem. David also went out to look for the Brothers but did not meet with any.

On Monday, May 1
Our dear hearts Christel and Andres arrived here. We rejoiced and were very dear to one another and spent the day listening to the joyous news that our dear hearts had brought with them and with love.

On May 2, Tuesday
We brought our business to Logan. The other brothers were not at home. He was content with everything that was proposed to him. We also began to plant our corn today.

On May 3, Wednesday
Brothers Anton and David went down the Susquehanna to the traders to fetch iron. Because our horses had run away, Brother Christel went out to look for them and came back in the evening but had not found them.

On May 4, Thursday
Two Indians arrived from Nescopeck, Nutimus's two sons, and brought work for the blacksmith's shop. They stayed in our house for quite a while and were quite friendly. They told us that their house and everything that they had had been burned by a bush fire because no one had been home who could have extinguished it.

On May 5, Friday
Christian spoke a lot with Nutimus's sons and told them about the Savior. They were very attentive and alert and very hungry to hear something of the little Lamb. They also had little in common with the local Indians but rather stayed with us for most of the time. Although there was much dancing and music, these two kept themselves apart. Armstrong, a Delaware, arrived here today also, and Brother Christian preached to him about the Savior and his little Side Hole.

On May 6, Saturday
Brothers Anton and David returned home again and just at the right time, because the water was already so high from the heavy rains that toward the

end of their journey they could not continue and, half a mile from Shamokin, needed to chop through a tree that lay across the water so that they could get away from the bank. Otherwise, whiskey showed itself to hold sway among the Indians.

On May 7, Sunday
We told Logan that our horses had run away and asked if he could help us out of our dilemma and lend us a horse for Catharina. He promised to fetch one for us and to allow two Indians who had to bring some things back from Tulpehocken for him on horseback to accompany us. Our Brother and Sister Anton [Schmidt] and Brother Christian prepared for a journey to Bethlehem in the early morning.

On Monday, May 8
Because the water was still very high, David rode to Eva Creek to see if it was possible to cross but found that it was impossible. So, the Brothers and Sisters had to stay here today.

On Tuesday, May 9
Our Brothers and Sisters left from here on their way to Bethlehem. Because Eva Creek was still very high, David and a Shawnee Indian carried a canoe on their shoulders to Eva Creek and put our Brothers and Sisters safely on the opposite shore and waded across with the horses. The farewell was a little painful, and David walked back home quite alone and in fact a little melancholy. Once he got home, whiskey had once again become the master over the people. Logan and John had resolved not to drink, and so they hid themselves the whole day. John locked himself in his storehouse, and Logan camped out in our garden under the trees and slept the night there. He told David that he was afraid of the drunken people, as they set off looking for him and wanted to get him to drink, but he did not want to do this.

On May 12
We received news through the Indians who had gone with our Brothers and Sister to Tulpehocken that they had arrived safely in Tulpehocken.

On May 13 and 14
It was quite rowdy in Shamokin. There were many people gathered, and they continued drinking. David visited Tachnechdorus [John Shikellamy] in his storehouse, where he had locked himself in. He said that the Delaware had been tormenting him so much and had been working on him the whole week, that they wanted to get him to drink, and that is why he had shut himself in.

Because he knew that it came from the devil. David said, yes, that was really true; it was just a deception of Satan, because when they were all a little sober again, then they would all be so sick that they had ruined their houses through drink. John said also that he was thinking of going to Philadelphia with the Five Nations, and he wanted to visit T'girhitondi there. Sawonagarat, an Indian, our neighbor, came down from Wyoming and brought news that the messengers of the Five Nations were there in Wyoming and that they were expecting them there any day now. We were in Bethlehem in our hearts a great deal over today and yesterday and were quite blessed and content in the little Side Hole.

On May 15, Monday
The Indian from Meniolagomeka who wanted to find his sister visited us again. But he had not met up with her and now wanted to go down the Susquehanna to Juniata on the hunt. David spoke to him a great deal about the Savior and told him that he should not forget what he had heard in Bethlehem. He said that he never wanted to forget it because, when he was in Bethlehem, he had felt something in his heart that he would never forget. He had also felt a great desire to be baptized, and, when he returned home again, which would happen in two months, he wanted to visit the Brothers and Sisters in Bethlehem again.

On May 20
Blackfish and Logan asked fervently that we plough a piece of land for them on which they could plant Indian corn, because they could not plough. They would like to pay us for this. We said, we would be happy to do it for them for nothing if only we had the time, but at the moment we were by ourselves that we didn't have the time.

In the evening three Indians came to us from the Nanticoke at Juniata. They are moving up to Wyoming, and more will follow. They stayed with us until late into the night; they were very hungry. We gave them something to eat, for which they were very happy and grateful. They wanted to lodge with us, but we said that we did not put up any Indians and had not ever done so yet. The Indians here had a big house, and they would prefer it if they stayed there overnight. They were shy, however, and did not want to go to the Indians; rather, they said if they were not permitted to stay with us, then they would rather go into the woods. Because a heavy rain and thunderstorm came, then we said that they should stay where they were; it would be rough sleeping in the woods; they would have no hut and no fire, and on top of that it was very dark. They were very happy.

On Monday, May 22
Seven canoes full of Nanticoke came through here, and many more on foot, traveling up to Wyoming. They are very good people and can also speak English well.

On Tuesday, May 23
Logan and Blackfish once again asked David fervently that he should plough for him. David said he would go out with Blackfish and show him how to do it; he could learn it and would plough four acres for him and the rest he could do himself.

On May 24
Shamokin became quite empty again. Everyone was going off to hunt.

On Saturday, May 27
Most of them came back from the hunt, and immediately everything was crowded and crazy, and they raced around throughout the whole day and night like never before. Many of the young men came to us and wanted to sleep in our house, said they were afraid of the drunken people. We turned them away gently. The womenfolk camped out on our land to be safe. We were quite happy with one another in the little Side Hole and commended ourselves to the little Lamb.

On May 28
Quite unexpectedly, our dear Brothers Kunz and Marcus Kiefer arrived here. They had spent the previous night in heavy rain, as they could not make a fire. Because they had got completely soaked by lying up on the top of the Spangenberg and had woven one tree through another to try to get some warmth because they did not know that they were so close to Shamokin. In the morning they had to cut down another tree over Eva Creek that was quite high so that they could get across. They told us that they had got lost up on the Thürnstein and had taken the wrong path when they were about thirty miles from Shamokin and had come upon the Susquehanna. We were so happy with one another and thanked the little Lamb that they had found their way. They also arrived at quite a bad time, as it was quite stormy and troubled because of the drunken Indians. They brought us many joyous tidings from Brother Johannes from [Saint] Thomas and also from the Brothers and Sisters who had come from Europe.

On May 29
David went up into the mountains to see if he could find the horses that we had lost last week and came back toward evening but had not found them.

A Delaware from Tgochari wanted to sleep here this evening. We tried to show him the best we could that he should go to the Indians, that they had a big house, and that our house was not for the Indians to lodge in.

On May 31, Friday
Brother Kunz left from here for Bethlehem. David accompanied him to his night camp. The drunken Indians ran around a lot this night. In the morning very early we heard straightaway that David, a Delaware Indian, had been killed this night by the Maqua, because he was supposed to have been a great magician and had cursed many Indians. His brother Daniel came and wanted to have a coffin measured up for him. We told him that we could not do it because we had never made one before. And then they buried him according to the Indian manner in the Delaware burial place. He was very beaten and stabbed all over his body.

On Thursday, June 1
David came home and discovered his two Brothers happy and content together. Everything was very quiet again in Shamokin, and the one who had killed the Indian walked around very proud and boasted that he had been such a hero.

On Saturday, June 3
Logan came very early and said that they all wanted to go on the hunt today. The reason for this was that Blackfish wanted to make an offering of three stag.

On Sunday, June 4
They returned home again, and they brought four stags, and three of them were sacrificed tonight, during which everything proceeded very solemnly. Even the bones were thrown into the fire so that no dog could eat them.

On Monday, June 5
Jeremias the Indian[2] arrived here from Bethlehem to visit us. He said that he and Christoph had been on a hunting expedition in the mountains. He was quite weak; he said that he soon wanted to return to Bethlehem, as he had already been in the woods too long.

On Tuesday, June 6
Jeremias left again. He was very content and was happy that he would soon be with the Brothers again. The Indians here wondered at him a great deal and could not take their eyes off him.

On Wednesday, June 8
Four canoes full of warriors arrived here.[3] They brought two scalps.

On Thursday, June 9
Thirty more warriors arrived by land. They brought three prisoners with them, two men and a little girl. When they were still a distance from the town, they called out in the war cry and made their presence known. The Indians here sent someone out to meet them and to invite them in, and the whole of Shamokin collected in front of the houses and let the warriors pass and their prisoners. They took them off them and tied them to a stake. They had to do a little dance first, and, once that was over, they led them in here, and everyone who could, and so desired, let forth a blow, began to beat them in a quite savage fashion, some with sticks, some with their fists, so that blood flowed. One of them was quite old and could not run quickly. He received many blows, and, as he ran, he fell from the many blows.[4] Once they were in the houses, they stopped beating them. They did nothing to the little girl. The womenfolk took her and treated her kindly. One's heart wanted to burst to see how they treated them. Once they were in the house, they bound up their wounds again, and, soon after, the Indians who lived around here gathered and made their prisoners dance around them and made fun of their enemies. In the evening the warriors danced with their prisoners. Three of the chiefs of the Five Nations came down here from Wyoming, where they had been staying for a while.

On June 10 and 11
We were visited by many warriors. They behaved very nicely and well, and most of them were quite gentle people and as big as giants. They discussed matters at length with David, asked a lot where we lived, what kind of people we were; then they asked at length whether we had anything to sell. We told them, however, that we were not traders but rather that the blacksmith worked for the Indians whenever they needed something done. We loved them and liked to help them. Most of them were Onondaga, even the prisoners who they had brought belonged to them.

On Monday, June 12

In the early morning Logan came and said that they would like the rest of the war party who were still down in the settlements drinking whiskey to come up to Shamokin because they wanted to travel to Lancaster with the three councils of the Five Nations who had come down here. That is why they had agreed to send two messengers down to fetch them. That is why David, in the name of John Shikellamy, Logan, and John Petty should write a letter to the settlements that they should not give them any more whiskey so that they would leave. David did this and wrote a letter in their name.

The three chiefs of the Five Nations visited us also. They were very polite and modest. We gave them a meal, and they also asked where we lived. They told us where they lived and that they were thinking now of going to Lancaster to hold a council with the government.

[illegible matter]

They also visited Anders in his blacksmith's shop. Most of the warriors left today. All in all there were about fifty of them.

On Tuesday, June 13

John left here with the three chiefs to go to Tulpehocken to Conrad Weiser's.

On Wednesday, June 14

Some warriors visited us again and told David all kinds of things.

On Thursday, June 15

Logan and all of Shamokin, with the exception of the Delaware, left here for Lancaster, and no one stayed home except Blackfish.

On Saturday and Sunday, June 17 and 18

It was very quiet in Shamokin, like it hasn't been in a long while. We were blessed hearts together in the little Side Hole and made ourselves quite comfortable in there.

On July 1 and 2

We were visited by many unknown Indians, who brought work to the blacksmith's shop. They were not very happy that they had to wait for two days but rather would have preferred that the smith work on the Sabbath and Sunday and did their work for them.

On July 3

The Savior protected David quite especially from a serious accident, as an Indian was trying out his flint, and David came to the Susquehanna at just that moment that it went off and heard the ball zoom past his head because the little Lamb had allowed it to so come to pass that he shot a few feet above the target; otherwise, he would have accurately hit the head or neck. The Indians were very surprised when they saw him.

On Friday, July 7
Warriors came here again from the war. They brought the news with them that one of them had recently been stabbed at the mill. The Swatane's eldest daughter, who had recently arrived here, visited us today, discoursed long with David, mourned her father's death greatly, because they had now become pathetic people, as she said. She asked where we lived and whether we all lived so closely together like the people here in Shamokin. David also told her that the Swatane had been in Bethlehem the previous autumn and that he liked it very much. We gave her some beans. She said she had nothing left to eat because the Indian corn in the area had all been eaten.

On July 13
The Nanticoke from Wyoming arrived here. One of them asked, how it could happen that they were not visited this year by our Brothers. We had otherwise visited them every year at least once. We told them that we thought someone from Bethlehem would come to visit them soon.

On the July 14
Some Cayuga from not far from Tioga arrived here. They brought work for the blacksmith. They were very well behaved and modest people. They discoursed at length with David.

On July 15
Two traders arrived here.[5] Shikellamy's grandchild had a young stallion, which they wanted because they said it belonged to them; that's why the traders wanted it. David was supposed to translate for them and help them strengthen their case, so that the Indian believed them. But David said he understood nothing of such things and did not want to get involved. The Indian understood Delaware; he could speak to him himself.

He gave the Indian a blanket and a pair of woolen stockings so that he should be content. Because we really needed salt and a few other things, and we would really have liked to borrow a horse from the Indian, we spoke to Shikellamy's daughter's husband about it. He was immediately willing and gave us his horse so that we could go to Tulpehocken to fetch some things.

On July 16
Quite late at night, Brothers Heinrich Frey and Anton Schmidt arrived here and brought us many glad tidings from Bethlehem.

On July 18
David and Heinrich Frey went down to Thomas McKee's to fetch our canoe, after we had lent it to some of his people, and he had not brought it back, although he had promised to bring it back in two days.

On July 19
David and Heinrich came home again but were not able to get the canoe, as they had taken it down the Susquehanna. They met Logan on the way, who was coming back from Philadelphia and who seemed very contented. He soon told us that he had seen T'girhitondi, Tecarihontie, Gallichwio, and many other of our Brothers in Philadelphia and had spoken with them.[6]

On July 20
Two of the chiefs of the Five Nations arrived here and brought news that the others were on their way down here and that they had left them in Tioga, but they would arrive here in perhaps five days.

On July 21
Because we were short of provisions, and the three Seneca who had been in Philadelphia did not arrive, our two Brothers Andreas Bezold and Marcus Kiefer went to fetch some from Tulpehocken with our two horses. John and his family arrived here and told David in a friendly fashion everything that he had seen and heard in Philadelphia.

On July 22
The two chiefs of the Five Nations who had recently arrived came to visit us. One is an Onondaga and the other a Seneca. They spoke at length with Ganosseracheri and told him many things.

On July 24
The three Seneca from Philadelphia arrived here.[7] They were very cordial. They asked to be allowed to lodge in our house, which we did then permit; because there were many of them, we said that we would now have little to eat and that our stores of provisions had all been depleted. But we still had Indian corn and beans, for which they were very grateful and said countless times

niàwo for it and had great sympathy for us. The whiskey began to hold sway in Shamokin.

On July 25
Our Brothers Andreas Bezold and Marcus Kiefer arrived from Tulpehocken and brought some provisions with them but had both become slightly ill on the way, and both got a strong attack of fever.

Four canoes full of warriors arrived here who were going into war. They were hardly here for more than a few hours, then everyone was drunk and raged throughout the night in a pitiful manner. It was a true yelling and shouting among them. But we were left in good peace by them.

On July 26
The drinking continued. The drunken Indians visited us often but tried to be as polite as they could and spoke with us in a brotherly fashion, for they all know that we are their brothers. We also spoke with the three Seneca and gave them the presents [shirts] and said to them, "This is what Brothers Tecarihontie, Gallichwio, T'girhitondi sent to you," and they and all the Brothers send their most cordial greetings and because they loved them dearly, they had wanted to show their love one more time. They told David various things, that they had been given a string of wampum as a sign of brotherhood by Brothers T'girhitondi, Tecarihontie, and Gallichwio, and they had given them a fathom of wampum to take to the council at Onondaga, which was to say as much that the Brothers should visit the Five Nations next spring. They were struck with gratitude and friendship and said that we should greet their brothers T'girhitondi, Tecarihontie, Gallichwio, and Annuntschi for them and say many *niàwo* in their names, which we promised to do and also told them that Brother Ganosseracheri and Rachwistonis were thinking of leaving tomorrow to see their Brothers, and they wanted to pass on their greetings at this time. They discoursed at length with Ganosseracheri, and, when they were done, they pressed his hand surprisingly and said he should do the same, and to kiss and embrace Brothers T'girhitondi, Tecarihontie, and Gallichwio and Annuntschi also. Ganosseracheri said yes, that will most definitely happen, and our Brothers would be very happy about this.

9

JANUARY 8–MARCH 5, 1750

CHRISTIAN RAUCH

On January 8
Brother David [Zeisberger] arrived in Shamokin again and met with Brother Anton and Marcus, who had been looking out for the Brothers for a while, healthy and content. It was very quiet and lonely here because none of our neighbors was home except the Delaware.

On January 15
A trader came here from Thomas [McKee] and lodged the night with us.

On January 19
David was unlucky and scalded his leg with a kettle of boiling water.

On January 22
Tachnechdorus's wife came to our house in the evening and said she had left him because they no longer thought as one. She complained that she had frozen both her feet before; last night she had lain in the bush and could not make a fire because it was already so late. We had to let her into the house to sleep.

On January 23
We told John's [Tachnechdorus's] wife that she should go over to the Delaware and lodge there because it was not seemly that she stay in our house. When the blacksmith's wife was here, then it would be more appropriate. She said, however, that she did not want to go to the Delaware because they were a bad people. Rather, she got her things together and went to Sgochari. We gave

her matches. Shawonogarati came here from John [Logan] and lodged overnight.

On January 25
We sent Brother Marcus to Tulpehocken because David's leg began to get really bad, and we did not know what to do, and we had no medicine for it, in the hope of meeting Brother Rauch along the way.

On January 29
Brother Marcus came back from Tulpehocken and had met Brother Rauch at Peter Kuchern's, who sent us a good plaster.

On January 30
The Cayuga, Hahotschaunquas, came from John's [Logan's] hunting cabin here with his wife and child. They would have liked to see us allow them to stay in our house, but we showed them to the big house and gave them something so that they could cook for themselves. He said to us that John had gone up to Sgochari and would soon be here.

On February 1
A trader came here from Thomas [McKee] and stayed with us overnight.

On February 2
John arrived here from Sgochari and brought his wife back with him.

On February 3
John and the Cayuga visited us. John complained that everything in his house had been burned, boards and everything. Who had done it? We said to him, the Indians who were here a while and who traveled through. Delaware and Shawnee and Tutelo had stayed in there, and because they had no wood at night, they had burned the boards and also the planks from our fence occasionally.

On February 5
John visited us and discoursed at length with David. He also said to him that Shawonogarati had said that David had said another man had gone with his wife to Sgochari. David said that was not true, as there were no Indians here when she left. At this John said that he had often found that Shawonogarati told many lies. David asked him also whether his wife had not said anything

to him of us. He said, yes, we had told her she should go to the Delaware; it was not seemly that she lodge here with us because we are all men, and the blacksmith's wife was not here. David told him that we allowed her to spend one night here because she had come late and because her feet were almost frozen because she could not make fire. He seemed quite satisfied with this and was very relieved.

On February 8
John and the Cayuga traveled to Thomas [McKee]. John said that he had heard that Thomas had beaten his wife and needed to go to see whether this was true. A Delaware from Jacob Vorsinger's circle came by here in the evening and stayed with us overnight. He is a good man and very friendly toward us; he loves us. [We] should visit the people sometime; they live on the flats this side of the Long Island in the West Branch.

On February 10
We had a peaceful and contented Sabbath. We were quite alone.

On February 11
One of Thomas's servants arrived here and brought a letter from Thomas to Brother Anton to fetch the belongings of a trader that he had left in our house and had then gone to Tulpehocken, and Thomas demanded in the letter that Anton should send a list of the belongings because he thought that he had gone through them. However, Anton answered him through the man that he could send him a bill because he did not know the belongings, but rather he preferred it this way.

On February 17
We had a quite blessed Sabbath, and in the evening a sweet meal of the Lamb [Communion] with one another. We felt as though the Savior was among us with his bloody little Side Wound, and we were quite content together.

On February 18
Four traders arrived here and lodged with the Delaware and got into an argument with one another. Three of them came to our door in the night as we were already sleeping and asked that we allow them to come in and sleep the night in our house. They could not stay together. We allowed them then to spend the night here. One of them was the one for whom the belongings were being fetched and came from Tulpehocken. Before this he had lived in Lancaster and had heard Brother Nyberg preach. He told us he had been

with one of our Brothers, Robert Ehrs, on the Swatara and praised him greatly. Brought us some tobacco from him. He said he had read the Greenland diary at his house.[1]

On February 24
John Petty returned home from the hunt with his whole family. He visited us soon and asked how much he owed us; he wanted to pay. We then told him, and he complained bitterly that the previous blacksmith, Andres Bez, had written more on his bill than he remembered having asked to be done. He knew what he owed Brother Anton, but the other blacksmith had lied. David spoke to him very earnestly and said he knew very well that the other blacksmith had not lied, and he knew well enough that we were not that kind of people who would try to deceive him, to try to get many hides off him, but rather that we loved them and really tried to help them. But in return they should really try to deal with us honestly and not blame us like this. But in the future we would act accordingly and not lend him anything. Other Indians paid right away when they had work done, but because they were our neighbors and brothers we had until now given them credit until they could pay. It had been an old debt; perhaps he had forgotten it. At this he said that he wanted to pay everything. It might be the case that he had forgotten something. He didn't know that Andres had done something for him. So God knew it; he wanted to pay so that he could be at peace with his conscience. David told him that he could well believe that the other blacksmith had not deceived him because he was our Brother, and we all knew him very well, and we knew very well that our Brothers did not lie. Yes, he said, he knew very well that we did not deceive; we were too good a people to do this; he had probably forgotten something. David said to him that we wanted to keep things with him in the future so that we would write him a bill when they had something done, and they would have to hold on to it, and when they paid it then they needed to find it again. Yes, he said, that would be good if we did it like that, and so he was quite happy again.

On February 25
Shamokin became quite tumultuous again, and everyone began to drink whatever was there. That was something quite new to us because this winter we had seen hardly any drunken Indians; rather, they were so quiet here like we had never experienced, but now the whiskey would find its way in again.

On February 26
In the morning John Petty came into our house half-drunk and complained again about the blacksmith, that is about Andres, that he had tricked him so.

David said to him that he did not want to talk to him about it now but rather save it for another time and let him leave again. David traveled up the river to Nescopeck to visit the Indians there.

On February 29
He came home again and had met up with the old man, Nutimus, and two of his sons in Nescopeck, who had welcomed him very cordially. David gave them greetings from our Brethren, especially from Brother Cammerhof, who had visited them this winter and told them that he had been in Bethlehem seven weeks ago and that there he had seen old Nutimus's sister. She had been very ill and had a great desire to be baptized in the Savior's blood before she died. She had asked the Brothers that she should drip with the blood, and Brother Cammerhof had then baptized her.[2] David said he would have liked to come to visit them long ago and would have brought the news to them, but, when he got to Shamokin, he had burned his leg and had not been able to walk. Now it was quite healed, but not completely, and so he had set off on his trip again. There were several other Indians there who were very friendly, and the house was full almost the whole time, because he was there. On the way he also visited Labachpeton's Village and had slept for two nights in his hunting lodge, and he had welcomed him cordially and had hosted him well. He had also had the opportunity to talk to him about the Savior. He is a very wise man and cares for us greatly.

Fig. 6 Indian medal used by Moravian missionaries to indicate their permission to enter and travel through Haudenosaunee lands. Unidentified maker, circa 1736, with alterations circa 1750. Silver, 2 3/16 × 1 15/16 in. Silver weight: 3 oz (troy) 1 dwt (95g). Gift of Miss Fanny Ogden, New-York Historical Society, 1923.36. Photo © New-York Historical Society. http://www.nyhistory.org.

On March 3
We had a contented Sabbath. We were almost alone in Shamokin.

On March 5
Everyone fell to drinking again, and in the evening there was a huge tumult among the Indians because they were beating their wives so that they had much to endure.

10

APRIL 14–JUNE 2, 1753

BERNHARD GRUBE

On April 14
Brother Grube, Christ, and Kobus van der Merck arrived from Bethlehem with the Daily Text, "Your garments have an odor as though they came from the air of Christ's tomb."[1] The Brothers in Shamokin were very happy about their arrival, as they needed some advice about several circumstances. That evening we were very blessed together. Our neighbors, the Indians, were very loud and quite drunk.

On April 15
We rested and Brother Grube told the other Brothers news about the Gemeine. In the evening we held a little Singstunde about the sufferings of Jesus.

On April 16
After the Morning Blessing, all the Brothers went about their work. Brother Pfeifer began the masonry work on the chimney in our house. Brother Grube stayed at home and cooked. At noon he invited Captain Logan and his Brother John Shikellamy to speak to him about the new fence that Brother Joseph had promised to have made for him a year ago. Brother T'girhitondi was now traveling over the big water to Brother Johannes and the other Brothers. Brother Tecarihontie[2] had returned from Greenland, etc. In the matter of the fence, we thought to take care of it in the following manner, because we did not have time to build a completely new one; that is, we wanted to take the best planks from their and our old fence and then erect a new fence with them; that would be just as good as a new one. He said the same thing to

them about the [original damaged] that means that we would soon leave. We had in mind to demolish it completely because we needed a lot from it in our new house, and we also did not like to see other people living in it. They were both satisfied with my proposition. Logan said he would move away from here a few miles up the West Branch. John, however, would stay here and build a little storehouse next to our new house (this will probably not happen because John has taken a Shawnee wife and will live not far from Logan).[3] In the evening John showed the Brothers the piece of land that was supposed to be fenced in.

On April 17
In the night the Indians began to drink again. We were quite disturbed in our sleep.

On April 18
This state of affairs continued. But we did not allow ourselves to be disturbed but rather in the morning and evening held our opportunities and were especially happy about the beautiful words of the Savior, "whosoever eats this bread"[4] and held the hope that we too would soon enjoy this.[5]

On April 19
On Maundy Thursday in the morning, things were still rather noisy because of the drunkards. At midday we held a little Quarter of an Hour meeting. Brother Grube told the other Brothers that we would celebrate Communion today. In the evening the Indians became quite quiet, and we held our Communion service peacefully, and during it read the sermons that the Savior had held to his disciples on his Passion. After that we held another Quarter of an Hour service and a Pedelavium and after that the [original damaged] and our bloody Lamb pervaded us in our very souls [original damaged] martyr Body and Blood, and so we went [original damaged].

On April 20
On Good Friday we sang [original damaged] verses on the Passion and thanked Him from our hearts that He spilled His blood for us poor little sinners on the Cross.
    In the evening three warriors from the Oneida country arrived to have their weapons repaired here. But we said to them that we were not working tomorrow or the next day because we had two great feast days and had to speak to our God. They were very understanding.

On April 21
On the Great Sabbath (Easter Saturday), we were quite still and thought a great deal of Jesus's Body in the tomb. The warriors came to visit us. I asked them if they knew Ganosseracheri. They said yes and were very friendly. Friedrich from Gnadenhütten is staying around here also for a few days but did not come to see us. In the evening we had a Singstunde, and after that we went to rest.

On April 22
Before dawn we visited our departed Brother Hagen's grave, sat ourselves down at it, and sang a few verses. In the evening we read an Easter sermon and held an Evening Hour.

On April 23
Very early after the Morning Blessing, Brothers Grube, Kobus, and Marcus Kiefer went in the canoe to the mill to fetch provisions. Grube and Marcus were going along for the first time. Today we went more than fifty miles and stayed the night in the shelter of a thick tree. We were happy and thankful to the Savior, that he had gracefully protected us this day.

On April 24
We traveled another sixteen miles and arrived at 9:30 a.m. at the place. We took the wagon from Quitapahilla [original damaged].

We could not continue, and, as soon as we were at the mill, a terrible northwesterly storm arose. Our little ship was in quite a lot of danger because of the waves and because we could not quite haul it up onto land. In the evening Brother Xanter arrived with the provisions, but we could not load them because of the storm, which lasted through the night. We could also not keep a fire and had to sleep with one another on the wagon but could hardly stand the cold.

On April 25
The storm continued. We made a little mound with the wagon's cover, behind which we could load the flour into the barrels. As we were done, Brother Xanter left again, and we gave him two packs of hides for Bethlehem. An hour later the storm quietened down a little, and we began to travel but immediately had to navigate a very dangerous drop but came through safely. We thanked the Savior for this, because many people have already met with misfortune there. For about twenty miles we had very strong currents. In the evening we lodged on an island opposite where white people live.

On April 26

We woke up early, and, after we had traveled several miles, we caught a good wind. We profited by raising our sail, which consisted of a blanket. It went well. We passed another dangerous drop (where David and Martin had been shipwrecked). We tied a long rope to the canoe, and one of us pulled on that, and the others worked the paddles, and so we got up them safely. Our sail pulled as good as a man, and it turned out that we covered seventy miles against the current in a day and a half. But we got quite weak from this. In the evening around 9 o'clock, we arrived safely in Shamokin. We found everyone drunk, but we were able to bring our things quite quietly to the house and were glad to be with our dear hearts, who were still at home. They told us how badly the Indians had behaved during our absence and that they had allowed the Brothers no rest day or night and that they had killed almost all our chickens and eaten them.

On April 27

Our dear hearts David and Heinrich Frey arrived from Bethlehem. The Indians started to drink again.

On April 28

Things were still very tumultuous. Several Indians came to visit David and welcomed him, especially the two young warriors, one of whom was an Oneida chief, whom David knew well and had been there when they had wanted to allow the Brothers to travel through their lands. He was very pleased to see David here. In the evening David held the Singstunde.

On Monday, Tuesday, and Wednesday the Brothers made a canoe.

On May 3

The dear hearts David and Heinrich Frey left here for Onondaga. We supplied them with provisions, and, after we had kissed them cordially, they left with their new little ship. Brother Grube accompanied them for a few miles, and at his departure they let off a few shots for joy. We would have loved to go with them to Wyoming. But it could not be at this time.

On May 7

Brothers Pfeifer, Schwarz, and Kobus left here for Bethlehem. They took some hides with them. We also gave them reports to take with them. This week the new fence for the Indians was finished.

On May 11
We started to plant Indian corn. But it goes very badly, as the ground has to be broken up first with the hoe. An Indian began to build our charcoal store.

On May 19
We celebrated a blessed Communion and beforehand had a thorough Prayer Meeting [*Bande*].

On May 20
We were quite blessed in Jesus's wounds.

On May 21
Eleven canoes full of Indians arrived here. They had lived for a while on the Juniata and actually came from Monocacy in Maryland and are called Conoy Indians.[6] They speak most like the Nanticoke; they can also speak good English, and they want to settle in this area.

On May 25
We were finished with planting Indian corn.

On May 29
We began to move into our new house. We transported most of our things there with the skid.

On June 1
We were finished. We also left hardly a nail in the old house, took everything that we could loosen. In time we will also take off the roof. Everything went well and without hindrance. The day before everyone was drunk.

On June 2
We held our first Sabbath in the new house. Had a contented Lovefeast and dedicated our new little *Saal* and thanked the Savior for this dear little place. Brother Grube composed a little hymn for the occasion.

11

JUNE 4–JULY 31, 1753

BERNHARD GRUBE

Brother Grube's Little Travel Diary to Quenischaschaque

On June 4
Brother Grube traveled to Quenischaschaque. After I had taken my leave from the Brothers, I traveled with our canoe up the West Branch. About four miles from here, I visited Captain Logan's new place. But he was not at home. One mile farther on I visited a Shawnee hut. There were many people there, also John Shikellamy's wife, who had planted here. I did not stay there for long but rather continued my travels. It was quite tough. There came then a great thunderstorm, and I got very wet. In the evening I was very tired, and, as I was looking around for a place to put up my tent, I heard Indians calling out on the other side of the river. I answered them, and, as I went onshore to make a fire, they came over to me, and one of them called out, "Brother, Brother!" And this was our Christian Renatus, who had been out hunting with another Indian. He said, "Brother! I am happy to see you visiting! I thought of you already today, whether or not you would soon come to visit me, and, as I saw your canoe from afar, so I thought right away, that is the Brother from Shamokin. Come a little farther with us to a better spot, and then let's stay together!" I traveled a little farther from there with them, and we found a good little spot for our night camp, and I had a very good opportunity to tell them something of the Savior, and we were quite contented together. They gave me some bear meat to eat, and I gave them some bread, and so I slept very well with my dear Indians.

On June 5
I rose early and departed. The Indians soon followed me. I had a hard job getting up the falls, and I had to drag the canoe several times. At noon I waited

for Christian Renatus, and, as I was sitting on the bank and eating something, an Indian approached me from the other bank and asked where I wanted to go, and, when I told him, he told me that he did not advise it, as it was impossible to get up there alone, as there were many falls and very fast water the whole way up, and when Christian Renatus came to me, he told me the same thing. I therefore resolved to leave my canoe with the Indian and to continue my journey on foot. It was about ten miles this side of Ostonwakin.

I then continued my journey, which was mostly on the right-hand side of the West Branch, and, as I got to Ostonwakin, I relaxed on the spot where earlier the Indian town had stood, and I refreshed myself with strawberries and thought a great deal about our dear disciple and his dear travel company who pitched their tents here ten years ago.[1] It is a pleasant area, but now no one lives here anymore. I could now easily bathe in the Ostonwakin, the last time, however, it was up to my armpits, and the current was very strong.

In the afternoon, around 5 o'clock, I arrived at the first little town on this side of Quenischaschaque, where the deceased Madame Montour's daughter Margaret and her family live.[2] She is a very rich woman, has thirty horses, several cows, and forty pigs. This year she planted eight acres of Indian corn. I [manuscript corrupt] . . . The old woman cried and complained to me about her son and her daughter's husband, who were shot last year in the war.[3] The latter was shot by a Maqua by mistake, as he wanted to take an enemy prisoner, who, however, ran away from him, and, as he wanted to capture him, the Maqua shot and hit them both so that they both died soon after. In the evening I heard a great wailing and crying in the hut, for the sake of the murdered warriors. The old woman and her daughter were both wearing mourning clothes, brown and black.

On June 6
I went to Quenischaschaque, and, as I came into the town, an Indian by the name of Thomas Freeman came up to me and said immediately, "Welcome Brother! I know who you must be, and I want to take you into the lodge." And so he took me to James David's house, where Christian Renatus lodged, who also came out to meet me and was very pleased. Soon several Indians arrived and asked whether this was the Brother about whom they had heard so much, and they were very friendly toward me. Then I was treated to bear meat. Thomas Freeman said, "The reason they wanted to see and speak to a Brother was that there were various Indians here who really wanted to know the way to blessedness and wanted to hear something about the Savior." Then they took me into his house and told me much about his life story.

I went back into my lodgings and had to lie down because I did not feel well [manuscript corrupt]. In the evening I had a contented conversation with my host, to whom I praised the love of the Savior to us men and what He did for us on the Cross; He wanted to make the poor Indians happy, etc. I also read him some verses in Delaware, and the people in the hut were all attentive.

This morning I saw about 20 warriors arrive who were traveling home again through the great wilderness. They had a boy and a girl with them as prisoners; the mother had died along the way. But they could not stay here because last winter almost all the corn had been eaten by a great number of warriors, and the people are badly dispositioned because of the many warriors who always pass through here. Many have not a single grain of corn to eat and have to fetch flour from Tulpehocken more than 100 miles away, and the old and weak have to suffer much hunger.

On June 7
The chief of the town visited me, Christian Renatus's eldest brother. After this I went to Thomas Freeman and had the opportunity to tell him something about our reason for being here, and why we love the Indians so much and wish from our hearts that they might get to know their bloody God on a Cross also. He cried at this and said, "I am already baptized by the Church of England in Maryland, but my heart still knows no peace." I spoke a little more with him and then returned home. In the evening I visited a sick man and spoke to him about the Savior, during which an old man with two children from Allegheny came to us in the house, and many Indians gathered around him to hear news about the French movements there. I went into the woods for a while and was blessed and happy.

On June 8
Most of the Indians gathered in the old governor's house and called me to them. As I got there, I felt in my spirit that the enemy wanted to play some. The old man began and asked why I had come here. He did not want to hear anything about our journey. He had heard that we had transported many Indians onto an island, and he had still more wondrous things to say. When he had finished, I answered him and said, "My friend! I did not come here for myself; rather, several Indians desired that I come and visit them. Your very own brother, Brother Christian Renatus, had desired this" (he was there and said yes). Our method is to say nothing of our way to anyone who does not feel a desire in his heart and wants to go there too. I was therefore quite surprised that he wanted to forbid me from coming here again, to visit my good

friends, and he had no power to do that, for most of the Indians were not of his mind. I was pleased, however, that he had spoken his mind, and he would not then mind me speaking mine, as I just had. I intended to leave tomorrow and did not know whether I would ever return here in my life. And so I went back to my lodgings. Soon several of the Indians came to me and were downcast about the old chief's words and told me that they did not think like him but rather that I should visit them more. Meanwhile, I was quiet and happy and spoke some with the Savior. In the evening I visited Thomas Freeman. There were several Indians with him who were very friendly toward me. As I went back to my lodgings, the old chief was in front of his house, and he said he had nothing against me returning and appeared quite friendly.

On June 9
I made myself ready for the journey and spoke some more with Christian Renatus about his staying on here. I told the other Indians, who wanted to know, that he was going back to Gnadenhütten. I distributed my remaining rations, and this was pleasing to them. I then left and several Indians accompanied me to Thomas Freeman, with whom I was supposed to travel part of the way until I got my canoe. Christian Renatus asked me something and said, "Hey Brother! Do you still have paper with you? I have to write a letter to my brothers in Gnadenhütten." And so we walked a little way together, and he dictated it to me. He also said to me, "O Brother! Come back soon to me. I would very much like it." I said, "I hope to see you soon at my home, on your way to Gnadenhütten." My host also asked me to visit him again soon, and they took me to Margaret. Thomas Freeman said that we should go a little onto land and say a prayer before we left, and so Margaret called me into her hut, as several others had gathered there. Thomas Freeman knelt down and prayed for a Quarter of an Hour, and everyone was very thoughtful during this. The old woman said repeatedly, "O Lord, o Lord!" We continued on, but it began to rain very heavily, and so we stayed the night with the Indians, where I had left my canoe. We had very little room to lie down.

On Sunday, June 10
I got up early and, as I went to the river to leave, I found that my canoe had gone. I asked one of the Indians who might have taken it. He said a Shawnee. But I should just go downriver a little to the Shawnee town, and I would find it there. And so I did this, and I found it. Then I paddled hard because I really wanted to get home that evening, and toward evening I arrived happily in Shamokin again. Brother Marcus Kiefer had come to meet me and met me just as I came on land. We rejoiced together as though we had not seen each

other for half a year. The Brothers told me straightaway how the time had been here and that they had been very plagued by the drunken Indians; especially two warriors from the Seneca country had behaved very badly. They had broken down the doors to the house and violently wanted to get food, grabbed the Brothers by the chest, and acted as though they wanted to kill them. The Brothers gave them bread and milk, but they were not happy with that, and one especially acted like Satan. Here patience and love are especially needed. Conrad Weiser's four sons had been here during this time but had not come into our house.

On June 12
We began to hoe our Indian corn. Logan, John, and a few other Indians went to Tulpehocken to Conrad Weiser's to fetch flour.

On June 16
We held a blessed Communion.

On June 17
Brothers Grube and Marcus Kiefer visited the Conoy Indians. There were mostly women at home. For the time being there is no work to [be] done with them.

On June 18 and the Following Days
We were busy with hoeing Indian corn. The shoemaker, Peter, who lives twenty miles away, arrived here safely in the morning on his way to Tulpehocken, with another man whose name is Ludwig Maus, and had some work done in the blacksmith's shop. The shoemaker asked me to visit him, and if I wanted to hold a meeting at his place on a Sunday that would be very welcome to him and his neighbors, for they had not heard anything about the Savior for a long time. He said he had a small child who was still unbaptized. I told him I could not promise anything because I was sent here not for the Christians but rather for the heathens, but because the man had so begged me I resolved to visit him on the 23rd after the Sabbath meal. Brother Marcus Kiefer accompanied me several miles, and as I arrived the people rejoiced greatly and asked me to hold a meeting on Sunday, which I could not refuse. They also lamented the fact that the small child, a few weeks old, was still unbaptized and asked me to baptize her.

[On June 21]
Brother Grube celebrated his 39th birthday with a little Lovefeast.

On June 24 [Sunday]
I held [a Quarter of] an Hour for the people from the area who had gathered and also baptized the shoemaker's little daughter. Anna Magdalene and the mother and father cried at this. All the people who mostly live by Jacobs Höhe in the valley asked me to visit them again soon. A few of them have heard our Brothers speak already. I soon got on my way again and climbed the steep mountains and in the evening arrived again in Shamokin. A few minutes later the two Indian Brothers Peter and David arrived who had been hunting and who wanted to visit us, about which we were very happy. They stayed the night with us.

On June 25
They left again into the woods, for there was much drinking here. Brother Grube wrote letters to Bethlehem. The drunken Indians said to Peter that he should preach to them, but he answered, if you were sober you would not say that. An Indian from Wyoming arrived here in the blacksmith's shop. He spoke a great deal about the Savior to another Indian. Our two Brothers Peter and David listened and said that the man spoke many truths about the Savior, and, as we inquired more closely as to who he was, it turned out that it was the brother of our Nathaniel from Meniolagomeka.[4] A handsome man. He also wants to visit his brother in Meniolagomeka after the hunt. Anton's biological brother was also here, but he soon left after he heard that smallpox was here.

On June 29
Ludwig from Nescopeck came down here and ordered something in the blacksmith's shop. He was going to the hunt.

On June 30
We had a quiet and blessed Sabbath.

On July 1
We heard that Logan had taken another wife and had left his old one, the Mohican woman. We visited the huts but found no one home except Schafmann, a good friend of the Brothers.

On July 2
We heard that French Andrew [Montour] had traveled through here on his way to Onondaga. We would have liked to write to our dear Brothers there ourselves but could not, as Andrew did not stop by here. These days five

warriors came down here; one of them was an Onondaga, a handsome man, to whom Brother Grube gave a letter for our dear David [Zeisberger], and he promised to deliver it properly.

On July 10
Ten warriors arrived here again with two scalps.[5] They came to us a lot because they were very hungry. We gave them some food to each according to our ability, and they were very grateful for it.

On July 14
We held a blessed Communion.

On July 19
Andrew arrived from Onondaga by way of Quenischaschaque and brought letters from our dear heart David, about which we were very happy. We would have liked to send them on to Bethlehem immediately, but none of us could be missed for so long. Andrew told us that he had made the journey from Onondaga to Quenischaschaque in five days but that he had a good horse.

During these days a boy from Shikellamy's family died of smallpox. The children here have mostly all had the smallpox and got through it quite well. We tended them with milk and did good things for them.

On July 28
We had a contented Sabbath and Prayer Meeting of the heart [*Herzensbande*]. In the afternoon we went to visit the Indians but did not arrive at the right time, as whiskey was then their master.

On July 31
Brother Grube traveled by water to Wyoming and left the two Brothers contented and well at home.

12

JANUARY 11–JULY 2, 1754

DAVID KLIEST

On Friday, January 11
I traveled with Brother Mattheus Otto from the dear and precious congregation in Bethlehem with true pangs of love, and, because it was already late, we could not make it farther than Macungie and stayed in the schoolhouse with Brother and Sister Neubert, who welcomed us cordially and with love.

On Saturday, January 12
We left there early, and around midday we reached Heidelberg. Brother and Sister Wagner welcomed us cordially also, as did many of the Brethren who live in the countryside who had gathered here for a sermon. After the sermon we took our leave and traveled from here to George Loesch. Brother Casper Rieth accompanied us for part of the way, and after he had got us onto the right path, he took his leave amicably and returned home. The dear Brother and Sister Loesch took us in with much love and warmth, and we stayed here overnight. They provided well for us with food for our impending journey. After we had said goodbye warmly, we departed here on January 14. Dear old Father Loesch accompanied us for 6 miles, and then we took our leave, and he returned home.

On Tuesday, January 15
We arrived in Shamokin, and, as we came toward our house, we heard our Brother Bachhof's voice, which made us very happy that he was still alive. The two dear Brothers Bachhof and Marcus Kiefer were very happy about our arrival and welcomed us warmly.

On Wednesday, January 16
We rested a little. Brother Otto[1] sorted out our little house apothecary a little and recommended a medicine for Brother Bachhof, which he should continue until his diarrhea was completely cured. After this had happened, Brother Otto and I went to the Susquehanna and visited the Indian huts. We found only two menfolk at home; the others were all womenfolk and children. We also visited the grave of our departed Brother Hagen. After this we returned home again and resolved that Brother Otto and I would leave the next day for Bethlehem. We closed this day with a tender and heartfelt Evening Blessing and laid ourselves down to rest in the wounds of the Savior.

On Thursday, January 17
Brother Bachhof complained that he was experiencing more of his diarrhea and for this reason had not been able to sleep all night, at which we perceived in our hearts that it would be better if Brother Bachhof were to go back to Bethlehem and I stay here. We proposed this to him, and it suited him. After we had breakfasted a little, we took heartfelt leave of one another. Brother Marcus Kiefer accompanied them and stayed alone at home. I felt in my heart and soul a little downcast that I had to stay here, but the dear Savior was tangibly close to my heart, and in my spirit I abided much with the congregation.

On Friday, January 18
I had quite a lot of visitors from the various womenfolk and children, for whom I had to partly sharpen their axes and who also wanted something to eat. This evening my dear Marcus Kiefer returning from accompanying [the others] and brought with him heartfelt greetings from Brothers Bachhof and Otto. I was happy that he was here again.

On the Sabbath, January 19
We celebrated a dear and peaceful Sabbath. At noon we had a Lovefeast, and I spoke some about the blessed path of the congregation and what the Savior had done for His people and what I had felt and known in my heart during the short time of my visit, which does not allow me to express in words very easily. After the Evening Blessing we laid ourselves down to rest in the wounds of our Husband.

On Sunday, January 20
We visited the Indians in their huts. We were also visited by two white people. They live only six miles away from here, on the other side of the Susquehanna,

by George Gabriel, who is a trader. They brought some work for me. One of them, a tailor, N. Ostermann, said that he had also been acquainted with Brethren in Switzerland in Bern, and after this he had visited Herrnhaag. That was in the year 1742. However, he had not received permission to stay there and blamed his bad conduct for being sent away. After that he had got married and has been in the country for five years but moved up here only recently. We closed the day with an Evening Blessing and laid ourselves down to sleep, content.

On Monday, January 21
We were most overjoyed with the arrival of our dear Brother David [Zeisberger], who brought with him both in letters and words beautiful and happy news from the dear congregation. Brother David also told us that on the way here he had learned that the dear hearts Gottlob [Hoffmann] and Nathaniel had returned from their trip to North Carolina safe and well, which was very dear for us to hear, and we thanked the Lamb for this. Our dear heart David also worked very hard; as he had found our house still so unfinished, he did what he could. He laid a beautiful strong floor in our house, for which he made the boards himself, and we helped as we could. Overall, he was able to help us with advice and deeds more than we had thought possible. He also held a beautiful Singstunde and Evening Blessing for us. In all these opportunities the Lamb felt close to our hearts. During this time we also had the Cup of Thanksgiving.

On February 17
We enjoyed the Body and Blood of the Martyr, at which we were unspeakably happy.

On February 18
We were a little sad because our dear heart David, who had been a blessing to us until now, traveled to the synod. We asked for the congregation to think of us in support of our bloody Husband.

In the month of March Indians came to us now and again asking for me to fix their [flintlocks]. Otherwise, nothing special happened.

On Monday, April 1
We heartily rejoiced at the arrival of our dear Brother David and Brother Gottlieb. They were most welcome. Our hearts were also gladdened by the pleasant news that they brought with them from the congregation both in

letters and orally.² During this week our dear heart David held many nice little Singing Hours and Evening Blessings. The Lamb was among us.

On the Sabbath, April 6
We held a Lovefeast, during which Brother David told us something of our dear Brothers and sisters in the Gemeine. This made us feel contented.

On Sunday, April 7
We held a quite blessed Communion. Everything around us was quite still. As though we were in the midst of the Gemeine.

On Monday, April 8
In the morning our dear heart David prepared himself to leave. Beforehand we held a little farewell Lovefeast, and then we took a heartfelt leave of him, gave him some little letters, and through these tried to remind the Brothers and Sisters to think of us.

This so-called Passion Week [*Marterwoche*] was an especially blessed week to us because the "Passion of the Lamb is a great joy to us. His Crown of Thorns and scourge a balsam to our souls. Our soul is well in itself when we think of Him, and He should plunge us into His Side Hole."

On the Sabbath, April 13
We spent the day in a blessed meditation on the Body of Jesus in the grave. We held at midday and in the evening a Singstunde and an Evening Blessing.

On Thursday, April 18
The Shawnee chief from the Great Island was here and brought me some work. He was happy to have found me here. He recognized me straightaway because I had repaired a gun for him two years ago in Bethlehem. He also asked about Brother Albrecht, who had stocked his gun two years ago to his complete satisfaction. He would have liked to have talked much more with me but could speak no English. But I could feel what was in his mind and heart, that he held us dear. His wife was also well-mannered.

On the Sabbath, April 20
A gunsmith arrived here from Lancaster and stayed with us overnight. His name was William Henry.³ He has often gone to the meetings of the Brethren in Lancaster. He went from here on the 21st to Thomas McKee. Today we were also visited by our neighbors who live by the trader, George Gabriel. He himself

was also here and brought some work, and then he complained that we came to visit him so little. He said that he held the Brethren dear and wished that we would come to visit him more often on Sundays. For his part, he was trying to build a closer connection with us, and he has many people at his house, and it would be good if we would come occasionally and see how it went with them and sometimes hold an exhortation. He asked very seriously that I should inform the Brethren in Bethlehem that they should also take care of him, because he lived not only for the temporal things of the world but also for the things of his heart. I told him that this was good. I would report this to the Brethren, and because we were here we wanted to come and visit him as much as the time and circumstances allowed. But to preach to people or to hold an exhortation to those who are comfortable in their condition was not our way of doing things. If we were to come to them and find someone there who yearned in their soul to get to know his God and Creator, then it would be a joy to our heart to speak to such souls. Today Mr. Conrad Weiser arrived here and stayed with the Indians in the town.

On Monday, April 22
He visited us and was very friendly. We offered him our house as a lodging and told him he was welcome here. But he replied that he was not able to be welcome, because whenever he was here the house was always full of Indians, and therefore neither we, nor he, would have any peace. We asked him to tell us whether we could serve him in any way. We wanted to do as much as we could for him from the bottom of our hearts. He said he would tell us.

Today Leonhardt, the Indian from Nescopeck, who had lived with the Brethren before now, was here. He was very drunk, identified himself right away, and asked for Brother Grube. He said he was going to war with the Catawba. I could not speak with him very much, as he was not in possession of much reason. We gave him some food and let him go on his way. The aforementioned gunsmith[4] from Lancaster returned today with a Jew by the name of Joseph Meuer and stayed overnight with us. The Jew is a silversmith.

On April 23
They traveled from here to Wyoming.

On April 27
They returned and stayed with us overnight. They also brought some pieces of hard coal with them, which they had broken off from the cliffs above the Susquehanna, and also two pieces of ore, which they wanted to test out at

their furnace. They told us that the Indians in Wyoming had told them that they had the ore tested in Bethlehem and that brass had been made with it. I said that I did not believe that was true. They said that they had heard from several people that we were melting down a lot of ore here and were becoming very rich from it. He had now discovered that people had been lying to him, because he could see for himself that we didn't have the slightest means to do this and no smelting oven.

On Sunday, April 28
In the morning they left here, and Mr. Conrad Weiser, who had stayed in Shamokin for a whole week and who had visited us almost every day and had shown himself to be very friendly toward us, came to visit us and say goodbye again. We closed the day with an Evening Blessing.

On Friday, May 3
The old Mohican, Blackfish, brought us two heartwarming letters from Bethlehem from our dear hearts David and Christian Seidel, which told us of the arrival of the dear and beloved Brothers and Sisters from Europe on the *Irene* and about their almost unheard of speedy and safe passage across the ocean.[5] We rejoiced and thanked the little Lamb for everything that He does for His people and the Gemeine. We desired that we would soon see Brother Joseph and the dear hearts who had accompanied him in the flesh so that we could greet them and welcome them cordially; in the meantime we would do this in spirit. We closed this day with a small service of song and Evening Blessing and also took part in the festival of thanks that was being held in Bethlehem and Nazareth and thanked the Lamb in our poverty as well as we could. We felt the Lamb's closeness in our hearts, and so we laid ourselves down to rest.

On the Sabbath, May 4
At midday we celebrated a Lovefeast and were in our hearts much occupied with the Gemeine. After this we visited the Indian houses but found few at home. We stayed a while in the house of Logan Shikellamy. He was friendly and asked whether Ganosseracheri would soon return here. We said that we did not know. He has sent us a letter yesterday with Blackfish, in which he reported that he was well and healthy and that our dear T'girhitondi had arrived safely in Bethlehem from over the water with some Brothers and Sisters. Logan and his wife were very happy to hear this. Furthermore, they asked how T'girhitondi's wife was doing. We told them that she was no longer

here but rather up with our dear God, at which they were surprised and looked very sad. They also asked about Joseph Powell and his wife and Sister Hagen. We gave them news of each person. Logan told us that they were thinking of leaving tomorrow with his Brother John to Onondaga, to speak the words that Mr. Conrad Weiser had entrusted with him to the Six Nations.[6] He was thinking of returning in two months. They would be traveling with the Six Nations via Albany to Philadelphia first, where he was hoping to see dear Brother T'girhitondi, which he was looking forward to. We closed this day with a little Singstunde and an Evening Blessing.

On Sunday May 5
Today Brother Kliest[7] wanted to visit, as requested, George Gabriel (who lives on the other side of the Susquehanna, six miles from here) and the people who live by him but could not get over the river because the wind was so strong that they could not hear his calls;[8] therefore, [he] went home again without accomplishing this task. We were all busy this week with planting Indian corn and lots of other things. Not many Indians came, just those who needed something. We were at peace, and our Lamb of God was in our midst.

On the Sabbath, May 11,
We held a Lovefeast and thought a great deal about the dear Gemeine in Bethlehem on this day with an Evening Blessing.

Sunday, May 12
We were visited by various Indians. We were at peace and closed this day with a little Singstunde and an Evening Blessing. Not many Indians came here this week, so we used our time to chop wood, in part for charcoal and in part as firewood. We chopped the wood near our house so that it would become a little more airy. It is necessary. Until now we have been much inconvenienced by the mosquitoes and sand flies.

On the Sabbath, May 18
We held a Lovefeast and closed the day with an Evening Blessing and laid ourselves down to rest in peace.

On Sunday, May 19
We visited the Indians in their houses but did not find many at home. In the evening we held a Singstunde and Evening Blessing, during which we were quite content. This week we built two bridges over the ditch, which is close to

our house and also had various visits from Indians. In our hearts we dwelt much with thoughts of the dear Gemeine and often looked out for the Brethren who were supposed to be coming to relieve us.

On June 11
We had the great pleasure of seeing and heartily welcoming our dear and long-awaited Brethren, namely Brother Boehmer and Brother and Sister Anton Schmidt and Lambert Garrison.[9] At the same time we received many cordial letters from the congregation of the Lamb, which awakened in our hearts a special feeling of love, and the desire now grew ever greater to see the dear Brothers and Sisters in the Gemeine in person and to greet them and kiss them. Brother Boehmer and the Schmidts told us many things, and we shared in our hearts all that the Lamb had done for His people and Gemeine.

On the Sabbath, June 15
Brother Boehmer conducted a sweet Lovefeast for us and regaled us with more stories from the Gemeine, at which we felt well contented. After the Lovefeast I went out to look for our horses that the Brothers and Sisters had brought but could not find them. We thought that they had probably started to make their way back. Therefore, I went as far as the shoemaker by the name of Peter Glück, who lived fifteen miles away from Shamokin and on the [Tulpehocken] path. I asked if they had seen anything of the horses, but they said no. Because it would now soon be night, at their insistence I stayed overnight. They were very friendly and cordial and offered me quite a few opportunities to speak to them about the love of the Savior for sinners, and I felt contented in their home. They also asked many questions about Brother Grube, who had baptized a child for them a year ago, which is a great blessing to them, and also told me that he had held a meeting for them and had spoken about the text: "Surely He hath borne our griefs and carried our sorrows, yet we did esteem Him stricken, smitten of God, and afflicted,"[10] which had made such an impression on them and their neighbors that they would never forget it. They would have liked to have seen me hold a meeting for them in the morning, but because I do not have orders from the Gemeine to do so, I excused myself with the promise that they were thought of by the Gemeine and that Brother Boehmer, who had been sent to us by the dear Gemeine and who now lived in Shamokin, would come and visit them as soon as he had time and speak to them about the Savior. They looked forward to this very much.

On Sunday, June 16

In the morning I said my heartfelt farewell and returned home. I arrived only toward evening, as I had left the path and had gone far into the woods to see if I could find the horses somewhere and had almost lost my way. The Brothers and Sisters were therefore even more overjoyed to see me again. Today Brothers Schmidt, Lambert Garrison, and Marcus Kiefer traveled with the canoe down the Susquehanna to fetch provisions. After an Evening Blessing, we laid ourselves down to sleep, content.

On Monday, June 17

Brothers Boehmer and Gottlieb went to our old place and carried the stones from the old chimney to the blessed Brother Hagen's grave and made a fence with them around the grave and finished the job in one day.[11]

On Wednesday, June 19

The afore-named Brothers returned with provisions. To our joy they were healthy and well. We held a blessed Singstunde and Evening Blessing.

On June 20

The Brothers traveled with the canoe down the Susquehanna again to fetch boards for our house at the sawmill. Shortly after that, it began to rain very heavily and continued to do so the rest of the day. We could not leave the house. We held a blessed Lovefeast for the Sabbath and our little Lamb of God was among us, and we closed the day with a sweet Singstunde and Evening Blessing.

On June 24

The water rose a lot.

On June 25

The water came into our house about four feet high, and we had to come in and out with the canoe. Toward evening we thought that if the water continued to rise, we should move to the hills. We noticed, however, that it had crested, and so we recommended ourselves to the wounds of the Savior and laid ourselves down to sleep.

On June 26

The water fell as quickly as it had risen on the day before. It had caused us some damage in our house and fields, but we had particular cause to thank our dear Savior for His gracious protection in our ark.

On June 27
We were busy drying out our house and nailing down our floorboards that had been raised by the flood and looking for our horses, which had run away again. But we did not find them. We closed this day with an Evening Blessing.

On Friday, June 28
In the morning we prepared ourselves to leave for Bethlehem. We held one more sweet Lovefeast on our departure, and after this we took heartfelt leave of one another and in fact not without a little tear, because it was painful for those Brothers and Sisters who had to stay, especially for Brother Boehmer, who was not yet used to the solitary lifestyle. He accompanied us for a little, as did Brother Anton Schmidt, then we exchanged a kiss, and they returned. At midday we arrived at the shoemaker's [Peter Glück]. They welcomed us very lovingly, gave us some food to eat, and told us that whenever we came by this way we should stop to speak with them and that we should cordially greet the Brothers and Sisters in the Gemeine from them and recommend them to their prayers and whenever other Brothers and Sisters came by this way who had never been there before we should tell them not just to pass by, for they would love to see anyone of our people. And if they could not show much love to us, so they would do it in their hearts. We thanked them for their love and took a heartfelt farewell. We continued on to Ludwig's Ruh and wanted to stay there but found little firewood and so continued on to the Thürnstein, where we found wood and so made ourselves a good fire and lay down to sleep.

On the Sabbath, June 29
We set out on our way again in the morning and toward evening arrived at our dear Brother and Sister Loesch's, who were very happy to see us and welcomed us lovingly. Soon after, the dear Brother and Sister Neisser arrived from Bethlehem and stayed with us overnight and told us much blessed news from the Gemeine.

On Sunday, June 30
Brother and Sister Neisser continued on to Lebanon and with them for the sermon Father Loesch, Kliest, and Marcus Kiefer. In the evening we returned again with the beloved Father Loesch and laid ourselves down to sleep.

On Monday, July 1
We took our leave in the morning and went on to Heidelberg, where we met Brother and Sister Wagner, healthy and well. They refreshed us with some

food, and after this we took our leave and made our way to Papsts's plantation, where we stayed the night.

On Tuesday, July 2
We left here and in the evening arrived in our dear Bethlehem. We thanked the Lamb for His gracious protection and company to this point and gave ourselves over to the care of the holy Gemeine like the poorest and neediest children.

13

DECEMBER 19–25, 1754

HEINRICH FREY AND GOTTLIEB ROESCH

Journey from Gnadenhütten to Shamokin

On December 19
Over the noon hour we began our journey to Wyoming after a heartfelt farewell from Gnadenhütten. Brothers Fabricius and Wesa accompanied us to the top of the Spitzberg, and from there they turned around, and because they had carried our bundles until then, we were especially aware of their love for us. Soon after this an Indian from Gnadenhütten met us (he said he was the husband of our Mariane, who now lives in Wyoming).[1] We heard later that that was true, although he was separated from her again. He went with us until the watchpoint, where he made his way to Nescopeck. He behaved with great friendliness toward us.

On December 20
We made good night quarters with a large fire, as it was so cold, just as we did yesterday evening in Johannes Ruh.

On December 21
Toward sundown we arrived in Wyoming on the Susquehanna, which was flowing fast with ice. After calling loudly for a canoe to cross, some boys and an Indian woman finally came to the edge of the water, but the latter let us know that we could not be ferried across because of the strong ice flow. Then Brother Heinrich called out once again that we came from Gnadenhütten. At that she gave us a friendly signal, ran off, and said that she would send someone right away who would get us across, and thereupon Joachim, Abraham's son, appeared, making his way over to us very painstakingly through the ice chunks

and fetched us and brought us to his father's house, where we were welcomed in a very friendly fashion, also by old Maria, who Brother Grube had baptized there, who along with others joined us quickly and appeared quite happy and cheerful. From among the menfolk in Wyoming, there was no one else at home but Abraham and Joachim, for we had come upon some Delaware huts already, where there were only womenfolk at home. The aforementioned Indian woman, who had come to the Susquehanna and had arranged our crossing, as we later heard, was the wife, Elisabeth, of our dear old Paxinos.

It was very cold in the night, so that when we lay down by a pretty big fire we still froze, and so it was for our host, Abraham, throughout the whole night. And because Abraham can speak good German and at this moment was quite cheerful and awake, we were able to converse well with Abraham, and we had a very nice night in Wyoming. Abraham told us that it would be his wish that a Brother would live in Wyoming. It would be a blessing for the whole area. He assured us though that the Shawnee and especially Paxinos's household loved us dearly. There were also a few Delaware places that longed for something and that kept themselves orderly and loved us too. Also the Minisink town, where Brothers Grube and Rundt had been, still felt that they were looking for something for their hearts.[2] Things were not going well at a few other Delaware villages, especially where Gideon was living. Abraham's little son Isaac, who had been very ill for a time, was really cheerful, and when Brother Rösler gave them greetings from Brother Reber in Bethlehem, he said himself that he would like to dictate a little letter for him, and Brother Rösler wrote it as was dictated to us. He asked whether the little Negro boy, Daniel, was still living in the boys' school [*Anstalt*]. He wanted to greet him especially. Brother Abraham asked us where Brother Post might be. And, as we answered his question, he said of his own accord that he wanted to dictate a letter to him before we leave, which he also did on the 22nd, when Brother Rösler wrote it word for word as Abraham said it in Mohican, and Joachim then in German. And because we saw that we had achieved what we had wanted to in Wyoming, so we started our journey back today. As we left, we reminded them of the impending birthday of our dear Savior, who had already done so much for their hearts, that they should in turn make use of this for the good of their hearts. (Brother Abraham had asked us soon after our arrival when Christmas Day was.) They gave us various greetings to convey to Bethlehem and Gnadenhütten, and so we went our way, quite content and comforted from the various blessed conversations about Wyoming and the whole affair of the Savior with the poor Indian people in this area and slept this night in Wamphallobank.

On December 23
We arrived in Nescopeck and visited with Nutimus, where no one but the *Paten* [Godfather] Nutimus was at home, who was very friendly, and at our request was quite willing to take us over the Susquehanna. As we arrived that evening at old Salomon's, it was good that we had crossed at Nescopeck, because if we had gone down the river on this side, we would not have reached them, because now in winter he lives a little away from the river in the woods and would not have heard us call [for a canoe]. He welcomed us at our arrival and professed that he would very much like it if we would come to his house. We had walked in the rain today. He and his wife and Johannes, the grandson, were alone at home. But it was not as comfortable for us here as it had been in Wyoming.

On December 24
We set off on our way to Shamokin again. At our departure he said that his heart was often in Bethlehem and Gnadenhütten, and he also sent greetings along with us. What we heard and felt there once again gave us cause for many conversations about the business with the Indians along the Susquehanna, at which we were content. By the evening we had come to about twenty miles above Shamokin, not far from Labachpeton's Village, where, after we had climbed our way through two big creeks, we made our night camp under the stars and celebrated the blessed night of the birth of our Creator and Savior. Around midnight it started to rain, and so we had to make a tent out of our blanket and sit under it, so then sleep was not permitted. But we were quite content and spent this night in quite blessed meditation, were with the Gemeine in our hearts, and the night had soon passed before we knew it.

On December 25
Toward evening we arrived in Shamokin on Christmas Day, quite happy at our dear Brothers and Sisters who had gone out to look for our arrival almost every hour. We rejoiced on both sides. And we thanked the Savior from our hearts that He had allowed this journey to end happily through the good works of His angels and His nearness.

14

APRIL 1–MAY 31, 1755

GOTTFRIED RÖSLER

On Tuesday, April 1
After Brothers Boehmer and Anton Schmidt left here for Bethlehem yesterday, Brothers Gattermeyer and Rösler, who are to be occupied here with Brother Wesa, began to settle into their affairs. We still had our dear Brother Christian Seidel and Heinrich Frey with us, who were, however, preparing for a journey tomorrow. The former held a short sermon and Evening Blessing for us on the Daily Text of the Savior: "Blessed are they who have not seen and *yet* have believed."[1]

On Wednesday, April 2
Brother Christian Seidel conducted the Morning Blessing for us, and after breakfast he departed from here with Heinrich Frey and the Indian Brother Joseph. Brothers Rösler and Wesa accompanied them for part of the way and carried their bundles for them. In the afternoon it rained very heavily, and because it had rained the whole of the previous night, we thought of our pilgrims a great deal, especially as to how they would cross the big creeks. In the evening, as it was still raining heavily, a family of Delaware came from the West Branch who asked us for night lodging. We gave them permission, and they were quite orderly and grateful, and we three Brothers laid ourselves down to rest, quite content after our Evening Blessing.

On Thursday, April 3
We had another Delaware Indian to take in, along with a white man from Thomas McKee's people, who came from the Allegheny. They were both very modest and wanted to acknowledge clearly everything they had enjoyed from us. Finally, he said that he had often thought of visiting Bethlehem.

On Friday, April 4
We were quite alone and content in our household. In the evening around our fire, we held beautiful discourses of the heart and closed the day with a blessed liturgy from the hymn, "O sacred head, now wounded."[2]

On the Sabbath, April 5
Toward midday we held our Sabbath Lovefeast. We had all kinds of visits today from Delaware Indians, who were either traveling through or else were hungry and looking for food. We fed the latter according to our means.

On Sunday April 6
Over breakfast we discussed how we wanted to celebrate our Sabbath Sunday. Right after this we prayed the church litany, during which we felt especially close to the Savior at the verse, "My God, you see them grazing."[3] Around midday French Margaret stopped in with several of her people and ordered something from me in the blacksmith's shop, and then she continued on her way. In the afternoon we delighted collectively in the first homily of the Litany of the Wounds.[4]

Monday, April 7
Today we were able to work in our garden for the first time and sowed all kinds of seeds. Not far from our house an Indian woman had camped with a few barrels of rum. That did not bode well for us, especially as an increasing number of Indians gathered and then, lo, in the afternoon, what we had predicted, began. There was quite a hubbub around our house And their comings and goings at our house made us quite uneasy.

On Tuesday, April 8
The noise that had begun yesterday and that had continued through the night went on. In the evening several came into our house, one of whom made a lot of noise and in his madness thought that he knew how to speak about Jesus in the thinking of the Dunkers[5] and Herrnhuters.[6] Later he was taken back to his wife by another Indian who had sobered up a little, and then we could sleep that night quite peacefully.

Wednesday, April 9
Today, on my 45th birthday, which I celebrated by myself at my work, in the blessed closeness of the Savior, it was quiet around the house again. We were visited by several Indians who were traveling by. An old Indian also came to me who lives about five miles from here on the other side of the Susquehanna. He complained to us that he otherwise lived in Jersey with Brainerd's people[7]

but had been forcibly taken away from there by his son and that he was very anxious here. He stayed the night with us, and we were quite comfortable with him. We told him something of the Savior and about Gnadenhütten, about which he knew a little. After a Singstunde, during which we cleaved ourselves anew to the wounds of the Savior with a few verses and celebrated Br. Rösler's birthday, we laid ourselves down to sleep, quite content.

On Thursday, April 10
In the morning we prepared a Lovefeast for ourselves as much as in commemoration of Brother Rösler's birthday yesterday. As for the description today of our dear Lord: an air of the heathen; Shamokin is surely such a valley of the heathen. There is no one now living here; one gets to see so few Indians here that I had not imagined this. After a blessed little Singstunde that Brother Gattermeyer held, we laid ourselves down contentedly to sleep.

On Friday, April 11
We were once again visited by all kinds of Indians. Brother Wesa visited the Delaware who had recently behaved so badly in his drunken state, and he had visited here again afterward and was quite withdrawn and, when he was drunk again, did not behave the way he had the first time. He can also speak some German. Brother Gattermeyer, who is beginning to learn some Delaware, used him for this purpose.

On the Sabbath, April 12
We held our Sabbath Lovefeast at noon, with lovely heartfelt conversations, and immediately afterward a blessed liturgy from the Pleurody.[8] We were ignored by the Indians who lived around us and quite undisturbed during this. Toward evening Peter Glück, the shoemaker, arrived with his son and brought us four bushels of maize flour. It was just at the right time, as our maize had just run out, and one of us would have had to go [for some].

On Sunday, April 13
Because we had our friends with us, we held an opportunity to speak about our good Shepherd, who gave His life for us and His martyrdom. The shoemaker told us afterward that, considering the sermon, he was no longer in agreement with his neighbors. A Lutheran pastor had been there several times already. They wanted to build a church and considered him to be a Moravian. He assured us of his love, even though he knew that he was not like us. Soon after this the Indians began to drink again, and because there was one among them who had something against the shoemaker, we made sure that he left

with his son because they soon would have found him in our house. Now our Sunday was at an end, as they made a terrible noise, which continued on throughout the night.

Monday, April 14
Today we had a difficult day, as our house was constantly surrounded by and full of drunken Indians. At first the men drank alone; after this the women began. Some Maqua arrived as well, some of whom also immediately started drinking. It would have been a great comfort to us if we could have gone into the woods, but we had to endure it. One could see so clearly how the poor heathen had been tyrannized by the god they had worshipped, and what they had learned from the white people until now, because one could hear, especially from one of them, all the most coarse words in the German language. In the evening it quietened down. It was as though a powerful storm had passed. We spoke with one another about what had happened and prostrated ourselves before the Savior and laid ourselves down to sleep after a little Singstunde.

Tuesday, April 15
During the past night one could hear screaming now and again. A drunken man knocked on our house one time but went on his way again. And thus we had contact from this sort of people the whole day, who were, however, quite quiet. In the evening a Maqua came with his wife and boy and stayed with us. He has been here many times. They came from Schohari above Tioga. They are baptized and live on the West Branch.

On Wednesday April 16
We had some visits from Indians. The Maqua, who are staying where our old house used to be, were reveling today. We could hear them quite well but were left in peace by them.

On Thursday, April 17
French Margaret returned and stopped in at our house at 4:30 in the morning. We treated her happily to breakfast with *sapan* and milk. They were also very friendly toward us. At midday Labachpeton was with us, and we talked about our people for a while. Drunken womenfolk of the Maqua came by too, but we did not let them into our house, and so they went on their way again.

Friday, April 18
Today Shikellamy's sons arrived, and the Delaware who had been around us began to set off for Tulpehocken again. Toward evening we unexpectedly saw

our dear Ahamawad [Christian Post], who had come from our dear Bethlehem and overjoyed us with letters, greetings, and other tales from there. He was quite wet from the rain and had gone through some difficulties and looked quite despondent so that we were worried about him.

On the Sabbath, April 19
We held our Lovefeast at midday, at which we had our dear Ahamawad, who entertained us with discourses and verses with a Sabbath-like feeling. Not long after this, he went to see white people across the Susquehanna to look for someone who would help him bring ten bushels of Indian corn up the Susquehanna that he had left about fifteen miles from here. In the evening he returned and had found someone.

On Sunday, April 20
We held contented discourses over breakfast, and after this we prayed the *Gemein-Litaney*, during which we felt quite at peace. After lunch Br. Ahamawad left here with our canoe to fetch the aforementioned corn.

On Monday, April 21
Today we were busy with our usual work in our garden and had to deal with hungry Indians visiting us almost every day.

On Tuesday, April 22
At noon Brother Ahamawad arrived with his corn. Because the Susquehanna is high, he had exhausted himself and had fallen into the water a few times.

On Wednesday, April 23
Logan and John Shikellamy had breakfast with us early. Another Indian and his wife, who is the daughter of Paxinos, came as well. Br. Ahamawad gathered all kinds of instruments together to take to Wyoming, and Brother Wesa had to do his part in this. Tonight a few Delaware Indians stayed with us, with whom we had all kinds of chances to hold discourses and told them also about the Greenlanders and our stay and purpose there as well.[9]

On Thursday, April 24
A young Christian man came to us. He was an Englishman. He said he came from Minisink, above Wyoming. He was wet and hungry, and we could not deny him his request for night quarters.

On Friday, April 26
The man who will go with our Ahamawad to Wyoming arrived. He lives about five miles from here and has traveled the path to Wyoming many times. Today, like many of the days before, we had talk of many hungry Indians here.

On the Sabbath, April 26
Our dear Ahamawad with his helper and our canoe set off to Wyoming early. We had spent the last week quite contentedly together. Before noon several Delaware Indian families who had come down the West Branch came to speak to us. They had ordered work in the blacksmith's shop and did not stay long so that we could enjoy our Sabbath tea and bread at noon undisturbed. Right after this we prayed the litany of the life, Passion, and death of our Lord, as we had amended ourselves with the help of Br. Rösler's new liturgy book. It tasted very good to us.[10]

On Sunday, April 27
Right after breakfast we prayed the *Gemein-Litaney*, and in the afternoon we delighted in the second and third homilies on the Litany of the Wounds. Yesterday and today we have been mostly alone and have made use of this as much as possible.

On Monday, April 29
A Maqua family came down the West Branch. They comported themselves in an orderly manner and were probably baptized. They asked us for something to eat and happily departed.

On Wednesday, April 30
A Delaware (who had spent this winter in Gnadenhütten) and his wife and two children stopped by. And after we had given them something to eat, they continued on their way. After our evening Singstunde we laid ourselves contentedly down to sleep.

On Thursday, May 1
During breakfast, we thought about the sermon of the Savior on the great Lovefeast, and it gave us cause for blessed meditations.

On Friday, May 2
Unlike yesterday, which was so good for us, because we had no visitors, today several white and brown people came by to speak with us. Toward evening the man who had helped our Ahamawad up the Susquehanna returned from

Wyoming. He brought us some news that was not so pleasant for us; namely, that a white man with his wife, children, and livestock were there where our old house had stood, who also wanted to plant there this spring. After this we heard that it was James Bottler, who had started a plantation a short way from here on the other side of the water on Indian land. Shikellamy's family did not stand for this and brought him here and wanted to keep him here, as we understood it, until the Five Nations arrived here, as everyone expected in a few months.

On Sunday, May 4
In the morning we prayed the Great Church Litany. In the afternoon James Bottler (who we mentioned the day before yesterday) with his wife and mother-in-law visited us. We were, however, very casual about this visit; we were quite friendly but did not allow ourselves to become engaged with him at all.

On Monday, May 5
Brother Rösler went to the shoemaker's to see if he might be going to Tulpehocken and to visit him as well, as he had wished. Brother Post had not spent the night there. They could not express how they felt as he spoke to them. Eventually, we came around to pleasant discourses, during which I was able to remind them of the old Lutheran doctrine, "By grace, without our good works, through Christ's merits and death alone we are saved" [Romans 3:23–25]. I felt quite at peace at their house.

On Tuesday, May 6
I returned home again. Nothing had occurred, other than we had had some requests from hungry Indians. This night we also had to take in two of them.

On Wednesday, May 7
The Maqua family (mentioned on April 29) arrived here from Tulpehocken with quite a case of Indian corn and stayed here overnight. The husband is called Jonathon, and they are all baptized. They comport themselves in a very orderly fashion and show themselves to be friendly. Logan and John asked us for Indian corn plants, which we also granted them.

On Thursday, May 8
On the remembrance day of the ascension and departure of our Savior from his visible presence in this world, we did some good for ourselves with the *Te Agnum* in the morning and in the afternoon a homily on the Litany of the

Wounds. Otherwise, we had few visitations other than a member of Shikellamy's family, who once again fetched Indian corn plants from us.

On Friday, May 9
We began to plant Indian corn, and because Brother Wesa had nothing to do in the blacksmith's shop, we managed to get half of it done.

On the Sabbath, May 10
We held our Lovefeast undisturbed, and after the same we delighted in the hymn, "O Sacred Head, Now Wounded."[11] Toward evening John Petty and others came from Shikellamy's relations and a crowd of their children. Those who came to us we fed with *sapan* and milk. They had also brought rum with them, which one could soon get to hear. We, however, were left in peace.

On Sunday, May 11
We had a visit early in the morning from two drunken men, one of whom was John Petty. We were also hardly alone the whole day. In the evening Schafmann came with his family. It is now quite lively here, as everyone who belongs to Shikellamy's family is here and is planting corn. Tonight we had to take in a white man for the night.

On Monday, May 12
We finished planting our Indian corn. Schafmann visited us. The rejoicing was mutual. He is very easy to love. There were also a few Shawnee there from Wyoming who had business in the blacksmith's shop. We asked about our Ahamawad, but they had nothing more to say to us than that he was busy with planting. More important, James Bottler is building himself a house where our old house stood. He has hired several white people to help him.

On Tuesday, May 13
Brother Wesa set off for Tulpehocken to Brother Loesch's house with hides that were still here from Brother Anton's time and that we do not know how to preserve because of the storms. He will also fetch some very necessary items for us from there.

On Wednesday, May 14
My dear Gattermeyers and I were busy in the garden and received few visitors today. Toward evening Brother Wesa returned home. He had left the hides

with the shoemaker because he was leaving soon for Tulpehocken, and he [the shoemaker] could take them there.

On Thursday, May 15
Our house was quite full tonight. There were two white men here who are living with the shoemaker and were looking for horses here. In addition, our much mentioned Mohican Jonathan was here. After him came some Delaware, who also wanted to stay overnight, but they saw that there was no more room for them.

On Friday, May 16
We had to guide some Indians who are living around us to planting Indian corn.

On the Sabbath, May 17
We felt as always a Sabbath blessing and the proximity of our dear Lord.

On Sunday, May 18
Holy Pentecost was a truly blessed day for us. The dear Mother, the Holy Spirit, allowed us to speak with Her and feel Her and have Her in quite a childlike fashion. We felt especially well as we prayed the church litany. Wesa and I went visiting in the town, and Logan, who was the only man we encountered alone at home, was very friendly. In the evening, after a blessed little Singstunde, as we felt the grace of the day, we laid ourselves down to sleep contented.

On Monday, May 19
I traveled to the shoemaker with Brother Wesa, who had several items of business with which I could help him.

On Tuesday, May 20
We returned home. Toward evening Caspar Rieth, the brother of Sister Anton Schmidt, who now lives in the vicinity, came to see us with another man. The former borrowed half a bushel of Indian corn to plant. They slept the night with us.

On Thursday, May 22
Another member of the aforementioned Mohican Jonathon's family slept with us.

On Friday, May 23

A trader and two Indians who had business in the blacksmith's shop came by to speak to us. The trader was from Oley. He knew many Brothers and had also gone to school at Brother Hussey's. The way he told us, he had been very unlucky in his trading. He came from the Allegheny, and there the French had taken everything from him. He ate a meal with us at night and then left.

On the Sabbath, May 24

After our Lovefeast we were refreshed by the seven final words of the Savior with the hymn from the new liturgy: "Christ, who makes us blessed."[12]

On Sunday, May 25

We prayed the litany in the morning. In the afternoon Brother Wesa set off on his way to the shoemaker's house because we had heard that the hides were still lying there and perhaps to take them to Tulpehocken ourselves.

On Monday, May 26

My dear Gattermeyer and I celebrated a Lovefeast on this day to commemorate the birthday of the dearest disciple and thought of him with tenderly loving hearts. As Brother Wesa did not return home, we concluded that he had gone on to Tulpehocken.

On Tuesday May 27

We began to hoe our Indian corn.

On Wednesday, May 28

In the morning we remembered that on this day three years ago our dear Christel had gone home and so, at the Collect we asked for eternal communion with him and the whole congregation in Heaven. We also sang in memory of that evening the "Song of Songs" before we went to sleep.

On Thursday, May 29

It was an extraordinarily hot day, which made us very warm as we hoed our Indian corn.

On Friday, May 30

As is usual for us every day, we had a great deal of demand from passing Indians, Maqua, and Delaware. Today we had very cool weather again, and Brother Rösler did not feel well.

On the Sabbath, May 31

During the previous night there had been such a hard frost that not only our beans, cucumbers, etc. but also our Indian corn had been ruined, and we had to plant everything all over again. The same thing happened to the Indians, and theirs had also got quite tall. For our Sabbath we profited happily from the Collect with the words of the Savior: "I sit in eternity at the slits of the wounds."[13] Toward evening we heard that Conrad Weiser was lodging in the town with another ten men and would soon leave here to go to the Great Island to build a fence for the much mentioned Maqua, Jonathon. This evening Brother Wesa also came home, which pleased us greatly that we could hear something about our dear hearts across the mountains.

15

JUNE 1–JULY 31, 1755

GOTTFRIED RÖSLER

On Sunday, June 1
In the morning we held a liturgy with the prayer to our Father. The rest of the day we spent in rest.

On Monday, June 2
We began to replace our frozen Indian corn. After we had planted a portion, we heard from a white man in our neighborhood who had business in the blacksmith's shop that it wasn't necessary to replant, as it would send up new shoots, so we stopped.[1]

On Tuesday, June 3
Toward evening our dear Brother Neusser and old Brother Loesch arrived here from Tulpehocken. Brother Wesa had ridden to meet them up to the shoemaker's. This visit, with the lovely letters and news from our dear Brothers and Sisters in Bethlehem and with the possibility of holy Communion, was cause for not a little rejoicing. After a short Evening Blessing that Brother Neusser held for us, we laid ourselves down to rest contentedly.

On Wednesday, June 4
After breakfast Brother Neusser went to our departed Br. Hagen's grave, to which Br. Rösler took them. In the afternoon he held a very pleasing *Gemeintag*, during which we rejoiced at the news of the foundation of the *Jüngerhaus* near Nazareth and the summary of the conference that was held there.[2] Toward evening we had a blessed Lovefeast and absolution and not long after our dear

bloody Husband fed and watered us sacramentally with His holy Martyr's Body and Blood and did many great things for us poor sinners. Halleluja!

On Thursday, June 5
Soon after breakfast, after Brother Neusser had held a farewell Quarter of an Hour service in the blessed afterglow of what we had enjoyed yesterday, he set off on his way again with his companion Father Loesch and was accompanied on horseback by Brother Rösler to Königsberg, ten miles from here. Conrad Weiser had returned with his company from Ostonwakin and had not needed to make the intended fence because he had found only one Indian family there, who were thinking of leaving there soon for Tulpehocken.[3]

On Friday, June 6
While all three of us were working in our Indian corn, Conrad Weiser visited us and acted in a very friendly fashion, and because he invited us to visit him in return, in the evening Brothers Gattermeyer and Wesa went to him, at which opportunity he told them that he was hard at work measuring the Shamokin property, which at Brother Ludwig's visit [Zinzendorf's] had been as good as his, but then it had not been the right time, which it was now.[4]

On Saturday, July 7
We were able to still feel what we had enjoyed this last week during our Sabbath celebration, as we also had in previous days during our joint singing of the verses. In the afternoon Logan came to us and wanted to tell us what was happening with the land. He wished that David [Zeisberger] would come because otherwise we did not understand one another properly.

On Sunday, June 8
This morning C[onrad] W[eiser] left here again. In the morning we prayed the *Gemein-Litaney*.

On Monday, June 9
The Mohican, Jonathon, was here with his whole family. He is moving from Ostonwakin to Tulpehocken. He brought all his household possessions to our house, also some hens with chicks, all of which he left with us, even though we objected strongly. French Margaret was also here.

On Tuesday, June 10
We made our first hay. Brother Wesa does not have a lot to do in the blacksmith's shop, and recently we have had few visits from Indians.

On Friday, June 13
Brother Ahamawad came with Brother Lechti from Wyoming. Brother Ahamawad's foot was very bad; they were hungry, and we had also had nothing to eat but Indian corn for quite a time. Then we decided to slaughter one of our calves, although we had not seen them for a few days, and we worried that they had been eaten by other people.

On Saturday, June 14
We five brothers had a blessed Sabbath Lovefeast together. In the evening the shoemaker came and brought us two bushels of maize flour again.

On Sunday, June 15
Because the shoemaker, Peter Glück, was here, Brother Post held a sermon on the lost sheep and his son, on the 15th chapter of Luke, from where the Gospel was taken today.

On Monday, June 16
In the pouring rain, French Margaret's grandson came, a very attractive man, and stayed the night with us.

On Tuesday, June 17
Brother Ahamawad wanted to set off back to Wyoming with Brother Lessly, but because it still looked a lot like rain they stayed here again.

On Wednesday, June 18
They began their journey in the morning. Because Brother Ahamawad cannot help Brother Lessly in the canoe up the Susquehanna, as his foot is still bad, Brother Wesa went along with them to help.

On Friday, June 20
Today, like yesterday, Brother Gattermeyer and I were busy making hay, because Brother Lessly had mown the meadow by our cornfield for us.

On the Sabbath, June 21
We were visited in the morning by a few hungry Delaware Indians. It was quite Sabbath-like for us the whole day.

On Sunday, June 22
We prayed the *Gemein-Litaney*, during which we felt quite content. In the afternoon two white men came by to speak to us; one of them was English

and the other was north German, with several Mohawk Indians. They were ordered to buy all kinds of things for the English army in the Allegheny. The Englishman appeared to be a very nice man. He told us that he had seen Brothers David [Zeisberger] and Christian Friedrich way upstream on the Susquehanna River, and also Brother Ahamawad in Wyoming. We treated them to some milk. Before they left the aforementioned Englishman said that if he could do something in return for what we had given them, then he would be happy. One could tell that he had already heard much about Bethlehem.

On Monday, June 23
Brother Gattermeyer and I had to make hay as well as perform our other tasks.

On Tuesday, June 24
In the afternoon, as we had carried the last of the hay inside, Brother Wesa returned from Wyoming, at which point we discovered that not only had they arrived safely but also they had seen our dear Christian Seidel and David there themselves, whom we should await here in a week.

On Wednesday, June 25
We began to hoe our Indian corn all over again. Until now it had appeared that nothing would come of it, but now with the almost daily rain it appears to be coming back.

On Thursday, June 26
In the afternoon we were truly overjoyed by the anticipated arrival of the two hearts Christian Seidel and David.

On Friday, June 27
It was simply a joy for us that the dear Seidel and David were here with us. The former told us several things about Bethlehem and other places, which we listened to with heartfelt interest.

On Saturday, June 28
Their presence made our Sabbath quite precious. During our Lovefeast our dear Seidel comforted us with the announcement of Communion during his visit, the news of which had an effect on our hearts. In the evening he held a blessed Quarter of an Hour service for us on the Daily Text with the Collect, "He will still come today,"[5] on the now not so seldom visitations of the Savior, as in the Old Testament.

On Sunday, June 29
In the morning we prayed the *Gemein-Litaney* and spent the rest of the day content. Before the Evening Blessing, Brother Seidel spoke more on the Daily Text, "O Death I will be thy plagues."[6]

On Monday, June 30
We spent the day hoeing our Indian corn, for which we also had the help of our dear Seidel and David.

On Tuesday, July 1
We continued hoeing our Indian corn. We had some requests from Indians. In the evening a few men came who asked for night quarters. One of them had already heard the Moravians preaching in Danesbury. Before our Evening Blessing the dear heart Seidel spoke a little about the day's description of our Beloved. "What kind of Husband is that? Briefly: He is the perfect one."[7]

On Wednesday, July 2
We finished hoeing the Indian corn. Toward evening we made our local Indians a meal of pancakes and *sapan* and milk, according to our means. There were eight of them, and they were very contented. Our dear David spoke with them during the meal in Mohawk. Tonight the two white men who had slept with us the night before stayed again. According to them, they were looking for land around here.

On Thursday, July 3
In the morning we prepared a Lovefeast because we were done with hoeing the Indian corn. In the afternoon Brothers David and Wesa went about 6 miles from here to fetch our canoe, which, since Brother Ahamawad's trip to Wyoming, had not been returned by the man who had taken him up there the first time. Brothers Gattermeyer and Rösler spent the time in heartfelt discourse and discussing other important matters with our dear Seidel while they were gone. This night we were alone, which we also put to good use.

On Friday July 4
We were content in one another's company, and nothing further happened.

On the Sabbath, July 5
During our breakfast in the presence of the Savior, we held some thorough discussions about the circumstances of our heart. Here each of us testified

in a sinner-like and blessed fashion as to why the Savior had bidden the Moravian Brothers to love one another. After this we spent the day in a Sabbath-like fashion and closed it with a blessed Lovefeast, Pedelavium, and, above all else, blessed enjoyment of the Martyr's Body and Blood of our dear Lord.

On Sunday, July 6
We held a blessed liturgy in the morning, remembering the feeling with which we had been blessed yesterday evening. In the evening we were gladdened by today's description of our Beloved: "The Maker of our Anticipation" [Vorfreude Macher] in a sermon that our dear Seidel held.

On Monday, July 7
He spoke in the evening on the Daily Text of the Savior: "Let both grow together until the harvest."[8]

On Tuesday, July 8
Our dear pilgrims prepared themselves for their trip to Wyoming, as they had also started to yesterday. In the evening our dear Seidel said a few words about our Beloved according to his description today: "He who consoled" [Der Trost sprach].

On Wednesday, July 9
After we held a farewell Lovefeast, our dear Seidel and David left us once again. Brother Wesa accompanied them to Labachpeton's village, where he brought our canoe back again.

On Thursday, July 10
In the morning I went to the shoemaker's house because we had no more flour, stayed there for a few hours, and returned in the evening. Shortly before me, Brother Wesa returned from accompanying the others.

On Friday, July 11
Nothing else happened, other than we spent the day on the work of our dear Ordinary [Zinzendorf].

On the Sabbath, July 12
The whole day seemed to us quite Sabbath-like.

On Sunday, July 13
In the morning we prayed the *Gemein-Litaney*. In the evening three Maqua came to us, who stayed the night with us and also made us a present of some deer meat.

On Monday, July 14
The Indians who had gone to John Harris's began to return with the flour that they had received as a present. Also, in the ten days that they were away, we had seen hardly any Indians.

On Tuesday, July 15
Labachpeton visited us and a few other Delaware, some of whom had business in the blacksmith's shop. They had also brought rum along, which they drank over on the island so that we could hear them, but we were left in peace.

On Wednesday, July 16
We once again had several visitors. We can clearly tell that they have flour again.

On Thursday, July 17
A few families of Delaware Indians came down the West Branch on their way somewhere else. But because it was so very hot, as it had been for a few days now, they camped from morning till toward evening in front of our house and also came in to talk to us a great deal. They were very well-mannered people.

On the Sabbath, July 19
We treated ourselves to something quite Sabbath-like. In the afternoon our dear Schafmann returned home from John Harris's and soon visited us after his arrival, at which point he received the greetings that had been left for him, but our dear Seidel and David and Brother Gattermeyer read him the short Maqua letter from the same, at which point he was assured in the special love of our Lord God, who spilled His blood for him and the whole world, to all which he listened with great attention.

We spent Sunday, July 20, blessed and undisturbed.

On Monday, July 21
Brother Wesa went to the shoemaker because he had still not brought us any flour.

On Tuesday, July 22
We had all kinds of visits from Indians. In the evening Brother Wesa returned and brought flour.

On Wednesday, July 23
A few Indian women had camped close to our house, who just wanted to ask us for some milk.

On Thursday, July 24
The shoemaker was at our house. He had work to be done in the blacksmith's shop, and then he went back home again.

On Friday, July 25
Brother Gattermeyer and I spent today mounding soil around our Indian corn.

On the Sabbath, July 26
Very early in the morning, our neighbor Bottler came to us and brought us quite frightful news about the war in the Allegheny[9] and thought that it was high time to move away from here, and a few hours later another man came who was staying in his house and repeated the same, and both became quite incredulous that they could see no fear in us. Why should we be afraid? There really are white people moving away from their places who live close farther down on the other side of the Susquehanna. We spent the day undisturbed in inner and outer calm.

On Sunday, July 27
We delighted among ourselves in the words from the Litany of the Wounds, "May the sweat from your Passion spill on us over our body and soul!"[10]

On Monday, July 28
Brother Wesa had thought of leaving here and going to Tulpehocken and on to Bethlehem. But Indians and white people kept coming who had work to do in the blacksmith's shop. So he delayed it till tomorrow.

On Tuesday, July 29
In the morning he left with a few crates of deer hides. Brother Gattermeyer and I are mounding the soil for our Indian corn along with the other work.

On Wednesday, July 30
Isaac Nutimus came to stay the night with us, with his Negro and three other Indians from Nescopeck. Brother Rösler had seen them all already in

Gnadenhütten. Brother Rösler took the opportunity to speak with them about Gnadenhütten, but they were not that open to this. Otherwise, they were friendly and well-mannered.

On Thursday, July 31
Brother Gattermeyer did not feel well (it was the beginning of the fever that he still has). Otherwise, we closed this month happy and blessed in proximity with the Martyr Lamb.

16

AUGUST 1–SEPTEMBER 30, 1755

GOTTFRIED RÖSLER

On Friday, August 1
Today's description of the Savior: "Christ is my life," gave us a blessed impression at the beginning of the month. Otherwise nothing much happened.

On Saturday, August 2
Today's description, "My Savior!," was especially tasty to us during our Sabbath celebration. In the evening Brother Wesa returned from Tulpehocken. He brought us letters, and, among other things, he also brought the *Memorabilia* of the months of June and July from our dear Bethlehem, which we read this evening and delighted in. One can hardly describe how good that tastes for someone in Shamokin.

On Sunday, August 3
Before breakfast Brother Gattermeyer visited our neighbor Schafmann and had the opportunity to say something to him of the blessing that we poor sinners have with the Savior. He was able to have a good talk with him, and we believe that the Savior is working also on his heart. We spent the rest of the day happy.

On Monday, August 4
Today we saw clearly that Brother Gattermeyer's discomfort was due to the fever, as it started again from the day before.

On Tuesday, August 5
A family of Delaware Indians camped in front of our house. They came from Tulpehocken and had horses laden with maize and Indian corn. They were

presentable and well-mannered people, and because it rained later they brought their things into our house.

On Friday, August 8
We had been busy the whole week with mounding soil for our corn and were finished with it today.

On Saturday, August 9
Toward midday Brother Lessly came to us quite unexpectedly with letters and news from our dear Bethlehem. We immediately enjoyed that which he had brought, and Brother Rösler was immediately invited to the synod in Warwick. In the evening we had Schafmann for supper with us, and that was very nice eating together.

On Sunday, August 10
Brothers Rösler and Lessly set off for Warwick with two horses.

On Tuesday, August 12
We sowed the seeds for our squash.

Wednesday, August 13
We spent in quiet. Last Sabbath, during our Lovefeast, we had thought about what had occurred 28 years ago with blessed memory, and we were quite happy afterward, as we heard that on this day on the Sabbath there was the actual celebration in Bethlehem.[1]

On Thursday, August 14
Tonight the Englishman from Danesbury who had been here last month stayed with us again. According to him, he had come to move to a place on the Susquehanna but had found it to be different than he had imagined and now had to sell the harnesses he had brought and so was going home from here via Gnadenhütten and Nazareth.

On Wednesday [sic], August 15
We meditated greatly and diligently about our Brothers and Sisters at the synod in Warwick.

On Saturday, August 16
We celebrated a very peaceful Sabbath. Brother Gattermeyer was also quite well today, apart from the fever, which he has been suffering from quite badly until now.

On Sunday, August 17
The Indians buried the remains of the old Conoy Indian by the name of Saeckwho, [who] had died in the previous spring near to John Harris's and whose bones they brought here yesterday.[2] Because they had also brought rum with them, a terrible noise and clamor soon began, which continued for several days and nights, as more and more Delaware Indians arrived and are around our house. But they have been quite modest in their behavior toward us.

On Thursday, August 21
It began to quiet down again. They wanted to bring the empty barrels of rum into our house, but we asked them to take them away. Toward evening Brothers Lessly and Rösler returned from the synod, to our joy, quite wet through from the rain. They immediately delighted us with several letters and regaled us with a few things so that we could participate fully.

On Saturday, August 23
Our Sabbath and especially our Lovefeast was spent mainly with stories about what had happened at the synod.[3]

On Sunday, August 24
Because Brother Lessly was thinking of returning to Bethlehem from here tomorrow, and Brother Wesa had resolved to accompany him to go to celebrate the Single Brethren [Choir] Festival, they spent the day getting ready for their journey.

On Monday, August 25
They left early and made their way via Nescopeck and Gnadenhütten.

On Wednesday, August 27
In the afternoon an Indian had lain himself down to sleep in front of our house so that in the evening, as we were eating, we woke him up to ask if we could give him some. We spoke to him but got no answer. He slept the night in our house, and when we woke up he laid himself down again in front of the doorway. Later he left again.

On Thursday, August 28
We were visited by many Indians.

On Friday, August 29
To celebrate the Single Brethren Day, Brother Rösler made himself quietly useful.

On Saturday, August 30

The description of the Savior today: "My psalms, O that I had a thousand voices!"[4] gave us a blessed impression during our Sabbath celebration. Despite the fact that it had not rained here for a while, the Susquehanna river had risen in the night so much that all the Indians' canoes had floated away. The river rose the whole day.

On Sunday, August 31

We read together the homily on the text, "O you holy five wounds."[5] It was a blessed Sunday celebration. In the afternoon Brother Gattermeyer went visiting in the town. He had the opportunity to enter into a nice discussion with a Delaware who had recently come from the Allegheny and who appears to be an upstanding man and has visited us several times already.

September

On Monday, September 1, and the days after this we spent happily in our usual work.

On Friday, September 5

We expected our [Br.] Wesa's return from Bethlehem, but our hope was for naught.

On Saturday, September 6

We held a very peaceful Sabbath. The whole day we did not see a single person.

On Sunday, September 7

To celebrate the Married Persons Choir Festival, Brother Gattermeyer made himself useful in peace and quiet. Brother Rösler went over to the town to visit Schafmann, who is helping his cousin, a very nice young Indian, to build a house. He did not meet up with him, however; instead, he rejoiced in the very kind behavior of his cousin and the grave of the departed Brother Hagen.

On Tuesday, September 9

The bridge close to our house that goes over the ditch to our cornfield fell down quite by itself. Because we really need this, we worked on this yesterday and today so that we can use it again.

On Thursday, September 11

The Mohican Jonathan arrived here with his family.

On Friday, September 12
Brother Gattermeyer had to fix something on the weapon of a warrior who is going to the Allegheny. There were many Indians and white people here for the same reason; the latter had dressed themselves completely as Indians, and Andrew Montour was their actual commander, who had quite clearly ordered that the aforementioned flints had to be fixed. If Brother Wesa had been here, he would probably have given him even more work to do. They did not stay here for long, and our John Shikellamy, and also John Petty, also left with them. During their stay here, a big black belt of wampum from the Six Nations arrived here, which is going to Philadelphia, with which they are unanimously letting their intention to fight against the French be known.

On Saturday, September 13
We were visited again by more warriors because some had stayed behind. But we were not disturbed in our Sabbath.

On Sunday, September 14
Because Brother Gattermeyer had to fix something on the aforementioned flints, we were a little disturbed in our Sunday blessings. Toward evening the wife of the Mohican Jonathan came and wanted to bring two kegs of rum into our house, and because she has all her other things here, she thought she had a right to do this. But she had to take them away again.

On Tuesday, September 16
We spent a quiet day at our usual work and reminded ourselves of the great work that had been accomplished on this day fourteen years ago, to our great blessing.

On Friday, September 19
On these days we received many visits from Indians. We also heard much tumult from the drunken ones but were not inconvenienced at all.

On Saturday, September 20
It was quite well, with our Sabbath quiet. In the evening our long-awaited Brother Wesa finally arrived safely, after almost four weeks' absence, and the letters he brought with him and the news from our dear Bethlehem made this evening quite a time of childlike rejoicing.

On Sunday, September 21
The Indians were celebrating again. We were about to be disturbed, but then it all subsided.

On Monday, September 22
The shoemaker was at our house and said that he was going to Tulpehocken. In the afternoon our Schafmann came by and said that he was going to go to Lancaster. We had a quite contented conversation with him and told him that he would soon come here for a visit. He said that he would soon go to Bethlehem.

On Wednesday, September 24
Two of Conrad Weiser's sons slept with us. They were very well-mannered, and we were also to them. They wanted to visit the Mohican Jonathan, and because he was out on the hunt, and they could not find anyone to look for him, they set off into the woods themselves to search for him.

On Friday, September 26
This morning we had the first and very hard frost. Because we were expecting the arrival of our dear Brother Seidel, Brother Wesa traveled to meet him with two horses in the mountain twenty miles away. But he returned alone.

On Saturday, September 27
To our joy, our dear heart Christian Seidel arrived in the afternoon with Marcus Kiefer, who was to stay here, and accompanied by Brother Samuel Herr. Their arrival made our Sabbath quite solemn, which in the morning we had not been able to observe because we constantly had Indians in the house. This evening our dear heart Seidel held a quite blessed Lovefeast, Pedelavium, and Communion, all in the unspeakable proximity of our dear bloody Lord.

On Sunday, September 28
We held a liturgy in the morning in the afterglow of yesterday's blessed joy. In the afternoon Brothers Rösler, Marcus, and Samuel Herr went over to the town and also visited the departed Brother Hagen's grave. Few of the Indians are at home. We spent the day contently, and Brother Seidel held a quite blessed liturgical Singstunde at the end of it.

Monday, September 29
Our dear hearts Seidel and Samuel considered their trip the next day, as did also our dear heart Gattermeyer, who for the time being is being relieved by Brother Marcus, prepared to leave with them also.

On Tuesday, September 30
After a heartfelt and meaningful Morning Blessing, they departed from us. Brother Marcus Kiefer accompanied them part of the way.

17

SEPTEMBER–OCTOBER 1755

GOTTFRIED RÖSLER

Brother Rösler's Account of His and Brother Philip Wesa's and Marcus Kiefer's Final Stay in Shamokin and Their Merciful Preservation in the War of the Wilden Against Pennsylvania, in the Year 1755

In recent years Shamokin had no longer been as it was when the Brethren [the Moravians] had first erected the blacksmith's shop there with the intention of spreading the Gospel among the Indians and had begun to live there. Since the passing of old Shikellamy (a decent man, who loved the people of God and who had visited Bethlehem and at whose invitation the business there had been started), only a few Indians continued to live there, from many nations like the Maqua, Cayuga, Tutelo, Conoy, Mohican, etc. but mostly bad people who had been ruined by the whites. The place had changed completely, and because so many Indians passed through there, the Brethren had become known to almost all North American Indian nations (as it was an established station of the Six Nations when they were at war against the Catawba). But they now had another warpath, and one only rarely saw an Indian from far off there, which is the real reason why the living of the Brethren was to be closed, and the blacksmith's shop moved to a spot of land purchased for that purpose between Gnadenhütten and Wyoming to fulfill its original purpose.

The way things came to pass, though, showed us that it pleased our dear Lord to end our plan there early because of the war with the Indians and to make an end with the blacksmith's shop and everything we had there, after He had protected us from the murders that had already begun there, His poor children, who lived there at the end, without any fear under His wings of grace and to bring us back to our dear Bethlehem to our people. And to this end, praising the good Lord, a detailed report is given.

In the last days of September in the aforementioned year 1755, many Indians who were unknown to us moved here, among them many white people who dressed as Indians. The Delaware, who lived in quite a number in several towns not far from here and who had come to live in peace with the Shamokin Natives, now began to move back and forth in and out of the Native town. Among them, a rather wealthy Indian had moved here from the Ohio country, after the battle that the English had lost, by the name of George Delaware, and he visited us regularly. We could tell from his behavior toward us that he had become very fond of us, and because his wife fell sick here, and he had a child of about a year and a half, whom he often brought to us, we had many opportunities to show our friendship to him in many ways, which we did faithfully.

On October 11, as I was all alone at home, he came and said that French Indians had been seen, and it would be good if we went into the woods and left the house alone this night; otherwise we could meet with misfortune. When he had gone, a local Cayuga, well known to us, came and asked me to give him some of the food I was cooking and said that he wanted to help us too, if the French Indians came and wanted to kill us. Although I was not able to take these words very much to heart and considered them to be childish chatter, as we were used to from the Indians, I could not remain completely ambivalent, and when my Brothers Wesa and Marcus Kiefer came home, I told them what had been said to me. I did not feel like leaving our house. We were strengthened by the words of the Savior for today and tomorrow and laid ourselves quite confidently down to sleep, "'And will God not avenge his elect?' God, who has chosen us dearly. He will do this and not hide Himself. He counts how often a Christian weeps."[1]

The next morning at dawn there were suddenly many gunshots coming from the Native town, which lay not a short English mile from our house and which frightened us somewhat. As we were now awake, aforementioned George Delaware came to us and answered the question, what kind of shots those were; he said the Indians had been on watch all night because of the French Indians and had let off shots for that reason. We were then much relieved.

However, in the ensuing days almost all the Indians from here moved away, and on the 16th we suddenly heard that about an hour away from us, on the other side of the Susquehanna, six plantations had been attacked by Indians—thirty-one people, some who had been pitiably murdered and some, especially the children and young women, had been taken away, and only one man, who had been shot several times, had escaped from there. Not only did we hear about this, but also the blood-covered murder weapons were brought into our blacksmith's shop, and one of the Tutelo Nation, who lived here, had also received a shot in his leg. We began to feel a little scared, but what could we poor children do? John Shikellamy, who was the chief here in Shamokin, along with his brother Logan, came and asked whether we were not afraid and wanted to move away. We answered that we were with them, and, as long as they stayed here, we wanted to stay too. At this he said nothing but came to our house often and repeated the same question.

In the meantime an Indian quite unknown to us had taken up lodging with us, who spoke no word of English, and thus we could not converse with him at all. However, he was a quite young, polite man, as he could see that we did not allow our dogs to stay in the house, and so he left his outside too and did not want to trouble us with anything. We gave him what we had to eat, and he did not leave the house for the five days that he was with us, until October 22, when very many Indians from all along the Susquehanna gathered in Shamokin, among them our friend Paxinos and other acquaintances from Wyoming and Nescopeck. As they came into our house, he gathered his things and left us amicably. Who this Indian was, and what his reason was for being with us, one cannot say. We thought quite a bit about him and asked among our local Indians about him but received no real answer. Perhaps he was given to us as a guardian angel [*Salve Garde*]. That the dear Father will know, who has shown us in many ways that He wants to protect us, and we could do nothing but rely on His counsel and support. But we wanted nothing more than to let our dear Brethren in Bethlehem know about our circumstances.

In the meanwhile, after the 16th we often conferred with one another, and on October 28 in the evening, as we were quite alone and sitting together by our fire, we talked about what could be done for us in our present circumstances. But nothing could be resolved. Our dear Marcus Kiefer firmly believed that there was no danger for us and that we could be quite calm. Brother Wesa was too anxious, but it was not his fault because in his blacksmith's shop he had to hear the most and had to work with the murder weapons. And I could say nothing except reassure them that the dear Lord, who had counted the hairs on our heads, would make everything right and allow no harm to come to us and support us at the right time with good counsel and deeds.

As we were talking thus, a young English trader came into the house and said that just now a belt of wampum had arrived in this town from the Allegheny Indians with the words that they were coming with a sharp axe, and we should get out of their way; otherwise, we would be hurt. Once he had left, we decided that one of us would go to Tulpehocken to Brother George Loesch and then from there go to Bethlehem with the express coach to tell them how things looked for us here. Because the others could not leave with a letter, the journey fell to me, and my Brothers helped get me ready for the journey that very evening. As we went to sleep rather late, to our great comfort we read together the [Daily] Text for today and tomorrow. (1) From the pages of the book [Old Testament], "Deliver me, I pray thee, from the hand of my brother, for I fear him" (Genesis 32:11). My God, who has promised me His protection at all times. Jacob remained alone. An angel of God came from Heaven. The words of the Savior: "The riches of all the world cannot repair the smallest damage to the soul. Be safe from all harm. Think of Lot's wife."

At this I became thoughtful and said to my Brothers, "Dear hearts, when you see that it is becoming really dangerous, come after me, because I see nothing here for which we should lose our lives. Above all, the words of the book, and the words of the Savior in the present time are such that it is as though they were spoken for us."

On October 24, before dawn, I set out, comforted by the notion that I would be back on the 28th! Brother Marcus Kiefer accompanied me a short part of the way, and, when we took farewell of each other, we still considered that the mission in Shamokin was not yet over. However, after I had come fifteen miles, where the first white people live on this side of the Susquehanna, I found everyone in fear and horror, and most of the people already fleeing. For although the first murders on the 15th had affected only six plantations, which stood on Indian land and the people there had been frequently warned, now those who lived on proprietary land in that area had also been told by the Indians that if they did not leave that they would suffer the same fate as the others.

I might have wished that my Brothers in Shamokin had known of these circumstances, but I could do nothing except continue my journey, and on October 25 toward evening I arrived safely at Brother and Sister George Loesch's house. They were exceedingly happy to see one of us, for, having listened to the talk, they had thought that we were already with the Savior. John Shikellamy had told the Brethren today in Shamokin to leave quite clearly, and Brother Wesa had set off to tell me and arrived at George Loesch's house on the 26th, just as I was writing, and because he had already resolved to go immediately to Bethlehem, he became the messenger who took the letter there.

Now our Marcus Kiefer was still in Shamokin. I could thus do nothing except try to travel there to fetch just him, because we could not even think of saving any of our belongings. So, on the 27th, in the morning, I set off. Whoever saw me tried to dissuade me from this trip. Brother John Jorden from Lebanon, who had also spent this night at the Loesch's, completely refused to consent to this plan. I assured him, however, that I was acting in accordance with my heart, and the dear Savior and angels would be my helpers, and so I set out. Sixty families who were fleeing over the mountains in the greatest poverty and sorrow met me on the way and told me with one voice that I was running into the arms of murderers, and many of them pleaded with me that I should turn around. Most of them knew that there was still one of us in Shamokin and said, "God will protect your Brother without you going to help him." A Baptist, who met me on this side of the Thürnstein Mountain [Pete's Mountain] said he had left many things behind but would not turn around; he was thinking of Lot's wife. At that it occurred to me that I had left Shamokin with exactly these words of the Savior. After this I met only with an English trader, who pleaded with me to turn around with the assurance that if my Brother were still there, then he was out of all danger, but if he had left Shamokin, then he had been definitely murdered. (The following day there were people who had gone back to fetch their things and had fallen into the hands of the murderers.) As I did not decide to turn back, he left me in pity.

I continued on only a few miles, and then it occurred to me to ask for counsel from my dear Lord and most loyal friend. The [Daily] Texts for today were Genesis 35:15: "And Jacob called the name of the place where God spake with him, Bethel." Luke 17:9: "When you have done everything you were told to do, you should say, 'We are unworthy servants; we have only done our duty.'" Night was about to fall, and I set myself down on the summit of the Thürnstein; my dearest Heart [Jesus] was unspeakably close to me and answered my question to the Lot, which I posed with the greatest humility. The answer was that I should turn back, which I then did with a comforted heart and found my quarters in the bush that night with the last family that came over the Thürnstein. On the 28th I arrived in Tulpehocken again and found refugees in Brother Loesch's house, and the whole area was in such a panic as though murder had broken out here and there already. I soon continued my journey, and, as night had fallen, I knocked on a stranger's door. I was very welcome because I could tell the people that even if there were danger, it was not so near, and they saw it as God's providence that they were able to sleep another night in peace.

On the 29th I came over the Heidelberg to Daniel Levant's house in heavy rain.[2] There I met Brother Heinrich Frey, who had been sent from Bethlehem to meet up with Anton Schmidt somewhere along the way to come to us in Shamokin. Because he heard that Brother Kiefer was still there, he continued on his journey, but it was not possible to get any farther through Tulpehocken than to Brother Loesch's. From there they turned back again, and on the 30th I arrived happy as a sinner and well at the Brothers and Sisters in Bethlehem with the beautiful words of the Savior: "Our citizenship, however, is in Heaven" (Philippians 3:20); that is the cause of all the joy of the church.

From October 25 Brother Marcus Kiefer was now all alone in Shamokin. Once Brother Wesa had left, he went one time into the Indian town, and there our once familiar Indians appeared quite murderous, and he felt very uncomfortable there. Finally, everyone moved away so that the town was completely empty. Then he was quite alone and began to pack up what he could of our things, along with the tools from the blacksmith's shop, and to bury them in the ground. In addition, our dear Schafmann visited him (he was a Conoy to whom the Brethren had given this name because of his sheeplike manner). He had built his house close to ours, had hardly any business with the other Indians, and far less had he become involved in any of the affairs of war with them. He and his wife had come and gone in our house like Brethren. We had wished him from our hearts baptism in the death of Jesus for which our Brother Christian Seidel had given permission this past summer. This fall 1755, as we heard, he departed this life not far from Harris's Ferry. We believe that because of the way in which he stayed close to us, that he will partake of this even there. He was a great comfort to our Brother Marcus Kiefer, and when he finally decided to leave for Bethlehem, this Indian accompanied him to Nescopeck. There they found all the Shamokin Indians, and many others besides, and also a beautiful feeling. Schafmann returned from thence to his family, and John Shikellamy offered himself to us as company all the way to Bethlehem, and they arrived there safely on November 15, where everyone was very happy to see Brother Marcus Kiefer, whom one had not thought to see again.

Before his arrival, ways to help him were considered, and in this most dangerous of times Brothers Schmick and Heinrich Frey dared to go to his aid in answer to the call of the Brethren and the Savior to Wyoming to see whether our friend Paxinos there had anyone who would go to him there, and he and his people were immediately willing to risk their lives for these Brethren, and some even set out. The fact that this Brother, M. Kiefer, arrived safely without this service, and the preservation of Brothers Schmick and Heinrich Frey on their dangerous journey and also Paxinos and his people's willingness to help, is to be considered as reason to praise the goodness of our dear Lord, who is the light of all things and who can do what He wills for the well-being of His children and Jesus in this world.

APPENDIX A

List of Missionaries and Blacksmiths at Shamokin

MISSIONARIES AT SHAMOKIN

Martin and Anna Mack (Jeannette, née Rau): September–November 1745; April 18–June 9, 1748.
Johannes and Anna Hagen: May 26–August 2, 1747.
Friedrich C. Cammerhof: September 29–December 31, 1747.
Joseph and Martha Powell: January 4–April 18, 1748.
David Zeisberger and Christian Rauch: November 30, 1748–January 31, 1749.
Christian Rauch: February 1–April 1, 1749.
David Zeisberger: April 3, 1749–March 5, 1750.
Bernhard Grube: April 14–July 31, 1753.
David [Daniel] Kliest: January 11, 1754–July 2, 1754.
Heinrich Frey and Gottfried Rösler: December 19–25, 1754.
Gottfried Rösler: April 1–October 30, 1755.

BLACKSMITHS AT SHAMOKIN

Anton Schmidt (also Rachwistonis) and Catharina Schmidt: 1747–55. See "Anton Schmidt."
Daniel Kliest: 1753–54.
Marcus Kiefer: 1755.
Peter Wesa: 1755.

APPENDIX B

Extracts of Letters from Frederick Cammerhof to Nicholas von Zinzendorf, Anna Nitschmann, and Johannes von Watteville, Numbers 4 and 5

Between 1747 and 1750, Frederick Cammerhof composed a series of letters to church leaders (Nicholas von Zinzendorf, Anna Nitschmann, and Johannes de Watteville) who had visited Pennsylvania in 1742.[1] In letter 4, dated April 1747, Cammerhof describes the council held in Shamokin with Shikellamy on the matter of the blacksmith's shop:

> On May 1, they were visited in the forest by some friendly Indians. Toward evening Shikellemy and his sons returned. He welcomed our Brothers warmly and bid them stay with him. He asked them then that evening if they would wait with the words they brought until tomorrow. They responded: <u>yes</u>.
>
> On May 2, Shikellamy went with his sons into the forest. They made a fire and called for our Brothers [to] come out and join them. When they arrived, he asked [that] they sit in the circle around the fire. Then Shikellemy spoke: Now is the time to hear the words you brought. Our Brothers began: we are sent by T'gerkedonti and his Brothers in Bethlehem, Nazareth, Gnadenthal, Gnadenhuetten, Frederickstown, Philadelphia and several other places to bring words to Shikellemy and his whole Council. And as a sign of this, we present you this Fathom of Wampom (at this point they handed them the wampum and a written document with a seal showing their legitimacy). They continued: Brothers, your Brother T'gerkedonti remembers you had requested a blacksmith and that he promised to send one. Last year, all the preparations were made to send someone, and he was ready to make the trip. But a terrible disease spread across Pennsylvania, and some other circumstances occurred, which hindered his departure. But we have come in his name to assure you of T'gerkedonti's and his Brothers' love for you. We want to know if you still want this blacksmith to come? We would further like to know in what manner this man would be housed and have other living

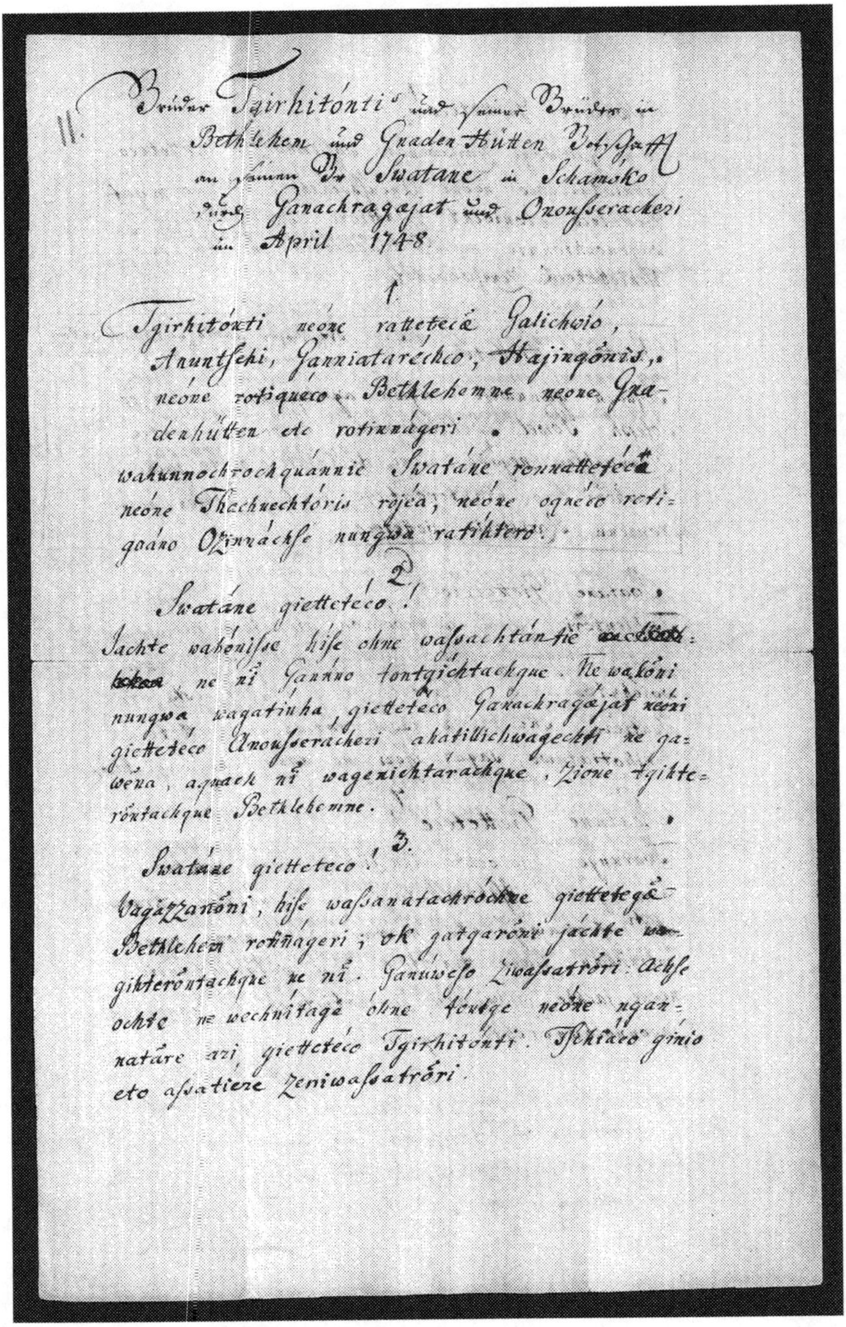

Bruder Tjirhitónti' und seiner Brüder in
Bethlehem und Gnaden Hütten Botschafft
an seinen Br. Swatane in Schamsko
durch Ganachragajat und Onousserachesi
im April 1748.

1.

Tjirhitónti neone ratteteca Galichoio,
Anuntjehi, Ganniatarecheo, Hajingónis,
neone rotiquero Bethlehemne, neone Gnadenhütten ete rotinnágeri.
wakunnochrochquánnie Swatane ronnatteseca
neone Thechrechtóris rójea, neone ognero roti-
goano Ozinnachse nungwa ratihteró.

2.

Swatane gietteteco!
Jachte wahónisse hise ohne wassachtónsie nockteti
boken ne ni Gannuo tontgichtachque. Ne walóni
nungwa wagatinha gietteteco Ganachragajat neri
gietteteco Onousserachesi akatillichwagechti ne ga-
wena, agnach ni wagenichtarachque, tjione tgitte-
róntachque Bethlehemne.

3.

Swatane gietteteco!
Wagazzanóni, hise wassanatachrochne giettetegá
Bethlehem rotinnágeri; ok gatgaróni jachte wa
gihteróntachque ne ni. Ganuwejo Liwassatróri achse
ochte ne wechnitagé ohne teutge neóne ngai-
natáre ari, gietteteco Tjirhitónti. Tjihtaeó ginio
eto assatiere Zeniwassatróri.

Fig. 7 Letter from August Spangenberg to Shikellamy in Onondaga. Courtesy of Moravian Archives, Bethlehem, Pennsylvania.

arrangements? For we love you and consider you our Brothers. Therefore we would like everything to occur smoothly and to begin on the right foot. We want to help you fulfill this wish. We also let the Governor in Philadelphia know your desire for a blacksmith and our intention to help you.

We think it would [be] good for the whole Council to tell us their thinking in this matter. We wanted to meet about this last autumn already, but our Brother Shikellemy wasn't here when we came. We hope earnestly that our good God and Lord, since He loves you all just as He loves us, and wants to have you know salvation, and teach you and instruct you in this as well as other matters. In order to confirm all these things we have spoken of, we present you with this additional Fathom of Wompum (with that they handed it over as a sign and gift for the Council). Then Shikellemy said: it would be good to gather his Council immediately and hear from anyone of them regarding the matter and fully discuss it. He also mentioned he didn't think it necessary to have the old Delaware King present, since he has no authority in the affairs of Shamokin. (+)

Next, Martin and Nathanael left. Shikellemy gathered his council members. After about 3 hours of consultation they called Martin and Nathanael back. They were told [to] sit in the Council circle. After they had set for a while and Shikellemy continued his conversation with his Indian council members, he took the wampum Martin had given him. He held it high in his hand. He explained to the others the meaning of this wampum. At this point each one of them took the wampum and spoke their thoughts and opinions. Finally Shikellemy took it back and kept it in his possession. (*)

Then Shikellemy began:

T'gerkedonti, my brother, we accept your words now as if you spoke them yourself. And as a sign that these things are true, I present this wampum (with that he gave it to our Brothers) and continued:

T'gerkedonti, my brother, I wish you'll do as I asked.

(+) Because he has lost his mental faculties. If they brought him to a fire, he would piss in it. NB. The fire in Onandago, the fire in Shamokin, etc. is called a *Council* and has great meaning.

(*) During the time the Indians were in discussion about this and considering a proposition, Br. Martin and Nathanael smoked their pipes. The Council laid their pipes down. When Br. Martin and Nathanael spoke again, the Indians took up their pipes in their hands and smoked.

We wanted a blacksmith, that is true. It is necessary for us. We are thankful it will happen. I've desired this for a long time, and I will treat him as my own flesh when he arrives.

T'gerkedonti, my brother, I hope he arrives soon.

The blacksmith will have his dwelling and shop right next to my house. In this way I'll be able to take good care of him and protect him from harm from drunken Indians.

T'gerkedonti, my brother, the blacksmith will be given a piece of land from my own, in order to feed himself and anyone else who might be with him.

T'gerkedonti, my brother, we have decided that Indians must pay for work he does for them. (NB. This term was the main condition of our Brothers in the original agreement.)

After Shikellemy had finished, he gave our Brothers another string of wampum. Martin and Nathanael discussed other things with them and reminded them of our other Brothers who had visited them previously. These were Anton, Nathanael, and especially Br. Ludwig and his sister,[2] with whom he had travelled to Wyoming. Shikellemy said: yes, he hadn't forgotten them yet, and as a matter of fact, thinks of them often. Martin then gave assurances of the Brothers' love despite the great distance between them; and our Brothers don't forget them either and wish them only goodness in body and soul. (vid. infra lit. . . . ** . . .) At that point the Council was ended. This body consisted of Shikellemy, his 3 sons, and 3 other Indians. They were all Maquaische, for Shikellemy didn't want any Delaware present. His son's wife was present. She was born into the Mohican tribe. She had to translate, interpret everything that was said from both sides. This was because Martin and Nathanael couldn't understand their tongue. (NB. This is quite unusual for Indians to have a woman take part at a Council meeting.) This woman is fond of us and already knows Mrs. Mack very well, because she lived there a year and a half. She inquired when Sister Mack would be returning to visit? Martin and Nathanael then went to visit all the Indians in their huts. Those who knew of the visitors' affairs, were friendly. In the evening we spoke again with the Mohican woman and her husband. We said how good the people have it, who believe in the Savior and feel His blood in their hearts.[3]

In the next letter to Zinzendorf, dated June 26, 1747, Cammerhof includes Spangenberg's complete response to Shikellamy:

> On the 6th of June our 2 dear Brothers Joseph Powell and John Hagen left for Shamokin. They are to construct the house and the smith shop there. As soon as it is done, the locksmith will come and take up residence and begin his work. They both departed with hearts full of blessed anticipation. We sent Br. David Bruce with them, since he has already been to Shamokin. He will then be able to find the way back with the horses. We determined that when they arrive in Shamokin, they should meet with Schikellimus and his Council and report again on the smith tools and their arrival, which have already been shipped, and the purpose for the shop. We prepared a beautiful Fathom of Wampum to this end, which they will take along. They will also take a written set of instructions, which I will explain here for you. They will serve as an answer to what I put forth for you in my last letter about Martin and Nathanael's trip to Shamokin. These are as follows:
>
>> Schikellimus, my Brother, I have some words to tell you and your brothers from Tkerkedonti, your Brother, and all his other Brothers in Bethlehem, Nazareth, Frederickstown, Gnadenthal, Gnadenhutten, Germantown, Philadelphia, New York, etc.
>>
>> Schikellimus, my Brother, Martin and Nathanael the Mohican have delivered your words and your Wampum to me. I accepted them as if you had brought them yourself.
>>
>> Schikellimus, my Brother, I was glad to hear you received my message warmly and have such a brotherly feeling toward me.
>>
>> Schikellimus, my Brother, our blacksmith is preparing to set out to you soon with his wife. All his necessary tools and equipment will [be] gathered at Lancaster.
>>
>> Schikellimus, my Brother, you sent me word that you will pick up this equipment at the Ferry and bring it up to Shamokin with your canoe. We will take it [to] the ferry with a wagon and send word when it is ready to be picked up.
>>
>> Schikellimus, my Brother, you sent word the smith should live close to your house, so you can look after him in case drunken Indians try to hurt him. Three of my Brothers are underway, one of whom already has lived among you. They want to see an appropriate place for the smith's house and will begin the construction of the house and his shop.

Schikellimus, my Brother, they will work hard to finish it as soon as possible. I hope you will do what I am asking and help them with this, especially providing men and horses as is needed.

Schikellimus, my Brother, you said you would provide a piece of ground from my own land, so he can plant his own things. Please do that. Give this ground to these Brothers so they can make a Fence and he can make use of it before winter.

Schikellimus, my Brother, you asked we do what you ask. Please let the blacksmith repair, improve the rifles of the *Streitern*/warriors who are going off to fight (against the Flatheads). He won't take anything in payment, for they have nothing with which to pay and they will need everything they have on their journey.

Schikellimus, my Brother, I love peace and not war. But since the warriors need their guns to shoot deer in order to live, I'll do what you have asked of me. The smith will not expect payment if they are going off to fight.

Schikellimus, my Brother, you said you will make sure all the Indians pay the smith for his work, even the fighters when they return from battle. Please see to this.

Schikellimus, my Brother, when the smith arrives with his wife, Br. Hagen will also stay with you and help him get started and assist him. Please treat them as my own flesh.

Schikellimus, my Brother, I have nothing more to ask or say. I am very fond of you and all your brothers. Live well.

Schikellimus, my Brother, as a sign of the truth of these words, I present this Fathom of Wampum.

These Instructions will be translated into the Maquaische language by Br. Pyrlaeus. Br. Hagen will bring these in writing.[4]

GLOSSARY OF TERMS

A

August 13—One of the two chief festival days of the Moravian Church. On August 13, 1727, refugees from Moravia (in the present-day Czech Republic) who were residing at Herrnhut, Germany, along with others who had joined them seeking religious freedom, underwent a memorable spiritual renewal in the nearby Lutheran parish church at Berthelsdorf. The group had been experiencing conflict within their community, and the August 13 experience gave them a new resolve to work together and go out in missions. The worldwide Moravian Unity commemorates August 13 as the spiritual birthday of the Renewed Moravian Church.

B

Brother (German: *Bruder*)—Male communicant member of the Moravian Church. This term is not applied to nonmembers of the church.

Brüdergemeine—Unity of the Brethren. This term officially designates the worldwide Moravian Church (both male and female members), also called the (Moravian) Unity.

C

Choir (German: *Chor*)—Segment of the congregation constituted of all the individuals of similar age groups or sharing the same sex or marital status. The term is derived from the French *corps*. At its peak the system included Children, Little Boys, Little Girls, Older Boys, Older Girls, Single Brethren, Single Sisters, Married People, Widowers, and Widows Choirs. During many years the Single Brethren, Single Sisters, and Widows lived, labored, and worshipped together in close fellowship within their respective Choir Houses. See Faull, *Speaking to Body and Soul*, 2017, and Petterson, *The Moravian Brethren in a Time of Transition*, 2021.

Choir Festival (German: *Chorfest*)—Special day of prayer and reconsecration put aside for each of the choirs of the congregation. Celebrations included the following:

March 25: Festival of All the Choirs
April 30: Widows Choir Festival
May 4: Single Sisters Choir Festival
June 4: Greater Girls Choir Festival
June 24: Young Boys Choir Festival
July 9: Greater Boys Choir Festival
August 17: Young Girls Choir Festival
Children Choir Festival succeeded the Small Boys and Small Girls Festival in 1820

August 29: Single Brethren Choir Festival
August 31: Widowers Choir Festival
September 7: Married Persons Choir Festival

D

Daily Text (German: *Lehrtexte*)—Intended as a word of awakening. The Moravian Church has published the Daily Texts annually since 1731. See also Watchwords.

deacon (German: *Diakon*)—First order of the Moravian ordained ministry. A Moravian deacon can administer the sacraments and rites of the church and serve as pastor of a congregation. The feminine term was sometimes applied to the wife of a minister, who was also ordained and assisted in the spiritual work among the women of a congregation. Until 1760 it could also be applied to unmarried women selected for service in the church.

G

Gemeine—Community. Among eighteenth-century Moravians the term carried several meanings: a congregation, a communal settlement, the worldwide Moravian organization, and the spiritual fellowship of Moravian Brothers and Sisters.

Gemeintag—Congregation Day. On this monthly festival day reports and letters were read from the *Gemeinnachrichten* (Congregational Accounts) to the congregation. The blessing and commission of missionaries also occurred on the Gemeintag.

Great Sabbath—The day before Easter. Moravian congregations frequently held services on the Great Sabbath to commemorate Jesus's day of rest in the tomb before Easter Sunday.

H

helper (German: *Helfer/in* or *Pfleger/in*)—A church official, usually responsible for the spiritual life of the congregation or one of its choirs, often the ordained pastor or one of his assistants. When the helpers meet as a deliberative body, it is termed the Helfer Conferenz, where the head pastor presides as primus inter pares.

J

Jüngerhaus—Disciple's house. After 1751 this was term used to denote Zinzendorf's household.

L

Lebenslauf—Memoir, or an autobiographical account of the life of a member of the congregation, which was supposed to give special attention to an individual's spiritual progress. The choir helper was usually the amanuensis of the account and added descriptions of the final illness and deathbed scene. The memoir was preserved and read at the departed's funeral.

Litany of the Wounds (German: *Wundenlitaney*)—Litany composed by Zinzendorf, his son Christian Renatus, and Zinzendorf's future son-in-law, Johannes Langguth (later von Watteville) in 1744. The *Litany of the Wounds* contains some of the most pervasive and realistic images of

Christ's life and Passion. Among Moravians it was a particularly popular and frequently sung litany that, through its drastic representation of Christ's wounds, enabled the individual to establish a more intimate relationship with the Savior. Despite being the subject of some of the heaviest criticism of the Moravian Church from its opponents, its influence stretches far beyond the 1740s, with imagery occurring well into the 1770s and 1780s.

liturgy—Formal prayer used in Moravian worship, including hymns and scripture verses interspersed to develop a spiritual theme.

lot—Method to make decisions. In the eighteenth century Moravians made frequent use of the lot in an effort to determine the will of the Lord in any situation in which their right course of action was not clear to them. They were convinced that they could in this way rely on Christ's guidance because of their acknowledgment of Him as the Chief Elder of their church. After a prayer the Elders would draw one of the three lots, with usually three possibilities: positive, negative, and blank. A blank was interpreted to mean "wait."

Lovefeast—Nonliturgical gathering during which rolls and tea, coffee, or cocoa were shared and hymns were sung or instrumental music was performed. This informal service was instituted by the Moravian Church in 1727 and has come to represent the New Testament agape. In the middle of the eighteenth century, it served both as a social gathering and as a happy religious service, offering the members of the Bethlehem congregation one of the few opportunities for relaxation. A Lovefeast could be observed by groups within the church fellowship or by choirs or by the entire congregation.

O

Ordinary—Presbyter or priest (second rank of ordained ministry) of a congregation (since 1745). The term sometimes applied specifically to Zinzendorf.

OS/NS—Old Style / New Style. In 1750 Great Britain introduced the Calendar (New Style) Act, which changed the start of the year from March 25 to January 1, starting after December 31, 1751. Great Britain also adopted the Gregorian calendar in place of the Julian. Thus, during the period covered by the Shamokin mission diaries, there can be two dating systems in use. Following standard historical practices, this work indicates OS or NS as cited in the manuscript sources.

P

Penn's Creek Massacre—An attack by the Lenape, or Delaware allied with the French forces, on the white settler colonists at Penn's Creek on October 16, 1755.

Q

Quarter of an Hour—Short service of song and prayer with a brief homily, commonly held in Choir Houses.

S

Saal—Place in which the congregation or one of its choirs met for worship. Even when separate buildings were set apart for worship, the use of this term persisted. Originally, the word resulted from a conscious effort to distinguish their meeting houses from the churches of other ecclesiastical bodies, the state churches in particular.

GLOSSARY OF TERMS

sapan—Porridge or soup made from ash-treated corn that is boiled, with berries (dried or fresh) mixed in. This nutritious staple is found among the Lenape and Haudenosaunee peoples.

Sea Congregation—Group of Moravians traveling on ships. In the eighteenth century, Moravians permitted their usual activities to be interrupted as little as possible while traveling. Thus, they organized themselves as a congregation, maintaining services, discipline, physical care of the individual travelers, and so on.

September 16—Day when Jesus Christ was appointed Chief Elder. On this day in 1741, during a synodical conference in London, leading Moravians became convinced that it was their Lord's will for them to no longer fill the office of Chief Elder of their denomination but to let their Savior be their head and Elder. This day thereafter was observed as a covenanting day for the ministers of the church.

Sifting Period (German: *Sichtungszeit*)—Period of deep divisions in the Moravian congregations across the Atlantic. This term is commonly used to denote the end of the 1740s, when a devotion to the Wounds and Passion of Christ was combined in religious services, imagery, and language with a stress on bridal mysticism and Zinzendorf's marriage theology. This devotion culminated in excessive religious enthusiasm and eroticized language. For example, adherents of the Sifting Period worshipping the Five Wounds of Christ can be witnessed in the imagery of the period and also in the various scathing critiques of the Moravian Church published in the religious tracts and broadsides in German-speaking countries as well as in Great Britain. In February 1749 Zinzendorf wrote his "Letter of Admonition" to the Moravian congregations, forbidding further use of the language of the Sifting Period. For an extensive and authoritative account of the Sifting Period, see Peucker, *Time of Sifting*.

Singing Hour (German: *Singstunde*)—Service devoted to singing. The congregation joins in a series of hymn stanzas, which the Brother or Sister in charge of the service has carefully selected to develop some specific devotional theme, thus making the service resemble a sermon in song. Ordinarily no address is delivered, although the service is opened with a prayer.

sinner (German: *Sünder*)—Someone who has acknowledged sinfulness in a given situation, assumed full responsibility for it, and has humbly repented. The adjective form "sinner-like" is frequently used in memoirs and mission diaries and has a positive connotation, suggesting humble reliance on the Savior's mercy.

Sister (German: *Schwester*)—Female communicant member of the Moravian Church. This term is not used for nonmembers of the church.

Society—Association of people affiliated with the Moravian Church and served by a Moravian minister but not fully organized as a Moravian congregation. Members of a society usually lived in towns, cities, or surrounding country areas, too far away to allow them to attend services regularly. Membership requirements were less stringent than those for a Gemeine.

speaking—Private interview with the pastor or Choir Helper. On stated occasions, especially prior to Communion, every communicant belonging to a congregation was expected to have an interview in which the individual's spiritual life and preparedness to partake of the sacrament was discussed. Speakings sometimes also took place when there were particularly pressing circumstances.

synod—Highest legislative body in the Moravian Church, composed of clergy and lay delegates from the congregations. In the eighteenth century, the worldwide church was administered from Germany, with delegates from other areas participating in the deliberations.

V

Vorsteher—Overseer or supervisor.

W

wampum—Traditional shell bead made of purple quahog (a hard-shelled clam) and white whelk shell, by the Eastern Woodlands Native Americans. Wampum has been used for centuries for ceremonial purposes in storytelling (as an *aide de memoire*), exchanging gifts, and recording important events. Settler colonists translated wampum's symbolic and ceremonial purpose into one of monetary exchange and produced wampum on an industrial scale themselves to facilitate trade with Native American nations.

Watchword—Daily Text of the Moravian Church, drawn from the Hebrew scriptures and chosen by lot.

NOTES

NATIVE AMERICANS IN SHAMOKIN

1. See, for example, Merrell, *Indians' New World*.
2. Diary of Powell, January 4–April 18, 1748, 121.4, folder 4, box 121, Moravian Archives, Bethlehem (hereafter cited as MAB); original in English.
3. Merrell, *Into the American Woods*, 22.
4. Radding, *Landscapes of Power and Identity*.
5. *Moravian Mission Records.* The present basis for arrangement of these materials is the work of the late Reverend Carl John Fliegel (1886–1961), research assistant at the Archives of the Moravian Church from 1952 to his death. A native of Germany, Fliegel read every word of approximately twenty-five thousand pages of these manuscripts, preparing a gigantic index consisting of an estimated thirty thousand cards with 135,000 entries.
6. The later codification of these initially orally transmitted instructions formed the basis of my 2002 NEH Collaborative Research Grant, "Instructions for Body and Soul: Pastoral Care in Eighteenth-Century Bethlehem, Pa." This project has now been published; see Faull, *Body and Soul*.
7. Marsh, *Lenape Among the Quakers*, 2.
8. See Richter, "Framework."
9. See Snow, *Iroquois*.
10. See Schutt, *Peoples of the River Valleys*.
11. For a full treatment of disease in the colonial period, see Fenn, *Pox Americana*.
12. See Mann, *1491*, 102–5, for this discussion.
13. Minderhout and Frantz, *Invisible Indians*, 62–64.
14. Marsh, *Lenape Among the Quakers*, 12–13.
15. Merrell, *Into the American Woods*, covers Shikellamy's role in colonial-Native affairs in some detail.
16. See Axtell, *White Indians*.
17. Dally-Starna and Starna, *Gideon's People*.

INTRODUCTION

1. "Heidencollegia," MAB.
2. Conrad Weiser was instrumental in the negotiations between the governor, the Six Nations, and the Moravians. Having met with Shikellamy in May 1746, he wrote to Spangenberg to say, "I explained the difficulties of transporting the blacksmith's tools up there, and he promised to have the same picked up from Joseph Chambers' place by water in a canoe. Joseph Chambers lives on the Susquehanna River seven miles above John Harris's ferry." Furthermore, Weiser had already negotiated the use of a small block house next to Shikellamy's house that could serve as a blacksmith's shop, and the Indians had promised to put a new roof on it for the Moravian smith. (Conrad Weiser to August Spangenberg, May 5, 1746, box 121.8.1, MAB). This letter reveals the

willingness of the Native Americans living in the area to provide the place for the blacksmith's shop and put on the roof before the smith came, challenging the idea that the Native Americans were passively waiting for help from the Moravians.

3. John Okely to August Spangenberg, November 9, 1746, box 121.8.4, MAB.
4. "Martin Mack's Journey to Shamokin," April 21, 1747, MAB.
5. Merrell, "Cast of His Countenance," 20.
6. See Reichel, *Memorials*, 1:96, 95–96.
7. Merrell, "Cast of His Countenance," 21; Merrell, "Shamokin," 16.
8. See Wellenreuther and Wessel, *Moravian Mission Diaries*, and Gambold and Gambold, *Moravian Springplace Mission*.
9. Other examples of research drawing on manuscript sources in the Moravian Archives in Bethlehem include Merritt, *At the Crossroads*, and Schutt, *Peoples of the River Valleys*.
10. Sachse, *Falckner's Curieuse Nachricht*, 132.
11. Bintz, *Texte zur Mission*, 37.
12. Zinzendorf, *Grafens von Zinzendorf*, 219.
13. Reichel, *Memorials*, 1:84.
14. Reichel, *Memorials*, 1:85, 1:93.
15. Reichel, *Memorials*, 1:93.
16. See Stockton, "Influence of the Moravians."
17. Jordan, "Journal of J. M. Mack"; "Lebenslauf des Bruders."
18. "Diary of Johann Martin Mack," MAB.
19. "Diary of Johann Martin Mack," MAB.
20. "Diary of Johann Martin Mack," MAB.
21. "Shamokin Diary," February 11, 1748, MAB.
22. On November 12, 1747, ten Iroquois representing the Ohio Indians came to Philadelphia. Logan and Weiser both supported the gifts to the Lake Erie Indians, and they were enthusiastic about this first direct contact with Indians living on the Ohio. Franklin published the Philadelphia treaty of November 1747 and gave detailed news reports of the Indians in the *Gazette* on November 12 and 19, 1747; December 3 and 15, 1747; and January 12, 1748. Scarouady had replaced the aging Canasetego as a key Six Nations leader. Scarouady told Weiser that if Pennsylvania encouraged them, the Six Nations would hold "a Council Fire on the Ohio in the spring, to which all the Indians around Lake Erie had already consented to come" (Van Doren and Boyd, *Indian Treaties*, xlvii). He demanded Pennsylvania help them make war. Pennsylvania agreed to do so and provided a list of goods that would be presented to the Indians, with more to come next spring for all the Ohio Indians.
23. "Shamokin Diary," February 28, 1748, MAB.
24. "Shamokin Diary," December 4–6, 9, 1748, MAB.
25. "Diary of the Bethlehem Congregation," July 1749, MAB.
26. A *Singstunde*, or "Singing Hour," is a short service of hymns focusing on a particular issue or event.
27. Johnson, *Court Zinzendorf*, 55, 57.
28. This attack by the Lenape, or Delaware, allied with the French forces, on the white settler colonists at Penn's Creek occurred on October 16, 1755. It was the first of a series of deadly raids by Native Americans on Pennsylvania settlements in the French and Indian War. The Lenape killed fourteen of the twenty-six settlers and took eleven captive. The tensions building along the Susquehanna River between European settler colonists and the Lenape were the result of repeated European encroachments on what had been agreed to be "Indian lands."

SECTION I

1. During the period covered by the "Shamokin Diary," there are two dating systems in use. The British used the Julian, or Old Style (OS), calendar, and the Germans, Dutch, and French

used the Gregorian, or New Style (NS), calendar. Following standard historical practices, this work indicates OS or NS as cited in the manuscript sources. An English version of Mack's account exists in box 28/217/12b/1, MAB. There are many differences between the two accounts, mainly in the choice of details to include and in stylistic smoothness. The account that exists in Mack's handwriting is the one translated here. A transcription of the English version can be found at "Mack Diary." For a discussion of student work involved in the creation of this text, see Faull and Jakacki, "Digital Learning." For all references to persons, see the biographical index.

2. Given the interdiction on the importation of rum to Shamokin, this is surprising. See Carter, *Shamokin Indian Traders*, 14–15. Allumapees had requested of the colonial authorities that traders not be allowed to bring large quantities of rum to the confluence. They agreed, and so only small quantities for personal consumption could be brought up the river. Shikellamy also wanted to make the confluence "dry" (Hazard, *Colonial Records*, 3:406, 501–2).

3. For all references to places, see the index of place names.

4. Bark huts were constructed by the Lenape from trees in the spring, when the bark was easier to peel off.

5. This island was Shamokin Island, now Packer Island.

6. The "old mother" is Madame Montour.

7. An important part of Moravian pastoral care in the towns and in the mission field was the "visit" to both those who were already members of the Gemeine and to those who were not. As Anna Mack was fluent in Delaware and Mohican, it was important she was present on these trips. Also she would be the one to speak to the women and not Martin Mack.

8. Presumably "across the water" is to the south side of the North Branch, as Anderius's mother's hut is on Packer Island (and she is Delaware). Today this is Sunbury.

9. In 1744 Conrad Weiser had the colonial authorities build Shikellamy a house at Shamokin (as requested by him) in return for his services in securing the Treaty of Lancaster. It is described as having been forty-nine and a half feet by seventeen and a half feet and covered with shingles. See Sipe, *Indian Chiefs of Pennsylvania*, 155.

10. "The enemy" is Satan.

11. This is Margaret Montour (1690–), also known as French Margaret.

12. Hockhocking, Ohio.

13. The source is unknown.

14. Brauer is David Brainerd.

15. Brainerd had a different approach to mission work. The Moravians worked with individuals, while the Presbyterians tended to preach to large groups.

16. "Opportunities" is the Moravian term for church services (*Gelegenheiten*).

17. A common practice in the diaries is to refer to the author in the third person.

18. Brother Joseph is August Gottlieb Spangenberg.

19. This remark is in contrast to what Mack writes in his memoir. See the introduction to this volume.

20. This is interesting evidence for the practice of multilingual singing in the Moravian missions. Recent research on this topic can be found in Wheeler and Eyerly, "Singing Box 33," and Woodward, "Incline Your Second Ear This Way."

21. Allumapees is the king.

22. Here "*wildes Volk*" has often been translated as "savage." However, this translation has taken into consideration the larger semantic field of "wild" that encompasses notions of wild to avoid the pejorative "savage." In the English version of this portion of the diary, Mack uses the phrase "as yet wild people." See also, for this usage and translation choice, Dally-Starna and Starna, *Gideon's People*.

23. Flatheads, or Catawba, also known as Esaw or Issa (Catawba iswä, "river"). The Catawba were in a state of warfare with northern peoples for a long time, particularly the Iroquois Seneca and the Algonquin-speaking Lenape, a people who had occupied coastal areas and had become vassals of the Iroquois after migrating out of traditional areas due to European encroachment. See Brown, *Catawba Indians*.

24. The Tutelo (also Totero, Totteroy, Tutera; Yesan in Tutelo) were Native American people living in present-day Virginia and West Virginia. They spoke a Siouan dialect of the Tutelo language thought to be similar to that of their neighbors, the Monacan and Manahoac Nations. Under pressure from English settlers and Seneca Iroquois, they joined with other Virginia Siouan tribes in the late seventeenth century and became collectively known as the Tutelo-Saponi. By 1740 they had largely left Virginia and migrated north to seek protection from their former Iroquois opponents. They were adopted by the Cayuga tribe of New York in 1753.

25. The Lenni Lenape or Lenape, or the Delaware people (or nation), had their historical territory in present-day New Jersey and eastern Pennsylvania along the Delaware River watershed, New York City, western Long Island, and the Lower Hudson Valley.

26. The war is the Iroquois against the Catawba.

27. Anderius's brother is Lewis Montour.

28. Andrew is married at this point to the granddaughter of Allumapees, also known as Sassoonan, "King" of the Delaware. See Merrell, "Cast of His Countenance," 19.

29. According to her biography, her people, the Oneida, lived near the Mohawk River, New York.

30. He was, in fact, his half brother, Lewis, Isabelle Montour's son by another man who was not her husband. See Vincens, *Madame Montour*, 234.

31. The provisions were from Brother George and Sister Loesch.

32. This is an interesting rejection of the theology of good works, which the Native Americans might have heard from missionaries from other denominations, such as the Presbyterians and Catholics.

33. This is possibly a description of the Lenape festival of "gamwing." See Jay Miller, "Old Religion."

34. Anna Mack was pregnant and delivered a son in Bethlehem on January 22 (OS), 1748. "Diary of the Bethlehem Congregation," January 22 (OS) / February 2 (NS), 1748, MAB. She was therefore riding back to Bethlehem eight months pregnant.

35. Joseph is a baptized Mohican from Shekomeko.

SECTION 2

1. Psalm 50:2 (King James Version).
2. Johannes Paul is Johannes Powell.
3. Maqua is Iroquoian.
4. "Gachrongi" is an Oneida expression of pleasure.
5. Psalms 22:29.
6. This term *Wilder* remains untranslated because of the complexities of the semantic field that encompass notions of "savage," "non-Christian," and "cultureless." See, for this usage and translation choice, Dally-Starna and Starna, *Gideon's People*, 1:ix.
7. The Daily Text for June 4/15, 1747, was "Darum, dass er für seinen Gott geeifert, und die Kinder Israel versöhnet hat (4. Mos. 25, 12.13). Das sichs Haus der Seelen, das ohne Grund geschwebt, auf seiner Merter pfählen, und ein creuz-geschlecht, voll von licht und recht, vor ihm wohnen möcht." (Numbers 25:12–13: Wherefore say, behold, I give unto him my covenant of peace: And he shall have it, and his seed after him, even the covenant of an everlasting priesthood; because he was zealous for his God, and made an atonement for the children of Israel.)
8. Moravians called Saturday the Sabbath. See Vogt, "Zinzendorf's Theology."
9. In the original "the Spirit" is "der Geist."

SECTION 3

1. "Diary of the Bethlehem Congregation," August 1747, MAB, supp. C.
2. Bloodletting was a common medical treatment for a variety of illnesses in the eighteenth century. A surplus of blood was thought to cause fevers, among other things. The Moravians appear to have performed this service for the Indians, although this is the first specific mention of this procedure in the "Shamokin Diary." In the agreement to the founding of the blacksmith's shop, however, there are explicit instructions not to bleed the Indians. Merritt makes the argument that the missionaries continued to bleed the Native people who requested it because it formed a connection between their beliefs (in body and soul) and those of the Native communities. See Merritt, *At the Crossroads*, 116–21.
3. "Mein Gott! du siehst sie weiden," hymn 325, in Zinzendorf, *Kleines Brüdergesangbuch*, 102.
4. The blacksmith Anton Schmidt; his wife, Catherine; and Christian Rauch arrived.
5. Christel is the diminutive form of the man's name Christian. In the Sifting Period the use of diminutives attached to names was widespread, reflecting the desire for childlike innocence in the eyes of God, perhaps. On the language of the Sifting Period, see Peucker, *Time of Sifting*, 58–92.
6. The "Society" is the Society for the Propagation of the Gospel.
7. One son was John Shikellamy, also known as John Logan and Tachnechdorus (Spreading Oak); another was Soyechtowa, or James Logan; and a third was Sagoechyata, or John Petty and Hetaquantagechty. See Merrell, "Shikellamy," 241.
8. The first site of significant falls on the Susquehanna is McKees Falls. The second set of rough water is at Dauphin, farther downriver.
9. The notion of the written word taking on the power of spoken utterances by the author, as if present, was crucial to understanding the rhetoric of formal councils. See Merrell, "I Desire All That."
10. William Penn (1644–1718) founded the colony of Pennsylvania in 1681. The land for the colony was given to William Penn's father by King Charles II of England as repayment for an outstanding loan. William Penn, a Quaker, served as governor and proprietor of the colony from 1681 to 1718. (Proprietary charters were granted to individuals as a direct result of their relationship with the king.) After Penn's death in 1718, his second wife, Hannah Callowhill Penn (1670–1726), governed the colony for a brief period, until Penn's will was settled and his sons John, Richard, and Thomas were granted shares of the proprietorship. Until the Treaty of Albany in 1754, the land near Shamokin on the western shore of the Susquehanna River was not owned by the Penn family. Until 1763 the Iroquois made alliances with both French-allied Indians and British-allied Indians. Their use of power was beyond any kind of protection for Moravian missionaries, as the Moravians refused to play one side off against the other. The power of Iroquoia with its confederation and "play-off diplomacy" was an ingenious system of "aggressive neutrality" the Iroquois applied to tip the balance between the French and British, if necessary. Both imperial governments rewarded the League of Six Nations (the Tuscarora had joined the league in 1722) handsomely to secure Iroquois neutrality. In the 1750s the league's hold on New York and Pennsylvania began to diminish; after the French and Indian War, the effectiveness of play-off diplomacy vanished. After wars had rent Indian government and identity asunder, remnants of the Iroquois, Delaware, and other tribes were less effective in dealing with state-styled governments. See Jennings, *Ambiguous Iroquois Empire*, 367–75, and A. Wallace, *Death and Rebirth*, 111–14. In 1768 the Treaty of Fort Stanwix expanded the boundaries of the proprietors' lands to include lands to the east, north, and west of Shamokin.
11. Conrad Weiser had overseen the building of Shikellamy's house at Shamokin in return for his diplomatic services to the Haudenosaunee in the 1730s. See P. Wallace, *Conrad Weiser*.
12. Until 1763 the Six Nations made alliances with both British- and French-allied Native Americans. This political gamesmanship resulted in both the French and British imperial

governments rewarding the Six Nations. However, after the 1750s their influence in New York and Pennsylvania began to decline. The building of the blacksmith's shop is an example of this strategy and reveals that the Moravians had no political power in these matters and maintained neutrality. See Jennings, "Pennsylvania Indians."

13. The Pedelavium was a rite in the Moravian Church, often performed during a Lovefeast or prior to Communion.

14. Deuteronomy 33:18.

SECTION 4

1. Many of the people living around the confluence at this time fell sick from the 1747 smallpox epidemic in Pennsylvania. See Webster, "Brief History."

2. Genesis 12:2.

3. Harris's Ferry, at present-day Harrisburg, was the closest ferry across the river.

4. His son is Christoph Weiser, with whom the missionaries stayed when they first set out for Shamokin in 1745.

5. David Zeisberger had already begun to learn the Onondaga language by living among the Six Nations. Shikellamy is clearly happy to have someone to speak to.

6. Of the Cayuga Nation, Shikellamy's wife (1695–1747) was the mother of James and John Logan, She was given the name of Neonoma, although this is disputed.

7. The closest mill to Shamokin in the 1740s is downriver, just north of Harris's Ferry. See Merrell, "Other 'Susquehanna Traders,'" 197.

8. "Our Annerl" is deleted in the original entry.

9. Both Anna Mack and Rachel Post could communicate quite fluently in Mohican with Shikellamy. See Heckewelder, *Narrative of the Mission*, 37–65.

10. Isaiah 58:12.

11. "My Annerl" is deleted in the original entry.

12. Isaiah 58:12. Obviously, the diarist has made a mistake, as this is the same as the entry for November 3.

13. This was a brief quarter-hour service for the married people that included a short reflection and hymns to celebrate their marriage as an image of the covenant Christ made with His church.

14. This refers to the first of "Reports from Cammerhoff," MAB. Even in Shamokin, the Moravians were kept informed about what was happening in the rest of the Moravian world through the network of worldwide communication. See Wessel, "Connecting Congregations."

15. "My Annerl and Catharina" are deleted in the original entries. The diarist is once again attempting to depersonalize his entries by removing the names, perhaps as the entries would be read by many in the worldwide congregation.

16. Shikellamy's son was James Logan, whose wife was a Mohican.

17. "No longer dead" is deleted in the original entry.

18. "Annerl" is deleted in the original entry.

19. This entry is included in the original manuscript as a separate inserted page, perhaps to serve as an example of how there could be misunderstandings in the relationships between the Moravians and Native Americans in Shamokin.

20. In 1745 James Logan accompanied Shikellamy and Spangenberg on a trip to Onondaga. See Spangenberg, "Spangenberg's Notes."

21. The "big man" refers to Zinzendorf.

22. Brother Ludwig is Zinzendorf.

23. The Litany of the Wounds was sung regularly on Fridays in Moravian Bethlehem in the 1740s. Focusing on the wounds of Christ, it promoted a pious attitude of devotion and grace for

Christ's sacrifice. It was quite controversial for its realistic depiction of the blood and wounds of Jesus. However, it was very popular in the missions. See Faull, "Faith and Imagination," 33–37.

24. They are referring here to the Moravian mission at Gnadenhütten, Pennsylvania.

25. The Watch Night service was a short service of prayer at the end of the year to reflect on the past and look forward to the future.

26. A vivid account of Cammerhof's journey to Shamokin with grain and other supplies is found in a published letter to Zinzendorf. See Jordan, "Bishop J. C. F. Cammerhoff's Narrative."

SECTION 5

1. The original was written in English by Brother Powell, who noted the wrong year. Spelling and punctuation are slightly modernized. A diplomatic transcription of this section of the diary can be found at Repko et al., "Joseph Powell Shamokin Diary." This section of the Shamokin mission diary served as a base text for an introductory course at Bucknell University in digital humanities. Students teamed up to transcribe and annotate Joseph Powell's section of the manuscript and then render the text in XML-compliant TEI. The tagging of names, places, and dates then allowed the students to visualize person-to-person networks, journeys, and timelines. See Faull, "Visualizing Religious Networks."

2. In November 1747 the western chiefs of the Six Nations discussed with the colonial authorities in Philadelphia their disappointment with the British—namely, that they were not fighting the French as hard as the Six Nations were. The colonial authorities assured the Iroquois that they were fighting the French hard at sea. The original discussions can be found here at "Treaty, Etc." See Shannon, *Iroquois Diplomacy*.

3. The T'girhitondi is Spangenberg.

4. The sale of alcohol to Native Americans was prohibited by an act in 1722, but the ban was not strictly enforced until a proclamation was issued by Lt. Gov. James Hamilton of Pennsylvania, on August 11, 1749. See Mancall, "Temperance," 107.

SECTION 6

1. "Anna Mack" is inserted in the margin in the original entry.

2. This sentence is inserted in the margin in the original.

3. This sentence is inserted in the margin in the original.

4. The Nanticoke are an Algonquin-speaking people from the eastern shore of the Chesapeake Bay in Maryland.

5. In this passage Zeisberger uses imagery and vocabulary redolent with the terminology of the Sifting Period, in which the wounds of Christ (especially the side wound) became an object of particular worship and veneration. See Atwood, *Community of the Cross*, 77–112, and Peucker, *Time of Sifting*.

6. David Zeisberger wrote a Delaware-English alphabet book and compiled a four-volume German-Iroquois dictionary and a Delaware-English dictionary. From 1772 to 1781, Zeisberger worked in five communities on the Muskingum River in the backcountry of Ohio: Schönbrunn, Lichtau, Neu-Schönbrunn, Gnadenhütten, and Salem. See Zeisberger and Horsfield, *Indian Dictionary*.

7. The diarists are referring to the June 1748 synod held in Bethlehem, Pennsylvania.

8. This sentence is inserted in the margin.

9. According to Zeisberger's Iroquois dictionary, *jachte* is the negative particle, and *ojaneri* means "benevolent," which would translate to "Traders are not good men." See Zeisberger and Horsfield, *Indian Dictionary*.

SECTION 7

10. "Virginia" was the term used to denote the lands that lay on the west side of the Susquehanna and to the south. Spangenberg was on a missionary trip that took him all the way south to what is today North Carolina.

11. Shikellamy is referring to the Single Brethren House in Bethlehem, which was erected in 1748.

SECTION 7

1. One of many names attributed to Shikellamy, "Swatane" is an Oneida word, denoting "The Light Bringer." See Merrell, "Shikellamy," 253n3. For an extended discussion of Shikellamy, see P. Wallace, *Conrad Weiser*, 272–76; Merrell, "Shikellamy"; and Schweinitz, *David Zeisberger*.

2. This tea was an herbal infusion.

3. Jesus Christ was elected Chief Elder of the church at the London Synod on September 16, 1741. See Hamilton and Hamilton, *History*, 73.

4. *Niàwo* is an Onondaga word denoting pleasure and thanks. As noted earlier, Zeisberger was a student of the Iroquoian languages and therefore noted the actual words in the diary. See Zeisberger, *Onondaga Grammar*, 19.

5. Zinzendorf, *Vier-und-dreyßig Homiliae*. For an examination of the sermons on the Litany of the Wounds, see Faull, "Faith and Imagination." For the most thorough account of the Sifting Period as a whole, see Peucker, *Time of Sifting*.

6. "Mein Gott du siehst die weiden / Breit aus die Flügel beyde," hymn 325, in Zinzendorf, *Kleines Brüdergesangbuch*.

SECTION 8

1. "Diary of the Bethlehem Congregation," April 15/26, 1749, MAB.

2. Jeremias was a Delaware from Wamphallobank who had just been baptized on March 15, 1749, in Bethlehem by Brother Johannes.

3. "From the Flatheads" is deleted in the original entry.

4. Zeisberger is describing the custom of "running the gauntlet," a practice Eastern Woodlands Native Americans used to test the mettle of their captives. The prisoner would be forced to run between two facing lines of Native people, all brandishing sticks and clubs or throwing stones. How a captive behaved while running through this gauntlet was closely observed. It is also thought that this was a way of expunging captives of their old allegiances before they were adopted into their captors' nations. See Zeisberger, *Northern American Indians*, 105.

5. "They accompanied" is deleted in the original entry.

6. In July 1749 representatives of the Seneca, with Conrad Weiser as interpreter, were meeting with the new governor of Pennsylvania, James Hamilton, in Philadelphia to report on illegal settlements by white people on Indian territory on the west bank of the Susquehanna River. Hamilton promised them that these settlements were not sanctioned by the colonial government and would be removed. Hamilton also was welcomed by the Seneca as a countryman, as he was born in North America and not Great Britain and would therefore understand their requests better. Hamilton ordered that the Seneca be given 100 pounds as a gift. See *Treaty Held*, 38–43.

7. The Seneca listed in the treaty meeting are Ogaushtash and Assuchquay. See *Treaty Held*, 38–43.

SECTION 9

1. The missionaries are most likely reading reports from Greenland that were included in the *Gemeinnachrichten*. A history of the mission was published later. See Cranz, *History of*

Greenland. For a thorough examination of the significance of this text, see Jensz, "Publication and Reception."

2. Nutimus's sister, Rahel, is referred to in the Fliegel Index as F#244. According to the "Catalogue of Baptized Indians" (MAB), she was baptized in Bethlehem by Brother Cammerhof on January 10, 1750, and died there five days later.

SECTION 10

1. "Deine Kleider riechen, Sie kamen aus der Atmosphäre des Grabes Christ Her."
2. Johannes de Watteville was sent to visit the missions in Greenland after his trip to North America and the Caribbean. See Egede and Stach, *Lives of Missionaries*, 180.
3. At the mouth of the Chillisquaque Creek, which Grube describes in his trip in 1754.
4. John 6:51.
5. The writer is referring to the impending sacrament of Communion during Holy Week at Shamokin.
6. The Conoy, also called the Piscataway, is an Algonquin-speaking North American Indian tribe related to the Delaware and the Nanticoke.

SECTION 11

1. For Zinzendorf's account of this trip, see his *Count Zinzendorf and the Indians*.
2. French Margaret's Town is located at the mouth of Lycoming Creek, where it runs into the West Branch of the Susquehanna River.
3. The two men were Lewis Montour and Echogohund.
4. This is probably Anton (F#249), son of Thamar (F#59), from Tenkanek (Tunkhannock), Brother of Nathaniel in Meniolagomeka, and husband of Johanna (F#250), who was Delaware and was baptized on February 8, 1750, in Bethlehem by Brother Cammerhof.
5. This sentence is deleted in the original.

SECTION 12

1. Brother Otto is John Mattheus Otto, Bethlehem apothecary and brother of Frederick Otto.
2. "On April 2, two of old Shikellamy's sons, John and John Petty, moved 30 miles away from here" is inserted in the margin.
3. See Gordon, "Entangled by the World."
4. The gunsmith was William Henry.
5. On April 15, 1754, many prominent Moravians arrived in New York on the *Irene*, a Moravian-owned ship: Brother Joseph (August Spangenberg); Bishop David Nitschmann; John Ettwein with his wife, Johanette, and their child, Christian; the painter Valentin Haidt and his wife, Catherine; and David and Regina Heckewelder, the parents of John Heckewelder. See Levering, *History of Bethlehem*, 277.
6. The words that Conrad Weiser had been entrusted to deliver to James Logan Shikellamy concerned the purchase of "the whole Province." As recorded in his letter to Richard Peters, dated May 2, 1754, Weiser describes finding only James Logan, "the lame one," at home in Shamokin, "almost naked," while his brothers were up at Canaseragy (now Muncy on the West Branch) after a falling-out over the failed expedition against the Catawba the summer before, during which two of Shikellamy's grandsons were killed. Going against the advice of Shikellamy's daughter and flaunting the peace that had been made between the Iroquois and the Catawba,

John Petty, Shikellamy's son, had led the young men to their death. Weiser reminds James Logan of this error and warns that he will ensure that Shikellamy's family will be left to sit among the "lice and fleas" if they do not help him deliver this message to Onondaga. For a full account of the embassy, see P. Wallace, *Conrad Weiser*, 355n.

7. The diarist is referring to himself in the third person.

8. Kliest was calling for a canoe to take him over the river.

9. Brother Boehmer is Martin Boehmer, and Brother and Sister Anton Schmidt are Anton and Catherina Schmidt. Lambert Garrison had just arrived on the *Irene*.

10. "Fürwahr, er trug unsere Krankheit und lud auf sich unsre Schmerzen. Wir aber hielten ihn für den, der geplagt und von Gott geschlagen und gemartert wäre." Jesaja 53:4.

11. "Our horses returned of their own accord today" is inserted in the margin.

SECTION 13

1. Mariane (F#227), a Delaware, was baptized by Cammerhof in Bethlehem in 1749.

2. The Minisink town was at the end of the Wyoming Valley. See Johnson, *Count Zinzendorf*, 56. Brothers Grube and Rundt had stopped there in July 1754, where they had participated in a sweat lodge and had preached in Delaware to the assembled people.

SECTION 14

1. "Seelig sind, die izt glauben." John 20:29.

2. "O Haupt voll Blut und Wunden." This German hymn, from a translation of a medieval Latin poem on the wounded body of Christ, is one of the staples of the Lutheran hymnal and the *Moravian Hymn Book*. It is best known for Johann Sebastian Bach's use of it as a recurrent theme in his 1727 "Saint Matthew Passion" and is sung especially on Good Friday throughout the Lutheran (and Moravian) Church.

3. "Mein Gott, du siehst sie weiden," *Kleines Brüdergesangbuch*, hymn 325. This hymn is also included in the church litany, an intercession for the church sung before the sermon on Sundays. See Peucker, *Herrnhuter Wörterbuch*, 63–64.

4. Zinzendorf, *Vier-und-dreyßig Homiliae*.

5. The Dunkers were a German Baptist sect from southwest Germany, some of whom settled near Germantown, Pennsylvania, in the eighteenth century.

6. The Herrnhuter, or Unity of the Brethren, were known in English-speaking lands as the Moravian Church.

7. Presbyterian minister David Brainerd was active in Pennsylvania and New Jersey in the 1740s and settled an "Indian Town" in Cranbury, New Jersey, in 1746. See Piper, *Tested by Fire*.

8. The Litany of the Wounds was composed by Count von Zinzendorf in 1744. The litany was extremely popular in the late 1740s, and many lines from it were quoted by members of the Moravian Church in their personal writings. The litany focused on the Passion of Christ and the five wounds he suffered. See Peucker, *Herrnhuter Wörterbuch*, 110.

9. Moravians had been conducting a mission in Greenland since 1733. See Cranz, *History of Greenland*. It is fascinating that the German Moravians are telling the Lenape about the landscape and peoples of Greenland in 1755 in North America.

10. The Litany of the Life, Passion, and Death of the Lord, composed in 1755, replaced the Litany of the Wounds, and focused more on Christ's life than on his wounds. It was designed to curb the excessive blood and wounds language of the Sifting Period. However, its effect on the diarist appears to have been quite strong.

11. "O Haupt voll Blut und Wunden." This hymn was composed by Paul Gerhardt (1607–76).

12. The Passion hymn is "Christus, der uns selig macht." Originally composed by M. Weisse in 1531, it is included in the new Litany of the Life, Passion, and Death of the Lord of 1755.

13. "Ich bleib ewig sitzen an den Wunden ritzen," is a line from a hymn by Zinzendorf et al., *Londoner Gesangbuch*, no. 640.

SECTION 15

1. According to the University of Minnesota Extension, if the growing point is below the soil then the corn plant can recover from a frost. However, if the plant has turned brown, then it is dead. See "Spring Freeze Injury."

2. On May 3, 1755, the cornerstone of Nazareth Hall was laid, which was to become the Boys School.

3. For an account of these travels from Weiser's point of view, see P. Wallace, *Conrad Weiser*, 379–81. According to Weiser, French Margaret had left her town for Virginia and her son Nicholas had gone to Ohio to scout the amassing French troops.

4. In 1739 the chiefs of the Iroquois Confederacy had supposedly granted Weiser many lands around the Susquehanna River confluence, but the proprietaries would not let him have it. Local oral history has it that Shikellamy gave Weiser the Isle of Que after they had both had a dream that this had come to pass. See Snyder, "Conrad Weiser."

5. "Er kommt auch noch heute." The Collect is taken from the Lutheran hymn, "Gottes Sohn ist kommen," by Johann Roh, in 1544.

6. "Der Hölle eine Pestilenz." Hosea 13:14. This text is also part of Bach's "Cantata for Quasimodogeniti," in "Halt im Gedächtnis Jesum Christ," Bach Werkverzeichnis, 67.

7. "Was ist das vor ein Mann? Kurz: Er ist es gar." This is typical of the kinds of devotional sayings that would be copied onto cards for private prayer.

8. "Lassets beyeinander bis zur Erndte." Matthew 13:30.

9. The neighbor is referring to Braddock's defeat on July 19, 1755, on the Monongahela River. See Preston, *Braddock's Defeat*.

10. "Dein Schweiß im Bußkampf, dünst uns über Leib und Seel," in Beyreuther et al., *Herrnhuter Gesangbuch*, 12, Anhang.

SECTION 16

1. August 13, 1727, is the date usually considered as the renewal date of the Unity of the Brethren, which took place in the parish church in Berthelsdorf, Germany.

2. The custom of reburying the bones of the dead in a new place of residence is attributed to the Nanticoke Indians, with whom the Conoy (Piscataway) Indians joined in the contact period on the Delmarva Peninsula of the East Coast of the United States, which is occupied by the vast majority of the state of Delaware and parts of the Eastern Shore regions of Maryland and Virginia.

3. In August 12–18, 1755, the Sixteenth Provincial Synod convened at Warwick. Bishop Spangenberg was president, and Bishops Boehler and Hehl were members. The project of founding a third exclusive Moravian settlement in Pennsylvania was announced. Warwick, which started on February 9, 1749, was to be the place and Lititz the name, after the old barony in Bohemia. See Schweinitz, *Moravian Manual*, 180.

4. "O daß ich 1000 Zungen hätte!" Text written by Johannes Mentzer (1658–1734), a friend of Zinzendorf's.

5. "O ihr heilig fünf Wunden, macht es wie Elijah," in Beyreuther et al., *Herrnhuter Gesangbuch*.

SECTION 17

1. Luke 18:7.
2. Daniel Levant's old mill house was in Maxatawny Township, between New Smithville and Kutztown.

APPENDIX B

1. The letters have been transcribed and translated by Edward Quinter as part of a larger project by Scott Gordon, professor of English at Lehigh University. I am grateful for permission to publish these extracts here.
2. Zinzendorf had been officially adopted by David Nitschmann before his trip to America, so Anna Nitschmann became his sister. See Faull, "Anna Caritas Nitschmann."
3. "Br. Cammerhof's Fourth Letter," MAB.
4. "Br. Cammerhof's Fifth Letter," MAB.

BIBLIOGRAPHY

ARCHIVAL SOURCES FROM THE MORAVIAN ARCHIVES, BETHLEHEM, PA

"Br. Cammerhof's Fifth Letter to Br. L. [Zinzendorf]." June 1747. Transcribed and translated by Edward Quinter, 9762a–63a, PP CJF. 1747–50.
"Br. Cammerhof's Fourth Letter to Br. L. [Zinzendorf]." May 22–24 (NS), 1747. Transcribed and translated by Edward Quinter, 9694b–98a. PP CJF. 1747–50.
"Catalogue of Baptized Indians." 1742–64. MissInd. Box 313.4.
"Diary of Bernhard Adam Grube, Daniel Kliest, and Others." April 14, 1753–December 25, 1754. MissInd. Box 121.6.
"Diary of Christian Rauch and David Zeisberger." February 1, 1749–March 5, 1750. MissInd. Box 121.5.
"Diary of Johannes Hagen, Johann Martin Mack, and Johann Christoph Friedrich Cammerhoff." May 26–December 31, 1747. MissInd. Box 121.3.
"Diary of Johann Martin Mack, from His Journey To and Stay in Shamokin." September 13–November 10, 1745. MissInd. Box 121.2.
"Diary of Joseph Powell, Johann Martin Mack, David Zeisberger, and Christian Rauch." January 4, 1748–January 31, 1749. MissInd. Box 121.4.
"Diary of the Bethlehem Congregation." 1747–49. Beth. Cong. 5–8.
"Diary of the Moravian Mission in Shamokin." Compiled by Gottfried Rösler. April 1–October 30, 1755. MissInd. Box 121.7.
"Die Heidencollegia." In "Travel Diaries, Other by Martin Mack." MissInd. Box 217.12b 809.
"Martin Mack's Journey to Shamokin." April 16–25, 1747. MissInd. Box 121.9.2.
"Messages to Shikellamy and Others by Christoph Pyrlaeus and Others." 1747–49. MissInd. Box 121.10.
"Reports from Cammerhoff to Zinzendorf, Anna Nitschmann, and Johannes von Watteville." 1747–50. PP CJF.
"Shamokin Diary." 1748. MissInd. Box 121.2.
"Travel Diary by Nicolaus Ludwig von Zinzendorf of His Second and Third Visits to American Indian Groups." August–September 1742. MissInd. Box 121.1.

PRINT AND ONLINE SOURCES

Anderson, Chad L. *The Storied Landscape of Iroquoia: History, Conquest, and Memory in the Native Northeast.* Lincoln: University of Nebraska Press, 2020.
"Andreas Brocksch." Moravian Lives. Accessed June 19, 2023. https://moravian.bucknell.edu/memoirs/andreas-brocksch/.
"Anton Schmidt." Moravian Lives. Accessed June 27, 2023. https://moravian.bucknell.edu/memoirs/anton-schmidt-sen/.
Atwood, Craig. *Community of the Cross: Moravian Piety in Colonial Bethlehem.* University Park: Penn State University Press, 2004.

Atwood, Craig, and Peter Vogt, eds. *The Distinctiveness of Moravian Culture: Essays and Documents in Moravian History in Honor of Vernon H. Nelson on His Seventieth Birthday*. Nazareth, PA: Moravian Historical Society, 2003.

Axtell, James. *White Indians of Colonial America*. Fairfield, WA: Ye Galleon Press, 1991.

Beyreuther, Erich, Gerhard Meyer, Gudrun Meyer-Hickel, and Nicolaus Ludwig Zinzendorf. *Herrnhuter Gesangbuch: Christliches Gesang-Buch der Evangelischen Brüder-Gemeinen von 1735*. In Zinzendorf, *Materialien und Dokumente*, vol. 3.

Bintz, Helmut. *Texte zur Mission*. Hamburg: Friedrich Wittig Verlag, 1979.

"Biographical Sketch of Rev. Bernhard Adam Grube." *Pennsylvania Magazine of History and Biography* 25, no. 1 (1901): 14–19.

Brown, Douglas S. *The Catawba Indians: People of the River*. 1966. Reprint, Columbia: University of South Carolina Press, 1966.

Calloway, Colin G. *New Worlds for All*. Baltimore: Johns Hopkins University Press, 1997.

"Cammerhof's Journal of 1748." *Pennsylvania Magazine of History and Biography* 29 (1905): 160–79.

Carter, John H. *Allummapees, King of the Delawares at Shamokin*. Sunbury, PA: Northumberland County Historical Society, 1998.

———. *Early Events in the Susquehanna Valley*. Millville, PA: Northumberland County Historical Society, 1981.

———, ed. *History of Sunbury*. Sunbury, PA: Northumberland County Historical Society, 1995.

———. "Indian Tribes of Shamokin." In Carter, *History of Sunbury*, 70–83.

———. *The Shamokin Indian Traders*. Sunbury, PA: Northumberland County Historical Society, 1995.

Cranz, David. *The History of Greenland*. 2 vols. London, 1767.

Dally-Starna, Corinna, and William A. Starna. *Gideon's People: Being a Chronicle of an American Indian Community in Colonial Connecticut and the Moravian Missionaries Who Served There*. Lincoln: University of Nebraska Press, 2009.

Donehoo, George P. *A History of the Indian Villages and Place Names in Pennsylvania*. Harrisburg, PA: Telegraph Press, 1928.

———. *The Indians of Pennsylvania*. Sunbury, PA: Northumberland County Historical Society, 1999.

———. *Pennsylvania: A History*. New York: Lewis Historical, 1926.

Egede, Hans, and Matthew Stach. *Lives of Missionaries: Greenland*. London: Society for Promoting Christian Knowledge, 1888.

Eshleman, H. Frank. *Annals of the Susquehannocks and Other Indian Tribes of Pennsylvania, 1500–1763*. Lewisburg, PA: Wennawoods, 2000.

———. *Lancaster County Indians: Annals of the Susquehannocks and Other Indian Tribes of the Susquehanna Territory from About the Year 1500 to 1763, the Date of Their Extinction*. Lititz, PA: Express, 1909.

Ettwein, John. "Reverend John Ettwein's Notes of Travel from the North Branch of the Susquehanna to the Beaver River, Pennsylvania, 1772." *Pennsylvania Magazine of History and Biography* 25, no. 2 (1901): 208–19.

Faull, Katherine. "Anna Caritas Nitschmann." In *Pietismus Handbuch*, edited by Wolfgang Breul, 197–202. Tübingen, Germany: Mohr Siebeck, 2021.

———. "Charting the Colonial Backcountry: Joseph Shippen's Map of the Susquehanna River." *Pennsylvania Magazine of History and Biography* 136, no. 4 (2012): 461–65.

———. "The Experience of the World as the Experience of the Self: Smooth Rocks in a River Archipelago." In *Re-imagining Nature: Environmental Humanities and Ecosemiotics*, edited by Alfred K. Siewers, 178–92. Lewisburg, PA: Bucknell University Press, 2014.

———. "Faith and Imagination: Nikolaus Ludwig von Zinzendorf's Anti-Enlightenment Philosophy of Self." *Bucknell Review* 38, no. 2 (1995): 23–56.

———. "Mapping a Mission: The Origins of Golkowsky's 1768 Map of Friedenshütten, Pennsylvania." *Journal of Moravian History* 7 (2009): 107–16.

———. "Masculinity in the Eighteenth-Century Moravian Mission Field: Contact and Negotiation." *Journal of Moravian History* 13, no. 1 (2013): 27–53.

———. *Moravian Women's Memoirs: Their Related Lives, 1750–1820*. Syracuse: Syracuse University Press, 1997.

———. *Speaking to Body and Soul: Instructions for the Moravian Choir Helpers, 1785–1786*. University Park: Penn State University Press, 2017.

———. "Visualizing Religious Networks, Movements, and Communities: Building Moravian Lives." In *Digital Humanities and Christianity: An Introduction*, edited by Tim Hutchings and Claire Clivaz, 213–36. Berlin: De Gruyter, 2021.

———. "Women, Migration, and Moravian Mission: Negotiating Pennsylvania's Colonial Landscapes." In *Babel of the Atlantic: Language and Cultural Politics in Colonial Pennsylvania*, edited by Bethany Wiggin, 101–27. University Park: Penn State University Press, 2019.

Faull, Katherine M., and Diane K. Jakacki. "Digital Learning in an Undergraduate Context: Promoting Long-Term Student-Faculty Place-Based Collaboration." *Digital Scholarship in the Humanities* (2015): 76–82. https://www.doi.org/10.1093/llc/fqv050.

Fenn, Elizabeth A. *Pox Americana: The Great Smallpox Epidemic of 1775–82*. New York: Hill and Wang, 2001.

Gambold, Anna Rosina, and John Gambold. *The Moravian Springplace Mission to the Cherokees*. Edited by Rowena McClinton. Indians of the Southeast. Lincoln: University of Nebraska Press, 2007.

"George Neisser." Moravian Lives. Accessed June 19, 2023. https://moravian.bucknell.edu/memoirs/george-neisser.

Gerstall, Vivian S. *The Silversmiths of Lancaster, Pennsylvania, 1730–1850*. Lancaster, PA: Lancaster County Historical Society, 1972.

Gordon, Scott Paul. "Entangled by the World: William Henry of Lancaster and 'Mixed' Living in a Moravian Town and Country Congregation." *Journal of Moravian History* 8 (2010): 7–52.

Grigg, John A. *The Lives of David Brainerd: The Making of an American Evangelical Icon*. Oxford: Oxford University Press, 2009.

Grinde, Donald A., Jr., and Bruce E. Johansen. *Exemplar of Liberty: Native America and the Evolution of Democracy*. Los Angeles: American Indian Studies Center, 1991.

Grumet, Robert S. *Historic Contact: Indian People and Colonists in Today's Northeastern United States in the Sixteenth Through Eighteenth Centuries*. Norman: University of Oklahoma Press, 1995.

Hamilton, J. Taylor. "The Confusion at Tulpehocken." *Transactions of the Moravian Historical Society* 4, no. 5 (1895): 237–73.

Hamilton, J. Taylor, and Keith Hamilton. *History of the Moravian Church: The Renewed Unitas Fratrum, 1722–1957*. Bethlehem, PA: Interprovincial Board of Christian Education, 1967.

Hamilton, Kenneth. "John Ettwein's Visit to Friedenshutten on the Susquehanna in 1768." *Settler* 4 (1957): 56–62.

Hanna, Charles A. "The Shamokin Traders and the Shamokin Path." In *The Wilderness Trail, or The Ventures and Adventures of the Pennsylvania Traders on the Allegheny Path*, 192–222. New York: Knickerbocker Press, 1911.

Harvey, Oscar Jewell. *A History of Wilkes-Barre, Luzerne County, Pennsylvania*. Wilkes-Barre, PA: Wyoming Historical and Geological Society, 1909.

Hazard, Samuel. *Colonial Records of Pennsylvania*. Harrisburg: Fenn, 1851–53.

Heckewelder, John. "History, Manners, and Customs of the Indian Nations Who Once Inhabited Pennsylvania and Neighboring States." *Memoirs of the Historical Society of Pennsylvania* 12 (1876).

———. *A Narrative of the Mission of the United Brethren Among the Delaware and Mohegan Indians, from Its Commencement, in the Year 1740, to the Close of the Year 1808.* 1820. Reprint, New York: Arno Press, 1971.

Heckewelder, John, and Peter S. Du Ponceau. "Names Which the Lenni Lenape or Delaware Indians, Who Once Inhabited This Country, Had Given to Rivers, Streams, Places, &c. . . ." *Transactions of the American Philosophical Society* 4 (1834): 351–96.

Higgins, Robert M. "An Indian Site in the Borough of Montoursville." *Journal of the Lycoming County Historical Society* 13 (1986): 28–34.

Hill, Ronald B. "A Brief History of the Andaste Nation." *Pennsylvania Archaeologist* 6 (1936): 35.

Hirsch, Alison Duncan. "'The Celebrated Madame Montour': 'Interpretess' Across Early American Frontiers." *Explorations in Early American Culture* 4 (2000): 81–112.

Hodge, Frederick Webb, ed. *Handbook of American Indians North of Mexico.* Bulletin 30. Pt. 2. Washington, DC: Government Printing Office, 1910.

Jennings, Francis. *The Ambiguous Iroquois Empire: The Covenant Chain Confederation of Indian Tribes with English Colonies.* 1984. Reprint, New York: Norton, 2013.

———. "'Pennsylvania Indians' and the Iroquois." In *Beyond the Covenant Chain: The Iroquois and Their Neighbors in Indian North America, 1600–1800,* edited by Daniel K. Richter and James H. Merrell, 75–91. Syracuse: Syracuse University Press, 1987.

Jensz, Felicity. "The Publication and Reception of David Cranz's 1767 History of Greenland." *The Library: The Transactions of the Bibliographical Society* 13, no. 4 (2012): 457–72.

"Johann Christopher Pyrlaeus." Moravian Lives. Accessed June 19, 2023. https://moravian.bucknell.edu/memoirs/johann-christopher-pyrlaeus/.

"Johann Matthaeus Otto." Moravian Lives. Accessed June 19, 2023. https://moravian.bucknell.edu/memoirs/johann-matthaeus-otto/.

Johnson, Frederick. *Count Zinzendorf and the Moravian and Indian Occupancy of the Wyoming Valley (PA), 1742–1763.* Proceedings of the Wyoming Historical and Geological Society. Wilkes Barre, PA, 1904.

Jordan, John W. "Bishop J. C. F. Cammerhoff's Narrative of a Journey to Shamokin, Pa., in the Winter of 1748." *Pennsylvania Magazine of History and Biography* 29, no. 2 (1905): 160–79.

———. "Journal of J. M. Mack [Diarium 21.8.-1.9.1753]." In *Historical Journal: A Quarterly Record of Local History and Genealogy, Devoted Principally to Northwestern Pennsylvania* 1, no. 3 (1887): 92–96

Journals: Shamokin, the Indian Capital, 1737–1755. Sunbury, PA: Northumberland County Historical Society Archives.

Kent, Barry C. *Susquehanna's Indians.* Harrisburg: Pennsylvania Historical and Museum Commission, 1984.

Kent, Barry, Janet Rice, and Kakuko Ota. "A Map of Eighteenth-Century Indian Towns in Pennsylvania." *PA Archaeologist* 51, no. 4 (1981): 1–18.

Kent, Barry, I. F. Smith III, and C. McCann, eds. *Foundations of Pennsylvania Prehistory.* Anthropological Series 2. Harrisburg: Pennsylvania Historical and Research Commission, 1971.

Kerber, Jordan E., ed. *Archeology of the Iroquois: Selected Readings and Research Sources.* Syracuse: Syracuse University Press, 2007.

"Lebenslauf des Bruders Johann Martin Mack, Bischofs der Brüder-Kirche und vieljährigen Missionars unter den Indianern in Nord-Amerika und unter den Negern in dänisch West-Indien, heimgegegangen am 9. Juni 1784 zu Friedensthal auf St. Crux." *Nachrichten aus der Brüder-Gemeine* 39 (1857): 767–81.

Levering, J. M. *A History of Bethlehem, Pennsylvania, 1741–1892: With Some Account of Its Founders and Their Early Activity in America.* Bethlehem, PA: Times, 1903.

Levine, Mary Ann. "The Fabric of Empire in a Native World: An Analysis of Trade Cloth Recovered from Eighteenth-Century Otstonwakin." *American Antiquity* 85, no. 1 (2020): 51–71.

"Mack Diary: English Original." *The Shamokin Diaries, 1745–1755.* Accessed August 1, 2023. http://shamokindiary.blogs.bucknell.edu/texts/mack-diary-english-original/.

MacMinn, Edwin. *On the Frontier with Colonel Antes, or The Struggle for Supremacy of the Red and White Races in Pennsylvania*. Camden, NJ: Chew, 1900.

Mancall, Peter C. "Temperance." In *Deadly Medicine: Indians and Alcohol in Early America*, 101–30. Ithaca: Cornell University Press, 1995.

Mann, Charles. *1491: New Revelations of the Americas Before Columbus*. New York: Vintage, 2005.

"Marcus Kiefer." Moravian Lives. Accessed June 19, 2023. https://moravian.bucknell.edu/memoirs/marcus-kiefer/.

Marsh, Dawn G. *A Lenape Among the Quakers: The Life of Hannah Freeman*. Lincoln: University of Nebraska Press, 2014.

"Martha Hussey." Moravian Lives. Accessed June 19, 2023. https://moravian.bucknell.edu/memoirs/martha-hussey/.

"Martha Powell." Moravian Lives. Accessed June 19, 2023. https://moravian.bucknell.edu/memoirs/martha-powell/.

Meginness, John. *Otzinachson: A History of the West Branch Valley*. Williamsport, PA: Lycoming County Historical Society, 1889. Reprint, Baltimore: Gateway Press, 1991.

Merrell, James. "'The Cast of His Countenance': Reading Andrew Montour." In *Through a Glass Darkly: Reflections on Personal Identity in Early America*, edited by Ronald Hoffman, Mechal Sobel, and Fredrika J. Teute, 13–39. Chapel Hill: University of North Carolina Press, 1997.

———. "'I Desire All That I Have Said ... May Be Taken Down Aright': Revisiting Teedyuscung's 1756 Treaty Council Speeches." *William and Mary Quarterly* 63, no. 4 (2006): 777–826.

———. "Indian History During the English Colonial Era." In *A Companion to Colonial America*, edited by Daniel Vickers, 118–35. Oxford: Blackwell, 2003.

———. *The Indians' New World: Catawbas and Their Neighbors from European Contact through the Era of Removal*. Chapel Hill: University of North Carolina Press, 2009.

———. *Into the American Woods: Negotiators on the Pennsylvania Frontier*. New York: Norton, 1999.

———. "The Other 'Susquehannah Traders': Women and Exchange on the Pennsylvania Frontier." In *Cultures and Identities in Colonial British America*, edited by Robert Olwell and Alan Tully, 197–219. Baltimore: Johns Hopkins University Press, 2006.

———. "Shamokin, 'the Very Seat of the Prince of Darkness': Unsettling the Early American Frontier." In *Contact Points: American Frontiers from the Mohawk Valley to the Mississippi, 1750–1830*, edited by Andrew R. L. Cayton and Fredrika J. Teute, 16–59. Chapel Hill: University of North Carolina Press, 1998.

———. "Shikellamy, 'A Person of Consequence.'" In *Northeastern Indian Lives, 1632–1816*, edited by Robert S. Grumet, 227–57. Amherst: University of Massachusetts Press, 1996.

Merritt, Jane. *At the Crossroads: Indians and Empires on a Mid-Atlantic Frontier, 1700–1763*. Chapel Hill: University of North Carolina Press, 2003.

Miller, Jay. "Old Religion Among the Delawares: The Gamwing (Big House Rite)." *Ethnohistory* 44, no. 1 (1997): 113–34.

Miller, Jennifer L. "'Our Own Flesh and Blood?' Delaware Indians and Moravians in the Eighteenth-Century Ohio Country." PhD diss., West Virginia University, 2017. https://researchrepository.wvu.edu/etd/8183.

Miller, Randall M., and William Pencak. *Pennsylvania: A History of the Commonwealth*. University Park: Penn State University Press, 2002.

Minderhout, David. "Native American Horticulture in the Northeast." *General Anthropology* 16 (2009): 1–7.

———. "Native Americans in the Susquehanna River Region, 1550 to Today." In *Native Americans in the Susquehanna River Valley, Past and Present*, edited by David J. Minderhout, 77–112. Lewisburg, PA: Bucknell University Press, 2013.

Minderhout, David J., and Andrea T. Frantz. *Invisible Indians: Native Americans in Pennsylvania*. Amherst, NY: Cambria Press, 2008.

Moravian Mission Records Among American Indians Records, Circa 1735–1900. New Haven, CT: Research, 1970.
Neff, George H. "How the Indians Lived at Shamokin." In Carter, *History of Sunbury*, 5–15.
Petterson, Christina. *The Moravian Brethren in a Time of Transition: A Socio-Economic Analysis of a Religious Community in Eighteenth-Century Saxony*. Leiden: Brill, 2021.
Peucker, Paul. *Herrnhuter Wörterbuch*. Herrnhut: Unitätsarchiv, 2023.
———. *A Time of Sifting: The Mystical Marriage and Crisis of Piety in the Eighteenth-Century Moravian Church*. University Park: Penn State University Press, 2015.
Piper, John. *Tested by Fire: The Fruit of Suffering in the Lives of John Bunyan, William Cowper, and David Brainerd*. Downers Grove, IL: Inter-Varsity Press, 2001.
Preston, David L. *Braddock's Defeat: The Battle of the Monongahela and the Road to Revolution*. Pivotal Moments in American History. New York: Oxford University Press, 2015.
———. *Native Americans' Pennsylvania*. University Park: Pennsylvania Historical Association, 2005.
———. *The Ordeal of the Longhouse: The Peoples of the Iroquois League in the Era of European Colonization*. Chapel Hill: University of North Carolina Press, 1992.
———. "War and Culture: The Iroquois Experience." *William and Mary Quarterly* 40 (1983): 528–59.
Radding, Cynthia. *Landscapes of Power and Identity: Comparative Histories in the Sonoran Desert and the Forests of Amazonia from Colony to Republic*. Durham: Duke University Press, 2005.
Reichel, William Cornelius. *Memorials of the Moravian Church*. Philadelphia: Lippincott, 1870.
Repko, Duke, Matt Lucas, John Edler, Ryan Clifford, Madeline Purdy, Jiayu Huang, Qijing Zheng, Nick Miller, and Claire Maree O'Bryan, eds. "Joseph Powell Shamokin Diary, January–April 1748." Bucknell University. Accessed June 24, 2023. http://www.students.bucknell.edu/projects/HUMN10001/MoravianDiaries/content/JosephPowell.xml.
Richter, Daniel. "A Framework for Pennsylvania Indian History." *Pennsylvania History* 57 (1990): 236–61.
"Rosina Neubert." Moravian Lives. Accessed June 19, 2023. https://moravian.bucknell.edu/memoirs/rosina-neubert/.
Runkle, Stephen A. *Native American Waterbody and Place Names Within the Susquehanna River Basin*. Harrisburg, PA: Susquehanna River Basin Commission, 2003.
Sachse, Julius Friedrich. *Falckner's Curieuse Nachricht von Pennsylvania: The Book That Stimulated the Great German Emigration to Pennsylvania in the Early Years of the Eighteenth Century*. Edited and translated by Julius Friedrich Sachse. Philadelphia: printed for the author, 1905.
Schutt, Amy C. *Peoples of the River Valleys: The Odyssey of the Delaware Indians*. Philadelphia: University of Pennsylvania Press, 2007.
———. "Tribal Identity in the Moravian Missions on the Susquehanna." *Pennsylvania History* 66 (1999): 378–98.
Schweinitz, Edmund de. *The Life and Times of David Zeisberger, the Western Pioneer and Apostle to the Indians*. Philadelphia: Lippincott, 1870.
———. *The Moravian Manual: Containing an Account of the Moravian Church, or Unitas Fratrum*. Bethlehem, 1869.
Shannon, Timothy J. *Iroquois Diplomacy on the Early American Frontier*. New York: Penguin, 2008.
Sipe, C. Hale. *The Indian Chiefs of Pennsylvania*. Lewisburg, PA: Wennawoods, 1997.
Snow, Dean. *The Iroquois*. Malden, MA: Blackwell, 1994.
Snyder, Charles Fisher. "Conrad Weiser in the Susquehanna Valley." *Proceedings of the Northumberland County Historical Society* 4 (1934): 5–72.
Spangenberg, August G. "Spangenberg's Notes of Travel to Onondaga in 1745." *Pennsylvania Magazine of History and Biography* 2, no. 4 (1878): 424–32.
Spittal, W. G., ed. *Iroquois Women: An Anthology*. Ontario: Iroqrafts, 1990.

"Spring Freeze Injury in Corn." University of Minnesota Extension. Accessed August 2, 2023. https://extension.umn.edu/growing-corn/spring-freeze-injury-corn.

Stockton, Edwin L. "The Influence of the Moravians upon the Leather-Stocking Tales." *Transactions of the Moravian Historical Society* 20, no. 1. Nazareth, PA: Whitefield House, 1964.

Thwaites, Reuben Gold. *The Jesuit Relations and Allied Documents: Travels and Explorations of the Jesuit Missionaries in North America (1610–1791)*. Edited by Edna Kenton. New York: Boni, 1925.

"A Treaty, Etc." Virginia Places. Accessed June 24, 2023. http://www.virginiaplaces.org/settleland/graphics/1747lancaster.pdf.

A Treaty Held with the Seneca Indians at Philadelphia, the 1st July 1749. Philadelphia: Franklin, 1749.

Van Doren, Carl, and Julian P. Boyd. *Indian Treaties Printed by Benjamin Franklin, 1736–1762*. Philadelphia: Historical Society of Pennsylvania, 1938.

Vincens, Simone. *Madame Montour and the Fur Trade (1667–1752)*. Bloomington, IN: Xlibris, 2011.

Vogt, Peter. "Zinzendorf's Theology of the Sabbath." In Atwood and Vogt, *Distinctiveness of Moravian Culture*, 205–31.

Waldman, Carl. *Atlas of the North American Indian*. New York: Checkmark, 2000.

Wallace, Anthony F. C. *The Death and Rebirth of the Seneca*. New York: Vintage, 1972.

———. *King of the Delawares: Teedyusung, 1700–1763*. Syracuse: Syracuse University Press, 1949.

Wallace, Paul. *Conrad Weiser: Friend of Colonist and Mohawk, 1696–1760*. Lewisburg, PA: Wennawoods, 1996.

———. "Historic Indian Paths of Pennsylvania." *Pennsylvania Magazine of History: Journal of the Historical Society of Pennsylvania* 76 (1952): 1–29.

———. *Indians in Pennsylvania*. 1981. Reprint, Harrisburg: Pennsylvania Historical and Museum Commission, 1993.

———. "We Came Out of the Ground." In *Pennsylvania: Seed of a Nation*, edited by Darrell Fields and Lorrie Fields, 8–19. New York: Harper and Row, 1962.

Webster, Noah. *A Brief History of Epidemic and Pestilential Diseases*. London: Robinson, Woodfall, Paternoster-Row, 1800.

Wellenreuther, Hermann. "White Eyes and the Delaware's Vision of an Indian State." *Pennsylvania History: A Journal of Mid-Atlantic Studies* 68, no. 2 (2001): 139–61.

Wellenreuther, Hermann, and Carola Wessel, eds. *The Moravian Mission Diaries of David Zeisberger, 1772–1781*. Translated by Julie Weber. University Park: Penn State University Press, 2005.

Weslager, C. A. *The Delaware Indians: A History*. New Brunswick, NJ: Rutgers University Press, 1972.

Wessel, Carola. "Connecting Congregations: The Net of Communication Among the Moravians as Exemplified by the Interaction Between Pennsylvania, the Upper Ohio, and Germany (1772–1774)." In Atwood and Vogt, *Distinctiveness of Moravian Culture*, 153–72.

Wheeler, Rachel, and Sarah Eyerly. "Singing Box 331: Re-sounding Eighteenth-Century Mohican Hymns from the Moravian Archives." *William and Mary Quarterly*, 3rd ser., 76, no. 4 (2019): 649–96.

Woodward, Walter W. "Incline Your Second Ear This Way: Song as a Cultural Mediator in Moravian Mission Towns." In *Ethnographies and Exchanges: Native Americans, Moravians, and Catholics in Early North America*, edited by A. G. Roeber, 125–44. University Park: Penn State University Press, 2004.

Zeisberger, David. *Essay of an Onondaga Grammar, or A Short Introduction to Learn the Onondaga Al. Maqua Tongue*. Translated by John Ettwein. Philadelphia: Lippincott, 1888.

———. *History of the Northern American Indians in Eighteenth-Century Ohio, New York, and Pennsylvania*. Edited by Archer Butler Hubert. 1910. Reprint, Lewisburg, PA: Wennawoods, 1999.

Zeisberger, David, and Eben Norton Horsfield. *Indian Dictionary: English, German, Iroquois, and Algonquin—the Delaware*. Cambridge: Wilson and Son, 1887.

Zinzendorf, Nicholas. *Count Zinzendorf and the Indians, 1742*. Lewisburg, PA: Wennawoods, 2007.

———. "Journey to Shamokin." In *Count Zinzendorf and the Indians*, vol. 11.

Zinzendorf, Nicolaus Ludwig. *Des Grafens von Zinzendorf Inhalt einiger öffentlichen Reden, welche im Jahr 1738 vom Januario bis zu Ende des Aprilis in Berlin an die Frauens-Personen daselbst gehalten worden*. Leipzig, Germany, 1743.

———. *Kleines Brüdergesangbuch: Hirten-Lieder von Bethlehem*. 1754. In Zinzendorf, *Materialien und Dokumente*, vol. 5.

———. *Materialien und Dokumente*. Series 1–4. Hildesheim, Germany: Olms, 1978–81.

———. *Vier-und-dreyßig Homiliae über die Wunden-Litaney der Brüder*. 1747. In Zinzendorf, *Materialien und Dokumente*, vol. 3.

Zinzendorf, Nicolaus Ludwig, Erich Beyreuther, Dietrich Meyer, and Gerhard Meyer. *Londoner Gesangbuch: Alt und Neuer Brüder-Gesang*. In Zinzendorf, *Materialien und Dokumente*, vol. 4.

REGISTER OF INDIVIDUALS

Abraham (Fliegel Index #1)—Husband of Sara (F#8), also Schawasch. A Mohican, he was baptized on February 23, 1742, in Oley, Pennsylvania (at the synod), by Christian Rauch, and died on November 10, 1762, in the Wyoming Valley.

Ahamawad—See Christian Post.

Allumapees (also Sassoonan)—Born around 1675 and died in 1747. This Delaware sachem signed away the land between the Lehigh River and Duck Creek to the British.

Annuntschi—See Christian Gottfried Seidel.

Bachhof, Rudolf Gottlieb—Born on January 6, 1717, in Lüneburg, Schleswig-Holstein, and died on September 21, 1776, in Friedberg, Salem, North Carolina.

Beata (F#83)—Wife of Zacheus (F#19) and sister of Maria (F#74). A Delaware, Beata was baptized as a widow in Bethlehem in 1746 by Brother Pyrlaeus and died on March 6, 1762, in Wechquetank.

Blackfish—Mohican and visitor to Gnadenhütten and Shamokin.

Boehmer, Martin—Married to Margaret and visitor at Shamokin.

Bottler, James—Settler on the North Branch.

Brainerd, Rev. David—Born in 1718, in Haddam, Connecticut, and died in 1747. He was an American missionary to the Native Americans who ministered among the Delaware of New Jersey. See Grigg, *Lives of David Brainerd*.

Brodhead, Daniel—Indian trader from Mennissing who had lived in the Wyoming Valley. According to Spangenberg and Cammerhof, he attended the synod in Germantown from May 10 to 14, 1747, with Justice Smout from Lancaster. Brodhead apparently was very fond of the Moravians. See "Br. Cammerhof's Fourth Letter," MAB. Cammerhof describes him as "respected and intelligent and is fond of the Brethren. He has attended our Synods regularly." Cammerhof, letter 7.

Bruce, David—Carpenter from Edinburgh and itinerant Moravian preacher to New Jersey, Pennsylvania, and Connecticut. He died in Wechquetank in July 1749.

Cammerhof, Johann Christoph Frederick (also Gallichwio, meaning a "Good Message")—Born in 1721 in Hillersleben, Saxony, and died in 1751.

David—Delaware and biological brother of Anton (F#249) and Nathan (F#83) from the Susquehanna.

Delaware, George—Rich Delaware from Ohio who was important to the Moravians for the final days of the Shamokin mission.

Dunn, Thomas—Iroquois and member of Shikellamy's extended family.

Elisabeth (F#372)—Delaware wife of Paxinos (chief of the Shawnee in Wyoming) and sister of Justina (F#203). She was baptized on February 17, 1755, in Bethlehem, by Spangenberg.

Fabricius, Georg Friedrich—Linguist and missionary at Gnadenhütten II. He was born on January 6, 1716, and died in the attack on the mission on November 24, 1755.

Freeman, Thomas—Indian at Quenischaschaque, 1753.

French Margaret—Either the daughter or niece of Madame Montour and a well-known visitor to the Moravians. In 1753 Brother Grube had visited her village on the West Branch, which was at the mouth of the Lycoming Creek. At that time she was in deep mourning for the death of her son and nephew in the failed skirmish against the Catawba.

Frey, Heinrich (Henry)—Born on May 12, 1724, in Philadelphia County and died on September 25, 1784, at the age of sixty, in Lititz, Lancaster County.

Friedrich (also Tschekana)—Mohican and son of Abraham (F#1) and Sara (F#8). He was baptized on August 16, 1749, in Gnadenhütten, by Frederick Cammerhof.

Gabriel, George—George Gabriel established a settlement in 1713 "at the mouth of Penn's Creek" (today Selinsgrove, Pennsylvania), which became known as Gabriel's Plantation. It is generally thought to be the first white settlement on the west bank of the Susquehanna River.

Gallichwio—See Johann Christoph Frederick Cammerhof.

Ganachragejat—See Johann Martin Mack.

Ganniatarechoo—See Johann Christoph Pyrlaeus.

Ganosseracheri—See David Zeisberger. Ganosseracheri means "on the pumpkin."

Garrison, Lambert—Arrived in America in 1754.

Gattermeyer, Johann Leonhardt—Born on July 19, 1721, in Regensburg, Bavaria, and died on November 24, 1755, in the attack on Gnadenhütten, Pennsylvania.

Genousseracheri—See David Zeisberger.

Gideon (also Tadeuscont and Honest John; F#259)—Delaware brother of Nicodemus (F#193) and Petrus (F#245) and husband of Elisabeth (F#260).

Glück, Peter—Shoemaker who lived fifteen miles south of Shamokin on the Tulpehocken path.

Grube, Bernhard Adam—Born in 1715 in Walschleben, Thuringia, and died in 1808. He married Elisabeth Büsse, née Krüger (1715–76) and was a Lutheran pastor in Erfurt before he arrived in America on the *Irene* in 1746. He served in Moravian missions broadly and between 1763 and 1765 accompanied and assisted the Christian Indians held in Philadelphia. See "Biographical Sketch."

Hagen, Johannes—Born in Brandenburg and died in July 1747 in Shamokin, Pennsylvania. He married Margaret Dissmann from Providence Township, then arrived in Georgia in 1740, where he worked as a missionary to the Cherokee. He went to Bethlehem in 1742.

Hahotschaunquas—Cayuga. Guide to Cammerhof and Zeisberger through Iroquoia.

Harris, John, Jr.—Born in Harrisburg, Pennsylvania, in 1716, and died on July 29, 1791. He was a storekeeper who operated a ferry across the Susquehanna River at the present-day location of Harrisburg. His father is considered to be the first settler to establish a trading post along the Susquehanna River.

Henry, William—Born on May 19, 1729, and died on December 15, 1786. Merchant, gunsmith, and member of the Moravian Congregation at Lancaster. Later he was a member of Congress and an important link between Bethlehem and Fort Pitt.

Hoffmann, Christian Gottlob—Born on December 12, 1715, and died on August 8, 1771.

Hussey, Robert—Born in 1713 in Wiltshire, England, and died in 1775. He married Martha Hussey (1719–90) and was a teacher at the Moravian School in Oley, Pennsylvania. See Martha's memoir in Faull, *Moravian Women's Memoirs*, and "Martha Hussey."

Isaac (F#101)—Son of Abraham (F#1) and Sara (F#8). A Mohican, he was baptized at Gnadenhütten II by Martin Mack on May 8, 1747, and died of smallpox in the Philadelphia Barracks on July 24, 1764.

Janekeaguhontis—See Anna Cammerhof.

Jepse (maybe Jephtha)—Esopus Indian from Shekomeko. He was baptized by the Moravians in 1743.

Jeremias (F#164)—Delaware from Wamphallobank. He was baptized on March 15, 1749, by Brother Johannes.

Joachim (F#44)—Mohican, son of Abraham (F#1), and married to Catharina (F#168). He was baptized on March 27, 1743, by Brother Büttner at Shekomeko, New York.

Jonathan (also Gayienquiligoa; F#13)—Mohican and baptized in Shekomeko by Brother Büttner in 1747. He had two sons, Jonathan and Philip. At the request of Tachnechdorus, Shikellamy's son, they went to Philadelphia to be taught to read and write at the academy. This would make them some of the earliest pupils of what was to become the University of

Pennsylvania. See P. Wallace, *Conrad Weiser*, 380.

Kiefer, Marcus—Born in 1719 and died in 1791. He was married to Magdalene Rubl and worked as a blacksmith at Shamokin.

Kliest, Daniel—Born on April 15, 1716, and died on May 1, 1792. He worked as a blacksmith at Shamokin.

Kuchern, Peter—Tulpehocken resident.

Labachpeton—Delaware chief and eldest son of Nutimus who resided at the confluence of the North Branch of the Susquehanna River and Catawissa Creek, Pennsylvania.

Leonhardt (F#213)—Delaware, brother of Jonathan (F#173) from Meniolagomeka, and husband to Lucia (F#288).

Lessly, Johann Friedrich—Born in Conestoga, Pennsylvania, on February 29, 1732, and died at the attack on the Gnadenhütten mission on November 24, 1755. He was one of the first members of the Single Brethren Choir in Bethlehem.

Logan, James (also Tshgahjute and Tajajute)—Shikellamy's second son. He was born in 1725 and died in 1780. His first wife was a Cayuga or a Mohican, who died in Shamokin in 1747.

Logan, John (also Tachnechdorus)—Born circa 1723 and died in 1780. He was the eldest son of Chief Shikellamy.

Mack, Jeannette (Jennetje)—Née Rau. Born in 1722 in Dutchess County, New York, and died in 1749. She married Martin Mack and worked as a missionary in Pennsylvania and New York. She learned fluent Mohican from the Native Americans who lived around her father's farm. The farm was visited in 1742 by Count von Zinzendorf, Anna Nitschmann, Benigna von Zinzendorf, and Martin Mack on their trip to nearby Shekomeko.

Mack, Johann Martin (also Ganachragejat)—Born in 1715 in Laysingen, Württemberg, Germany, and died in Saint Croix in 1784. He married Jeannette Rau on September 14, 1742. A cofounder of Bethlehem, he arrived in Georgia in 1736 and from 1742 was an assistant to the missionary Christian Rauch at Shekomeko. He was entrusted with the overall direction of mission work in North America in 1745 and served as a missionary in the Caribbean in from 1762 to 1784.

Maria (F#362)—Mohican. Relative of Abraham (F#1). Awakened in Wyoming Valley by Zinzendorf, she was baptized on July 28, 1754, by Brother Grube in the Shawnee town. She died in the fall of 1755, north of Wyoming.

Mariane (F#227)—Delaware. She was baptized by Frederick Cammerhof in Bethlehem in 1749.

McKee, Thomas—Born in 1695 in Antrim, Ulster, Ireland, and died in 1772 at McKee's Fort, Pennsylvania. He married Tecumsapah Mary McKee (Straight Tail) and was a Susquehanna trader and Crown Indian interpreter for the Delaware and Shawnee.

Meuer, Joseph (also Meyer)—Silversmith in Lancaster. He is identified in Gordon, "Entangled by the World," 14n18, and Gerstall, *Silversmiths of Lancaster*, 85.

Meurer, Johann Phillip—Born on March 25, 1708, in Ingweiler, Alsace, and died on April 15, 1760, in Bethlehem, Pennsylvania. He and his wife had five daughters. In February 1742 he traveled with the First Sea Congregation to Pennsylvania and arrived in Bethlehem in June 1742. He was ordained in the church of Tulpehocken and served there until 1746, then went to Donegal, Lebanon, Swatara, and York and served the congregation until 1756.

Montour, Andrew—Anderius, Sattelihu, Eghnisara, and Henry Lewis Montour-Tausseson. Oneida and Algonquin ancestry, with a French grandfather. He was born in his mother's village of Ostonwakin (near current Montoursville, Pennsylvania) around 1720 and died in 1772. The son of Madame Montour, Andrew was an important Métis interpreter and negotiator in the Virginia and Pennsylvania backcountry in the latter half of the eighteenth century; he later led the village before settling farther west.

Montour, Lewis—Isabelle Montour's son and Andrew's half brother. He was killed in the French and Indian War.

Montour, Madame Isabelle/Elisabeth—Usually referred to as "Madame" or "Mrs." Montour; may have been Isabelle (or Elisabeth) Couc. Métis with Algonquin and French Canadian ancestry, she was born in 1667 (or ca. 1685) and died in 1753. Perhaps she was Isabelle Couc's niece, who was born around 1685 and whose given name is uncertain. She was an influential interpreter, diplomat, and local leader. See Vincens, *Madame Montour*, and Hirsch, "Celebrated Madame Montour."

Montour, Margaret (also French Margaret)—Sister or niece of Madame Montour. She was born in 1690 and married Katarioniecha (Peter Quebec), a Mohawk. She resided at a village called French Margaret's Town (Wenschpochkechung, also known as Quenischaschaque), on the West Branch of the Susquehanna, at the mouth of Lycoming Creek (now Williamsport, Pennsylvania). The couple had at least five children: Catherine (French Catherine), Esther (Queen Esther), Nicholas, a son who was killed about 1753 fighting the Creeks, and Mary (or Molly). Like her mother, Margaret attended treaty conferences and often interpreted.

Nathaniel (F#14)—Mohican and husband to Zippora (F#5) and then to Rebecca (F#9). He was baptized at Shekomeko by Christian Rauch on October 10, 1742, and died in 1756.

Neisser, George—Born in 1715 in Sehlen, Moravia, and died in Philadelphia in 1784. He joined Spangenberg, Wesley, and Ingham on a trip to Georgia in 1735 and was a Moravian minister in New York and Philadelphia. See "George Neisser."

Neshanockeow—Spreads rumors about the Moravians.

Neubert, Daniel—Born in Königswalde bei Annaberg, Sachsen, in 1704 and died in 1788.

Neubert, Rosina—Née Hauer. Born in Kunewald, Moravia, in 1705 and died in 1785. She married Daniel Neubert. See "Rosina Neubert."

Nitschmann, Anna—Born in 1715 in Kunewald, Moravia, and died in 1760. She was the daughter of David Nitschmann. She was an influential leader in the Moravian Church. At the age of fifteen, she was made the Eldress of all the women in Herrnhut. She arrived in Pennsylvania in 1740, returned to Europe in 1743, and married Count Zinzendorf in 1757.

Nutimus (also Nootimes)—"King" of the Delaware. He was signatory to a deed in 1749 that was enclosed in the proceedings of councils at Easton, July 21–August 7, 1757.

Nutimus, Isaac—Son of King Nutimus of the Delaware. He was reported to have had three Africans living with him, one of whom was his wife. See Johnson, *Count Zinzendorf*.

Okely, John—Member of the Philadelphia Moravian Church. He arrived on the ship *Catherine* in May 1742 as part of the First Sea Congregation.

Otto, John Matthew—Born in 1714 in Meiningen, Germany, and died in 1786. He trained to be a surgeon, then traveled to Bethlehem in 1750. See "Johann Matthaeus Otto."

Paxinos—Shawnee leader. Born in Minisink, after 1744, and died in 1761 in Ohio. He married Elisabeth, a Delaware Moravian convert. After the outbreak of the French and Indian War, he and his people moved north to Tioga (Athens, Pennsylvania). He attended the Easton Treaty in 1757, where he brought fifty-seven Indians. In 1760 he went with his family to Ohio. Cornstalk was his grandson.

Petrus (also Young Captain Harris)—Delaware. Son of Harris on the Pukapuchke, half brother of Nicodemus (F#193), and husband of Theodora (F#246). He was baptized on January 31, 1750, in Gnadenhütten by Cammerhof and died on August 27, 1764, in the Philadelphia barracks.

Post, Christian Frederick (also Ahamawad)—Born in 1710 in Conitz, Polish Prussia, and died in 1785 in Germantown, Pennsylvania. He arrived in Bethlehem in 1742 and served as a missionary in Shekomeko in 1743 and then in Pachgatgoch. During the Seven Years' War, he served as messenger between the colonial government and the Delaware and Shawnee. From 1761 to 1762, he worked as an independent missionary to the Delaware in Ohio and then as a missionary on the Mosquito Coast, Nicaragua.

Powell, Joseph—Born in 1711 in Whitchurch, England, and died in 1774. Originally a follower of George Whitefield, he joined the Moravians in Bethlehem in 1742. He was a missionary in Shamokin in 1747–48 and later in Wechquanach, Connecticut.

Powell, Martha—Born in 1704 near Oxford, England, and died in 1774. A member of the Fetter Lane Congregation in London, she married Joseph Powell in 1742 and became a member of the First Sea Congregation. She served in various country congregations in the mid-Atlantic region and in 1759 went as a missionary with her husband to Jamaica for six years. In 1765 she returned to Bethlehem and finally worked in Maryland, at Carrols's Manor. See "Martha Powell."

Pyrlaeus, Johann Christoph (also Ganniatarechoo)—Born in 1713 in Saxony, Germany, and died in 1785. He married Susanna Benezet, studied at the University of Leipzig, and went to Bethlehem in 1741 with Zinzendorf. An accomplished linguist, he traveled widely in Mohawk country. See "Johann Christopher Pyrlaeus."

Rachwistonis—See Anton Schmidt.

Rahel (F#244)—Delaware and sister of Nutimus. She was baptized on the Monocacy Creek, near Bethlehem, in January 1750 by Cammerhof and died in Bethlehem on January 15, 1750.

Rauch, Christian (also Tschigochgoharong)—Born in 1718 in Bernburg, Anhalt-Bernburg, and died in Jamaica, West Indies, in 1763. He married Anna Elizabeth Robbins in 1742 and was the first Moravian missionary to go to Shekomeko in 1740.

Renatus, Christian (also Tepackhoshi, or Jo Growdon; F#117)—Delaware from Meniolagomeka. He was married to Salome (F#142) and baptized on November 26, 1748 at Gnadenhütten II by Cammerhof.

Rieth, Caspar—Uncle of Anna Catharina Schmidt, wife of Anton Schmidt.

Salomon (also Tamekappi and Keposch; F#133)—King of the Delaware at the Forks (Bethlehem). Baptized on January 24, 1749, in Bethlehem, by Brother Johannes, and died in the spring of 1756 in Tioga (Athens, Pennsylvania).

Sawonagarat (also Shawonogarati)—Neighbor to the Shamokin mission.

Schafmann—Conoy. Friend of the Moravians.

Schäffer, Michael—Born in 1696 and died in 1760. He hosted several conferences during the early period of Moravian activity in the commonwealth. See J. Hamilton, "Confusion at Tulpehocken."

Schmidt, Anna Catharina (Rieth)—Born in 1727 in Heidelberg, Pennsylvania, and died in 1762. She lived with Conrad Weiser, where she met Anna Nitschmann in 1741. She was introduced to Zinzendorf, joined the Moravians. married Anton Schmidt in 1747, and lived in Shamokin until January 1755.

Schmidt, Anton (also Rachwistonis)—Born in 1725 in Presburg, Hungary, and died in 1793. He married Anna Catharina Rieth, with whom he had three sons and one daughter. He emigrated with his family to America, lived in Oley, joined the Moravians in 1746, and moved to Bethlehem in 1747. He worked as a blacksmith at Shamokin from 1747 to 1754. In January 1755 he moved back to Bethlehem and worked in Christiansbrunn on the farm. He married a second time to Beata Yselstein, with whom he had another six children.

Seidel, Christian Gottfried—(1718–1759). Missionary to Native Americans in New York and Pennsylvania.

Shikellamy (also the Swatane)—Thought to be French Métis, taken prisoner, and adopted by the Oneida. Later he was an Oneida chief with oversight over the Six Nations in the Pennsylvania and Ohio regions. He oversaw the area around the confluence of the North and West Branches of the Susquehanna River at Shamokin (present-day Sunbury). He died in 1748 in Shamokin.

Shikellamy's wife (also Neanoma)—Cayuga and first wife of Shikellamy and mother of James Logan (Soyechtowa), John Logan (Tachnechdorus), John Petty "Unhappy Jake" (Arohot), and others. She was born in 1695 and died in 1747.

Spangenberg, August Gottlieb (also Brother Joseph and T'girhitondi)—Born in 1704 in Klettenberg, Saxony, and died in 1792 in Berthelsdorf, Saxony. He received his name on a trip to Onondaga. He studied theology at Jena, served as a teacher at the Halle orphanage of August Hermann Francke, and joined the Moravians. From 1733 on he was closely associated with Zinzendorf. He served as the head of the

American branch of the Moravian Church.

Tachnechdorus (also John)—Born in 1718 in Butternut Creek, New York. He was Shikellamy's eldest son and married Vastina (Shawnee/Quaker), from the mouth of Pequea Creek.

Tecarihontie—See Johannes de Watteville.

T'girhitondi—See August Gottlieb Spangenberg.

Tianoge—Cayuga. Friend to Spangenberg and Zeisberger.

Van der Merck, Jacobus—Born on December 18, 1728, in Esopus, New York, and died on January 24, 1773, in Bathabara, North Carolina. Briefly active in Pennsylvania, he then moved to North Carolina, where he was the builder of a mill in Bethabara and worked as a gun stocker. Before he moved to North Carolina, he married Christina Loesch, the daughter of the Loesches in Tulpehocken.

Wagner, Elizabeth (née Fliery, or Thiery)— Born on October 4, 1710, in Muhlhausen, Switzerland, and died on May 8, 1770. She married Anton Wagner, who later became one of the clergy serving the Heidelberg Congregation.

Watteville, Johannes de (also Brother Johannes). Born on October 18, 1718, in Walschleben, Thüringen, Germany, and died on October 7, 1788, in Gnadenfrei, Germany (present-day Piława Górna, Poland).

Weiser, Christoph—Born in 1699 in Aspach, Stuttgart, and died on June 16, 1768, at Emmaus, Lehigh County. He was the son of Conrad Weiser.

Weiser, Conrad—Born in 1696 and died in 1760. He was a Palatinate immigrant to Pennsylvania. He learned Mohawk as a youth and, from the early 1740s, was an Indian agent for Pennsylvania and an interpreter and diplomat between the Pennsylvania Colony and Native Americans. See P. Wallace, *Conrad Weiser*.

Wesa, Philip—Born on November 11, 1723, and died on March 18, 1758, in an accidental fall from a carriage. He worked as a blacksmith.

Zeisberger, David (also Ganosseracheri)— Born on April 11, 1721, in Zauchtenthal, Moravia (present-day Suchdol nad Odron in the Czech Republic), and died in 1808 in Goshen, Ohio. He was a Moravian clergy and missionary among the Native Americans in the Thirteen Colonies. He moved with his family to the newly established Moravian Christian community of Herrnhut, on the estate of Count Nicholas Ludwig von Zinzendorf in the German electorate of Saxony in 1727. He learned the trade of shoemaking, was ordained deacon of the Moravian Church in 1749, married Susan Lecron in 1781, and studied Mohawk, Onondaga, and Algonquin languages.

Zinzendorf, Nicholas Ludwig von (also Brother Ludwig and Disciple)—Born in 1700 in Dresden and died in 1760. He was educated at the Francke Pedagogium in Halle and studied law at University of Wittenberg. He traveled to North America in 1741–43, where he founded the Herrnhuter Brüdergemeine and the Moravian Church in America. He married Erdmuth Dorothea Reuss (1700–1750) and later Anna Caritas Nitschmann (1715–60).

REGISTER OF PLACE NAMES

Allegheny—Lands beyond the Allegheny Mountains, in what is today Ohio.

Berthelsdorf—Home of Count Nicholas von Zinzendorf, located three miles from Herrnhut. It was in the Lutheran parish church here that the Moravian Pentecost of August 13, 1727, occurred (see the entry for August 13). Zinzendorf's manor house had been newly renovated and served as the architectural model for his residence in Herrnhaag, as well as for Nazareth Hall in Nazareth, Pennsylvania.

Bethel—Former Moravian congregation located about eighty miles southwest of Bethlehem, Pennsylvania.

Bethlehem—Town in Pennsylvania named by Count Ludwig von Zinzendorf on Christmas Eve 1741. It was the center of Moravian mission activities to the Native Americans in the American colonies.

Blue Mountains—Located at Lorberry Junction, Swatara Creek.

Canaseragy (also Canaserage)—Shawnee and Chickasaw village on the West Branch at the mouth of the Muncy Creek. This was the line that the Five Nations demanded should not be crossed in the land purchases of the 1750s. In 1755 Conrad Weiser held a conference here, with twenty representatives of the Native American nations; six of these warriors were Chickasaw. Plants grown here were used for medical purposes by the Native Americans.

Chillisquaque Creek—Site of a Shawnee village. The name means "Place of the Snowbirds." It was a stop along the Great Shamokin Path, located upstream from Shamokin on the West Branch of the Susquehanna River.

Christiansbrunn—Located about two miles from Nazareth, Pennsylvania. This settlement was composed of Single Brethren.

Danesbury—Today East Stroudsburg, Pennsylvania, on the Pennsylvania–New Jersey border.

Easton—County seat of Northampton County, Pennsylvania.

Eva Creek—Today Shamokin Creek, just south of Shamokin (Sunbury).

French Margaret's Town—Today Williamsport, named after French Margaret, daughter or niece of Madame Montour and wife of Peter Quebec. Margaret prohibited the use of rum in her village, which was a widespread custom among the Native people. She was also politically active, attending many treaty meetings with Conrad Weiser and Shikellamy. See also Quenischachachque and Hockhocking.

Gnadenhütten—Moravian mission on the Mahoning and Lehigh Rivers, in today's Lehighton. Gnadenhütten (cabins of grace). Founded in 1746 and established as a mission to the Lenape by Moravians from Bethlehem, Pennsylvania, lower on the Lehigh River. During the French and Indian Wars (Seven Years' War), Native allies of the French killed eleven missionaries and Lenape (Delaware) Christians at Gnadenhütten on November 24, 1755. They destroyed the mission village, and only four of the fifteen residents escaped. This is the name given to another mission settlement in Ohio, which was established in 1772.

Gnadenthal—First farm operation in Nazareth, Pennsylvania.

Great Island—Also known as Mechek-menatey or Cawichnowane (on the Lewis and Evans map), an important gathering place near Lock Haven for the Iroquois, where many paths converged. It was a convenient location for councils and camping. These paths led to places such as the Allegheny River, Juniata River, and Lycoming Creek. The soil on this 325-acre area of land was extremely fertile, which provided a good location for the Native Americans to plant corn.

Harris's Ferry—Closest ferry to Shamokin across the Susquehanna River, at present-day Harrisburg.

Heidelberg—Pennsylvania, Berks County.

Herrnhaag—Town in Wetteravia, western Germany. Looking for a place that could serve as a refuge for the Moravians in Herrnhut should they be expelled from Saxony, Zinzendorf obtained permission in 1738 from the Count Ysenburg-Büdingen to buy land in his territory and establish a congregation. It became a settlement congregation and was the location for much of the religious enthusiasm and theological experimentation during the Sifting Period (approx. 1738–52). The new Count of Büdingen demanded religious and financial concessions from the Moravians. The Moravians refused and evacuated from Herrnhaag.

Herrnhut—Town in Upper Lusatia region of Saxony in southeastern Germany. In 1722 Count Zinzendorf allowed Moravian refugees to settle at Herrnhut and became the first of a series of settlement congregations. In the years after 1722, Herrnhut became the home base for evangelistic efforts in Europe and for mission enterprises worldwide. As the Moravian Church took on a denominational structure, Herrnhut became the headquarters.

Hockhocking—Also known as French Margaret's Town, on the headwaters of the Hocking River at what is now Lancaster, Ohio.

Jacobs Höhe—Jack's Mountain.

Königsberg—First mountain south of Shamokin. Today it is called Little Mountain.

Labachpeton's Village—Site of a former Delaware village near the mouth of the Catawissa Creek on the North Branch of the Susquehanna. This place is named in honor of the Delaware chief Labachpeton, friend to the British. See Donehoo, *History of the Indian Villages*, 90.

Lancaster—Part of the 1681 Penn's Woods Charter of William Penn and laid out by James Hamilton in 1734.

Lebanon—Settled by European colonists in 1720, many with the family names of "Steitz" and "Light," along a creek that was then named "Steitz Creek."

Lititz (originally Warwick)—Town in Lancaster County that served as a center for Moravian itinerant preachers.

Long Island—Island in the West Branch of the Susquehanna River, today Jersey Shore, Pennsylvania.

Ludwig's Ruh—Frequent night camp on the Tulpehocken Path, today near Hegins, Pennsylvania.

Macungie—Place name used as early as 1730 to describe the region that is now Macungie and Emmaus, Pennsylvania. Derived from "Maguntsche," this Lenape word means either "bear swamp" or "feeding place of the bears."

Meniolagomekah—Indian town in Monroe County, eight miles south of Wind Gap. Native Americans were removed from this village in April 1754 to Gnadenhütten on the Mahony at the request of the white owner of the land, Richard Peters, who wanted the area cleared of them. See Donehoo, *History of the Indian Villages*, 107.

Minisink—Referred to as the "Forks of the Susquehanna," where the Lackawanna Creek enters the North Branch of the Susquehanna. See Donehoo, *History of the Indian Villages*, 109.

Moncleir Bank—See Wapwallopen.

Moravia—Region of the Czech Republic. This area, along with Bohemia, served as the point of origin for the members of the Unity of the Brethren.

Nescopeck—Town on the North Branch of the Susquehanna.

Oley—Location of the Moravian church and school building, built about 1742, in Berks County, Pennsylvania. The school operated from 1742 until 1776.

Onondaga—Home of the council fire of the Six Nations of the Haudenosaunee, near present-day Nedrow, New York.

Ostonwakin—Today Montoursville, known as Isabelle Montour's village and refers to the Loyalsock Creek. This town was visited by Zinzendorf in 1742 but abandoned by the late 1740s.

Philadelphia—Seat of the colonial government.

Quenischachachque—Also known as French Margaret's Town, on the west branch of the Susquehanna at the mouth of Lycoming Creek (now Williamsport). John Heckewelder and Peter S. Du Ponceau, in "Lenni Lenape or Delaware Indians," claim that this is also the Lenape name for the West Branch, meaning the "river of long reaches." See also French Margaret's Town.

Quitapahilla—Branch of the Swatara Creek in Lebanon County. The Tulpehocken trail between present-day Reading, Tulpehocken, and Shamokin was frequently used by Weiser, Cammerhof, Shikellamy, and Teedyuskung on their way to councils in Philadelphia. For a detailed description of the trail, see "Cammerhof's Journal of 1748."

Schoharie (also Sgochari)—Town in upstate New York, southwest of Albany.

Second Mountain—Lorberry Junction, Swatara Creek, Pennsylvania.

Shamokin—Today Sunbury. Shamokin was a central point where many paths converged, making it a popular gathering place. Shikellamy, the Oneida viceroy of Shamokin, lived here when sent by the Confederacy of the Six Nations to perform governing duties. Both Native Americans and white settlers resided here in relative peace until conflict rose over the illegal settlements on Six Nations' hunting grounds. The attack on settlers at Penn's Creek in 1755 caused further unrest and tension. Native Americans abandoned the town in 1756. It then became the site of Fort Augusta and later Sunbury.

Shamokin Island—Now Packer Island. Lies in the North Branch of the Susquehanna River between present-day Sunbury and Northumberland. It is the site of the Shikellamy State Park Marina. According to Canasetego in 1736, Shamokin Island was one of the two designated places in the province remaining for the Delaware. See A. Wallace, *King of the Delawares*, 37.

Shekomeko—Moravian mission village in the Hudson Valley of New York State.

Spangenberg (also Königsberg)—First mountain south of Shamokin. Today it is called Little Mountain.

Spitzberg—Mountain near Shamokin.

Teockhansoutehan—French Indian town.

Thürnstein—Mahantango or Pete's Mountain, Pennsylvania.

Tioga—New York.

Tulpehocken—Site of Womelsdorf, Conrad Weiser's home, and frequent stop on the journey to Shamokin.

Wahochquage—Possibly Oquaga, Ouaquage, Broome County, New York.

Wyoming, Pennsylvania—Derives from the Lenape Munsee name meaning "at the smaller river hills." According to the Jesuit Relation of 1635 (see Thwaites, *Jesuit Relations*), the Wyoming Valley was inhabited by the Scahentoarrhonon people, an Iroquoian-speaking group; it was then known as the Scahentowanen Valley. By 1744 it was inhabited by Lenape, Mohican, Shawnee, and others who had been removed out of eastern areas. From the 1740s to the 1760s, the valley was the site of Moravian mission work among the Native Americans living there. The Moravians envisioned a settlement for Christian Indians and a replacement for the blacksmith's shop that had been at Shamokin, but the violence of the French and Indian War prevented this plan from being fulfilled.

INDEX

Abraham (Mohican man), 143–44, 213
    Friedrich, son of, 214
    Isaac, son of, 144, 214
    Joachim, son of, 143–44, 214
    Maria, relative of, 215
act
    Calendar, 189
    Sale of alcohol, 73, 199n4 (section 5)
    Scalp Act, xxv
agriculture. *See* horticulture
Ahamawad, 150–51, 153, 159–61, 216
    See also Post, Christian Frederick
alcohol, xxi
    brandy, 17, 69, 74, 75
    drinking, 12, 96–98, 103, 105–6, 113, 119, 149
    "drunken Indians," 26, 31, 78, 82–83, 94–96, 113, 184–85
    drunken man/men, 149, 153
    drunkenness, drunken state, 12, 19, 148
    drunken people, 10, 107
    drunken woman/women, 42, 83, 149
    rum, 17, 31, 37, 58, 97, 147, 153, 163, 168, 170, 195n2
    whiskey, 93, 94–96, 100, 105, 110, 113, 117, 131
    See also liquor
Allegheny (lands)
    illegal liquor trade, 73
    unrest and war in 127, 155, 160, 164, 170, 174
Annuntschi, 79, 80, 83, 88, 113, 213
    See also Christian Gottfried Seidel
apothecary, 133
Armstrong (Delaware man), 103, 104
Axe maintenance, 49, 65, 84, 133

Bachhof, Rudolf Gottlieb, 132, 133, 213
baptism, 7, 28, 29, 177
bark, 12, 18, 75, 101, 195n4
beans, as present, 43, 111
    See also horticulture
bear
    fat, 4
    meat, 82, 125, 126
    skin, 36, 98

Beata (Delaware woman), 63, 213
Berthelsdorf (Saxony), 187, 203, 217, 219
Bethlehem (PA)
    as commercial center, 8, 16, 122, 135, 137
    as center of mission, 181, 185
    flight back to, xvi, 16, 172, 174–77
    Native baptism in, 103, 118
    Native travel to, 74, 103, 108, 171
    Shikellamy's journey to, xxvi, 14, 74, 111, 172
Blackfish (Mohican man), 100–101, 106–8, 110, 137, 213
blacksmith
    building the shop 35–41
    complaints over, 87, 110, 117
    demand for services, xxi, 48, 55, 61, 63–64, 84, 87, 109, 164
    establishment of shop, 1–4, 183–86, 193–94n2
    tools, xvi, 3, 40, 45, 62, 177, 185
blessing (liturgy)
    evening Blessing, 133–38, 140–41, 146, 157, 161
    morning blessing, 120, 122, 146, 171
    Sabbath blessing, 154
    Sunday blessing, 170
blood
    communion, 46, 90, 134, 157–58, 162
    human blood/bloody, 25, 26, 88, 109, 173
    of the Lamb, 20, 46–47, 58, 60, 63, 65, 121
    verses, 65, 69
bloodletting (opening veins), 43, 44, 49, 62, 75, 80, 197n2 (section 3)
bloodthirsty, 26, 31
Blue Hill/Mountain, ix, xvi, 17, 36
Boehmer, Martin, 139–40, 141, 146
Bottler, James, 164, 213
    illegal settlement, 152, 153
Brainerd/Brauer, David, 20, 21, 29, 147
Brodhead, Daniel (Native American), 40, 213
bread, white peoples, 58, 62, 72, 84, 85, 87, 92, 125, 129
    communion, 16, 46
Brother Joseph, 27, 31, 36, 48, 50–51, 74, 120, 217
    See also Spangenberg, August Gottlieb

224 INDEX

Brother Ludwig, 59, 64, 158, 184, 218
　See also Zinzendorf, Nicholas Ludwig von
Bruce, David, 35, 36, 37, 40, 41, 42, 185, 213
burial, 51–52, 57, 58, 108, 168, 203n2 (section 16)
　Shikellamy's, xxvi, 14, 92

Cammerhof, Johann Christoph Frederick, 55, 66, 68, 103, 118, 181, 213
　See also Gallichwio
Canada, Canadian Lands, 27, 31, 32
Canaseragy, Canaserage, ix, 39, 201n6 (section 12), 219
canoe
　building, 101, 123
　with warriors, 5, 24, 27, 75, 109, 113
Catawba/Cattobat, 3, 38, 68, 76, 98, 136, 195n23, 201n6 (section 12)
　See also Flatheads
Cayuga, xix, xx, xxvii, 102, 111, 115, 116, 172, 173, 198n6 (section 4)
celebration (Moravian), 100, 133, 145, 147, 148, 158, 166–67, 168, 169, 187
　See also blessing; Communion; Lovefeast; Quarter of an Hour
celebration (Native), 28, 31, 75–76, 170
charcoal, 51, 53–57, 124, 138
Cherokee, 19, 31, 214
Chief (Native), xxiii, 109–10, 112, 123, 127, 128, 135, 174
　Chief Shikellamy (Oneida), xv–xvi, xix, xxv, 5, 8, 14, 217
　Iroquois Chiefs (Six Nations), 3, 199n2 (section 5), 203n4 (section 15)
Chief Elder, Christ as, 90, 189, 190
choirs, 7, 63, 168, 169, 187–88
Christel, 44–46, 93, 94, 97, 100, 103–4, 197n5
　See also Rausch, Christian
Christel (Christian Renatus von Zinzendorf), 155
Christian Renatus (Delaware) 125–28, 217
Communion, 46–47, 116, 121, 135, 157, 160, 171
　See also blood
conference (missionary), xii, 32, 33, 46, 51, 80, 157
Congregation Day, 10, 157, 188
　See also Gemeintag
Conoy, xxii, 124, 129, 168, 172, 177, 203n2 (section 16)
corn (Indian), 26, 126, 127, 150, 152, 158, 164, 166–67
　exchange with brandy, 69
　field, 159, 169
　gift, 16, 152–53
　harvest, 21–23
　hoeing, 84, 86, 87, 129, 155, 160–61
　pounding corn, 55
　ruined crop, 86, 156, 157
　council (Native), 36, 38, 45, 181, 185, 194n22
　Great Councils of the Five Nations, 101
　with Shikellamy, 3, 46, 181, 183–85
　See also maize
Cross, 19, 25, 36, 121, 127
　cross air, 44, 54, 55, 59, 82, 90
custom (Native), xii, 14, 23, 31, 37, 200n4 (section 8), 203n2 (section 16), 219

Danesbury, Moravian preaching in, 161
Daniels, Samuel (Delaware man), 70
David (Delaware man), death of, 108
David (Indian brother), 130
Delaware
　Allumapees, Sassoonan (sachem), 195n2, 196n29, 213
　burial, 108
　feast, 28
　George, 173, 213
　Greenland and, 150
　king, 183, 216 (see also sachem)
　people/Nation, xix, xxiii, 12, 16, 197n10, 221 (see also Lenape)
　town/villages, 29, 144, 173
　visits from, 58, 71, 86, 97, 147, 163, 169
　Wilder/Wilden, 37, 38
　witchcraft, 57, 103
　woman/women, 5, 56, 65, 72, 74, 102 (see also Packer Island)
doctor
　the Lamb as, 49
　Indian, 56
dogs, 108, 174
Dunn, Thomas (Iroquois), 99, 213

Elisabeth/Elizabeth (Delaware), 144, 213, 216
enemy, xxiii, 1, 70, 83, 109, 126, 127
　See also Satan
Eva Creek, 33, 66, 105, 107

Fabricius, Georg Friedrich, 143, 213
Fathom of wampum. See Wampum
fever, 44, 113, 165, 166, 167, 197n2
First Sea Congregation, 1, 215, 216, 217
Five Nations, xix, xxvii, 30, 102, 103, 152
　as political actor, xxiii, xxv, 1, 106, 219
　visit from, 109–10, 112
　See also government, creation of Native structure; Iroquois; Six Nations
Flatheads, 24, 50, 79, 186, 195n23
　See also Catawba/Cattobat

flesh, 24, 68
  as family, 67, 184, 187
  sustenance, 13, 70, 72, 73, 76 (*see also* meat)
flintlock/flint, 14, 31, 92, 110–11, 134
  repairs, xxi, 3, 16, 55, 56, 63, 65, 84, 101, 134, 170
  See also gun; rifle
Freeman, Thomas (Native American), 126, 127–28, 213
French and Indian War, xv, 5, 189, 197n10, 219, 221
  onset of, xxiv–xxv, 216
French Andrew. *See* Montour, Andrew
French Indians, xv, 173, 197n12, 221
French Margaret. *See* Montour, Margaret
French Margaret's Town. *See* Quenischaschaque
Frey, Heinrich, 80, 143, 146, 214
  during the escape 176–77
  travel to and from Bethelehem, 82, 83, 94, 95, 112, 123
Friedrich (Mohican), 122, 214
fruit
  berries, 190
  blueberries, 44
  cherries, 58
  strawberries, 126

Gabriel, George, 134, 135–36, 138
Gallichwio, 83, 87, 95, 112, 113
  See also Cammerhof, Johann Christian Frederick
Ganachragejat, 87
  See also Mack, Johann Martin
Ganniatarechoo, 83
  See also Pylaeus, Johann Christoph
Ganosseracheri/Genousseracheri, 79, 88, 101, 102, 112, 113, 122, 137
  See also Zeisberger, David
garden, 5, 76, 105, 147, 150, 153
Gattermeyer, Johann Leonhardt, 146, 148, 161, 163, 169, 214
  evangelising, 166
  illness, 165, 16, 167
  work, 153, 159–60, 170
Gemein–Litaney, 150–51, 158, 159, 161, 163
Gemeine, 19, 28, 38, 48, 64, 137, 142, 145, 188
  Bethlehem, 34, 42, 135, 138, 139, 141
Gemeintag, 41, 188
  See also Congregation Day
Gideon (Delaware), 144, 214
Glück, Peter, 129, 139, 141, 148, 159, 214.
  See also shoemaker
Gnadenhütten, ix, 144, 145, 148, 165, 172, 188, 219
  Delaware visitors, 50, 52, 63, 103; Armstrong, 128; Christian Renatus, 151
  displacement to, 220
  greetings from, 79, 181, 185
  Indian visitor, 143
  Mohican visitors: Blackfish, 101; Friedrich, 122
  rumours about Moravians, 75
  Shawnee visitors, 50
  Travel from and via, 16, 143, 167, 168
Gnadenhütten, Ohio, 5
Gnadenthal, 79, 181, 185, 219
government (colonial), 102, 103, 110, 216
  imperial governments and Six Nations, 197n10, 197–98n12
  in Philadelphia, xxiii–xxiv, 200n6 (section 8)
  Shikellamy and, xxv, 1
government, creation of Native structure, xx, xxiii, 197n10 (section 3)
  See also Five Nations; Iroquois; Six Nations
governor, 13, 15, 72, 127, 183, 193n2 (Introduction), 197n10 (section 3)
  Hamilton, 14, 200n6 (section 8)
  Thomas, 1
Great Island, ix, 8, 135, 156, 219
Great Sabbath (Easter Saturday), 122, 188
Greenland, 117, 120, 202n9 (section 14)
Grube, Bernhard Adam, 15, 120, 123, 129, 130, 131, 136, 139, 144, 202n2 (section13), 214
  diarist, 120, 125
  fetching provisions, 122
  liturgical work 121, 124
  travel to Quenischaschaque, 125–28
gun, xxi, 5, 70, 135, 186
  See also flintlock; rifle
gun smith, 135, 136, 214
gun stocker, 218

Hagen, Anna, 49, 54, 138
Hagen, Johannes, 31, 32, 33, 45, 46, 47, 214
  accidents 39, 40
  beginnings in Shamokin, 3, 185, 186
  diarist, 13, 35, 42
  grave in Shamokin, 122, 133, 140, 157, 169, 171
  sickness, 44
Hahotschaunquas (Cayuga man), 115, 214
Harris, John Jr., 163, 168, 214
Harris, Mrs., 66, 72, 74, 75, 76
  request for help, 71
Harris's Ferry, ix, 3, 8, 39, 40, 45, 76, 185, 220
  as landmark, 177, 198n7
Haudenosaunee, xii, xvii, xix, 8, 118, 220
Haudenosaunee Confederacy, xxvii, 1
Heidelberg, 35, 132, 141, 176, 220
Henry, William, 135, 214
Herrnhaag, 134, 220
Herrnhut, 9, 187, 220

INDEX

hides, 19, 38, 117
  as payment, 3
  for Bethlehem, 122, 123
  to Tulpehocken, 153, 155, 164
  See also skins
Hockhocking. *See* Quenischachachque
Hoffmann, Christian Gottlob, 134, 214
holy spirit, 22, 24, 29, 33, 83, 85, 154
homily, 169, 189
  Homilies on the Litany of the Wounds, 96, 97, 147, 151, 152 (*see also* blood; Litany of the Wounds)
horse/horses, 74, 80, 82, 131, 167, 171, 185
  borrow, 37, 111
  lack of, 35, 62
  laden, 19, 33, 97, 166
  runaway, 104, 105, 108, 139–41, 202n11 (section 12)
  Schäfer's, 36–37
  shoeing, 17, 56, 57
  sign of wealth, 126
  to fetch things from Tulpehocken, 30, 86, 105, 111, 112
  work, 36, 39, 42, 186
horseback, 9–10, 105, 158
horticulture, Moravian
  beans, 5, 156
  cabbage, 85
  corn, 79, 82, 104, 124, 138
  fruit-trees, 74
  turnips, 39, 45, 52, 55, 57, 61, 63, 65
horticulture, Native, 72, 101, 102, 125, 153, 154, 220
hostility against Moravians, 30, 72
hunting, hunt, 30, 93, 94, 101, 106, 108
  away for the hunt, 40, 53, 125, 171
  blacksmith repairs, 55, 56, 64, 65, 67
  cabin/lodge, 115, 118
  fresh meat, 72, 73
  grounds/lands, 15, 221
  return from the hunt, 99, 107
  Shikellamy's sons, 70, 94, 95, 98
  husband, 19, 39, 69, 75, 111, 126, 152
    Christ as, 30, 64, 90, 96, 98, 134, 157
Hussey, Robert, 153, 214
huts, missionary visits to, 18, 22, 23, 28, 64, 95, 130, 133

Indian/Indians
  at the blacksmith's shop, 70, 81, 105, 109, 117, 155 (*see also* hunt)
  "drunken Indians," 26, 31, 63, 82–83, 94–96, 107–8, 113, 149 (*see also* alcohol)
  fashion (hair), 43

  from Gnadenhütten, 143, 151
  in/from Bethlehem, 18, 108
  in Shekomeko, 23
  medal, 118
  nation/s, 10, 13, 58, 72, 98, 101, 172
  traders, 42, 213
  See also alcohol; French and Indian war; horticulture; hunt; *and specific tribes*
iron, xxi, 71, 79, 104
Iroquois, xix–xxi, xxiii–xxvi, 1–3, 4–6, 194n22, 196n24, 197n10, 203n4 (section 15)
  Catabaw war, 195n23, 201n6 (section 12)
  Isaac (Mohican), 144, 214
  See also Five Nations; Haudenosaunee Confederacy; Six Nations

Jacob's Höhe, 130, 220
James Logan (agent), xxiv, xxv
James Logan/Soyechtowa, 101, 112, 120–21, 125, 215
  alcohol, 96, 105, 110
  business, 93–94, 104, 138, 201n6 (section 12)
  as co-chief at Shamokin, 174
  father's death, 92
  house, 69, 120, 125, 137
  hunt, 93–94, 96, 98, 108
  land, 16, 138, 158
  meeting with colonial government in Lancaster 110
  Mohican woman's husband, 59, 61, 62, 64, 65, 78, 84, 184
  new wife, 130
  request for plough, plants, 106, 107, 152
  visits from, 93, 98, 100, 103, 150
Janekeaguhontis, 87, 214
  See also Cammerhof, Anna
Jannische, 81
  See also Mack, Anna
Jepse/Jephtha (Esopus), 40, 214
Jeremias (Delaware), 108, 109, 200n2 (section 8), 214
Joachim (Mohican), 143, 144, 214
John Shikellamy, 16, 115, 120–21, 138, 150, 215
  alcohol, 105, 110
  escort Kiefer, Marcus to Bethlehem, 177
  hunt, 70, 73
  McKee, Thomas, 72, 116
  new chief, 103, 174–75
  Onondage, 130
  Philadelphia, 106, 112
  visits from, 96, 98, 103, 150
  Weiser, Conrad, 102, 110
  See also Tachnechdorus

John Shikellamy's wife, 98, 102, 114, 121, 125
John Petty, 110, 153, 170, 201n6 (section 12), 217
    drink/rumpus 96, 117, 153
Jonathan/Gayienquiligoa (Mohican), 154, 158, 169, 170, 171, 214
Jonathon (Mohawk), 152, 156
Juniata (river), 106, 124, 220

Kiefer, Marcus, 107, 122, 128–29, 132, 133, 172–77, 215
    burying the tools, xvi, 177
    fence for Shikellamy, 82–84
    injury, 85
    provisions from Tulpehocken, 112–13
    provisions by canoe, 122, 140
king, 22, 24, 26, 45, 183, 216, 217
    God as king, 25
    Charles II of England, 197n10
Kliest, David (Daniel), 16, 132, 138, 141, 215
Königsberg (mountain), 158, 220, 221
    See also Spangenberg mountain

Lapachpeton (Delaware), 97, 149, 163, 215
Labachpeton's Village, ix, 118, 145, 162, 220
Lancaster, xix, 6, 116, 171, 220
    commercial center, 97, 135, 185
    council with colonial government, 110
    Massacre in, xxv
    Treaty of, 195n9
land, 88, 90, 128, 158
    claim, xxiv, 16
    in search of, 161
    Moravian land, 88, 107, 172, 186
    Native land/s, 15, 72, 101, 152, 175, 189, 203n4 (section 15), 213, 220 (*see also* Canada, Canadian lands); travel through, 118, 123
    proprietary land, 15, 175, 197n10
    purchase, xxii, xxiii, 219
    removal from, xxiv, xxvi, 220, 221
    Shikellamy's, 80, 83, 121
    Shikellamy's grant of land to the Moravians, 184, 186
    travel by, 51, 76, 79, 85, 109
    treaty, xxiv
    treaty of Fort Stanwix, 197n10
    white man's land, 15, 220
    working the land, 39, 40, 106
    See also territory; Walking Purchase
language, xix, 5, 6, 66, 218
    barriers, 4, 16, 158
    Cayuga, 103
    Delaware, 15, 111, 127, 148, 195n7, 199n6 (section 6), 202n2 (section 13)

English, xv, 4, 19, 25, 83, 98, 107, 124, 135, 174, 199n6 (section 6)
    song book, 76
    German, xv, 4, 144, 149
    Iroquois, xx, 4, 199n6 (section 6), 199n9 (section 6), 200n4 (section 7)
    Lenape, 15
    Maqua, 36, 163, 186
    Minisink, 15
    Mohawk, 3, 161, 218
    Mohican, 12, 21, 30, 144, 184, 195n7, 198n9, 215
    Oneida, 196n4 (section 2), 200n1 (section 7), Onondaga, xv, 198n5 (section 4), 200n4 (section 7), 218
    Sifting time, 190
    Singstunde (English, German, Mohican), 12, 21
    skills, 36, 101, 102
    Tutelo, 196 n24
    See also Zeisberger, David
Lechti (Brother), 159
Lehigh River, xix, 8
Lehighton, xvi, 188
Lenape, xix, xxi–xxiv, 4–6, 12–13, 189, 196n25, 219
    See also Delaware; Gnadenhütten
Leonhardt (Delaware), 136, 215
Lessly, Johann Friedrich, 159, 167–68, 215
letter/letters, xxii, 16
    as spoken power, 197n8
    dictated, 128, 144
    from Conrad Weiser, 59, 193n2 (Introduction), 201n 6 (section 12)
    from Thomas McKee, 116
    Maqua, 163
    of recommendation, 13, 72
    on behalf of Logan, 93
    on behalf of Shikellamy's sons, 110
    to Logan, 94
    to Shikellamy, 35, 182
    via Native Americans, 27, 78, 59, 131, 137
    writing, 21, 79, 95, 130
    See also words
liquor/licker, 30, 69, 73, 82
    See also alcohol
Litany of the Wounds, 64, 67, 164, 189, 198n23, 202n8 (section 14)
    See also homily: Homilies on the Litany of the Wounds.
Loesch, George (Tulpehocken), 34, 132, 141, 174, 175–76
Long Island, 116, 220

Lovefeast, 16, 21, 46, 90, 189
  birthday, 70, 129, 148, 155
  Christmas day, 63
  farewell, 135, 141, 162
  hoeing, 161
  new year's eve, 65
  Sabbath, 55, 67, 124, 133, 139, 153
Ludwig's Ruh, 36, 141, 220
lumber, 3, 37, 40

Mack, Anna (Annerl, Jeannette, Jennetje), 11–12, 16, 21, 58, 72, 215
  and Shikellamy, 54, 56, 60, 62, 64
  evangelising, 18–19, 22, 26, 28, 55, 57, 59, 64
  first arrival in Shamokin, 18
  language proficiency, 195n7, 198n9
  lodging with Anderius 12–13, 31–33
  pregnancy, 31, 196n35
  sickness, 19–20, 60
  travel to Bethlehem, 33–34
  work, 55
  See also Jannische
Mack, Johann Martin, 3, 14, 17, 19, 21, 77, 79–81, 90, 215
  blood-letting, 49, 62
  diarist, 10, 17, 48, 78
  evangelising, 21–22, 57, 83, 86
  first arrival in Shamokin, 18
  lodging with Anderius 12–13, 31–33
  memoir as contrast with diary, 10–12
  and Shikellamy, 48, 50, 55–56, 59–60, 62, 64, 78, 91, 183–85
  travel to Bethlehem, 33–34
  Weiser, Conrad, 50
  work, 51, 52, 56, 59, 62, 65, 84, 85, 88
  See also Ganachragejat
Macungie, 132, 220
maize, xx, 148, 159, 166
  See also corn
Maqua (Mohawk), 98, 101, 102, 151, 155, 172, 184
  killing, 108, 126
  revelling, 149
  visits from, 94, 149, 163
  See also language; Mohawk
Maria (Mohican), 144, 215
Mariane (Delaware), 143, 202n1 (section 13), 215
Maryland, xviii, xxi, xxiii, 124, 127
  McKee/Magee, Thomas, 71–72, 81, 97, 112, 135, 215
  McKee's people, 68, 114, 115, 146
  wife beating, 116
meat, 5, 12–13, 16, 26, 61, 93
  beef, 59

deer, 28, 55, 163 (see also venison)
  See also bear; flesh
medicine, 115, 133
Meniolagomeka(h), 103, 106, 130, 220.
Minisink (Mennissing), 144, 150, 202n2 (section 13), 220
  See also language
Meurer, Johann Phillip, 34, 215
mill, 53, 75, 122, 140, 198n7, 204n2 (section 17)
Mingo, Mingoes, 72, 75
Mohawk, xix, xx, 160
  See also language; Maqua
Mohican, xix, xxiii, 30, 52, 69, 172, 221
  the Mohican woman (James Logan's wife), 57–62, 64–65, 67, 78, 81–82, 84–85, 130, 215; as translator, 184
  See also language
Montour, Andrew/ Anderius/French Andrew4, 8, 17, 130, 170, 215
  providing lodging for Moravians, 11–12, 18–21, 26, 27–28, 31–33
Montour, Lewis, 27, 126, 215
Montour, Madame (Isabelle/Elisabeth), 8, 11, 12, 33, 126, 195n8, 215
Montour, Margaret/ French Margaret, 147, 149, 158, 159, 213, 216

Nanticoke, xix, xxii, 45, 83–84, 106, 107, 111, 124
Nathaniel (Mohican), 59, 130, 185, 201n4 (section 11), 216
Neisser, George, 141, 216
Nescopeck, ix, 86, 130, 136, 143, 168, 174, 177, 220
  Nutimus and his sons, 104, 118, 145, 164
Neshanockeow, 30, 72, 216
Neubert, Daniel, 132, 216
Neubert, Rosina, 132, 216
New York, xix, xxiii, 8, 185, 196n24, 197n10, 198n12 (section 3)
  See also Shekomeko
Nitschmann, Anna, 8, 181, 216
Nutimus (Delaware), 104, 118, 145, 217
Nutimus, Isaac, 164, 216
Nutimus's sister, 118
  See also Rahel

offering (sacrifice), 108
Ohio, xxv, 5, 102, 173, 194n22
Okely, John, 1, 216
Oley, 155, 213, 214, 217, 220
Oneida, xix, xx, 84, 121, 123
  See also language

INDEX

Onondaga, xv, xix, 31, 101, 102, 123, 130, 131, 182
  council at, xx, xxiii, 103, 113, 138, 198n20, 202n6 (section 12), 220; Shikellamy as mediator, xxiv, xxxvi
  people, 109, 112, 131
  See also language
ore, 136–37
Ostonwakin, 27, 50, 102, 126, 158, 221
  Creek, 101, 126
Otto, John Matthew, 132, 133, 216

Packer Island, 5, 12, 195n5, 195n8, 221
Passion (of Christ), 121, 135, 151, 164, 189
Passion week, 135
Paxinos (Shawnee), 16, 144, 150, 174, 177, 216
Pedilavium, 46, 121, 162, 171, 198n13
Penn, William, xvii, xxiii, xxiv, 197n10
Penn's Creek, 5, 16
Penn's Creek Massacre, xv, 5, 16, 189
Pennsylvania (colonial), xix–xx, xxii–xxv, 6, 172, 181, 189, 194n22, 197n10, 200n6 (section 8)
  frontier, 4, 5
  governor in, 1
  Moravians in, 7–9, 15, 198n12 (section 3), 203n3 (section 16) (see also Bethlehem; Gnadenhütten)
  Scalp act, xxv
Peter (Indian brother), 130
Peter Cutfinger (Delaware), 69
Philadelphia, colonial government seat, xxiii, 6, 72, 183, 221
  conferences Six Nations 15, 136, 138, 170, 194n22, 199n2 (section 5)
  conferences Five Nations, 106, 112
  governor of, 1, 200n6 (section 8)
  land claims, xxiv (see also Walking Purchase)
  Shikellamy as intermediary, xxv
  Treaty with Six Nations, 72
Philip (Native man), 45, 102
pipe (tobacco), 14, 28, 36, 37, 92, 183
plan ("Heathen"/Indian), 1, 27, 32, 33, 65, 85, 88
  contrast with Brainerd, 28–29
  end of, 172
  presented to the lot (Lamb), 51, 58, 61
  waiting for Lamb's guidance, 19, 28
Plantation, 3, 5, 15, 142, 152
  attacks on, 173, 175
  European, on Native land, 16
  Shamokin as, 36, 39
Pleurody. See Litany of Wounds
Pontiac's Rebellion, xxv
Post, Rachel, 1, 54
  language proficiency 198n9

Post, Christian Frederick, 1, 50, 54, 144, 159, 216.
  See also Ahamawad
poverty, 7, 137, 175
Powell (Paul), Joseph, 3, 35, 44, 93, 138, 216
  blood–letting, 44, 80
  building the mission, 3, 39–40, 185
  diarist, xv, 13, 66, 199n1 (section 5)
  evangelising, 67, 79–80, 88
  refusal to help Mrs Harris, 14, 71
  religious discussions w McKee, 68
  and Shikellamy, 36, 68, 78
  sickness, 38, 45–46, 70
  work, 44, 66–67, 73, 76, 79
Powell (Paul), Martha, 16, 87, 217
provisions, 36, 39, 40, 49, 51, 79, 80
  fetching of, 40, 122–23, 140
  from Tulpehocken, 27, 113
  from Quitapahilla, 79
  shortness of, 42, 112
prisoner/s, 109, 126, 127, 200n4 (section 8)
pumpkin, 28, 214
Pyrlaeus, Johann Christoph, 186, 217
  See also Ganniatarechoo

Quaker, xv, xxii, 1, 197n10, 218
Quarter of an Hour, 51, 68, 90, 121, 130, 189
  evening, 52, 59, 60, 63, 79, 85, 88
  farewell, 158
  Married persons, 55, 56, 62, 63, 64, 198n13 (section 4)
  morning, 67, 91
Quenischaschaque (French Margaret's Town and Hockhocking), ix, 125–28, 131, 221
Quitapahilla, 79, 122, 221

Rachwistonis, 3, 113, 217
  See also Schmidt, Anton
Rahel (Delaware), 201n2 (section 9), 217
  See also Nutimus's sister
Rauch, Christian, 44–46, 93–99, 100, 104–5, 114–15
  See also Christel; Tschigochgoharong
Rieth, Caspar, 132, 154, 217
rifle, 186
  See also flintlock/flint; guns
Roesch, Gottlieb, 134, 140, 143
Rösler, Gottfried, 144, 151–52, 155, 157–58, 161, 164–65, 166–69, 171, 172

Saal, 124, 190
sachem, xvii, xxii, xxiii, 8, 213
Saeckwho (Conoy), 168
Salomon (Delaware), 145, 217

INDEX

sapan (porridge), 149, 153, 161, 190
Saponi, xix, xxiii, 196n24
Satan, 19, 26, 31, 66, 106, 129
Sawonagarat, 106, 217
scalping, scalps, 5, 68, 76, 102, 109, 131
Scha(a)fmann (Conoy), 99, 130, 217
    death of, 177
    protection from, 16, 177
    visits from, 102, 153, 163, 167
    visits to, 130, 166, 169
Schäffer, Michael, 16, 17, 35–37, 217
Schmidt/Smith, Anna Catharina, 54, 67, 79, 93, 217
    evangelising, 68
    sickness, 49, 58, 69–71, 73, 75, 79
    work, 55, 76
Schmidt/Smith, Anton, 3, 49, 68, 98, 116, 153, 217
    departure for Bethlehem, 146
    and Shikellamy, 51, 56–57, 61–63, 184
    blacksmith shop, 48, 52, 55, 67, 72, 75, 117
    fetching iron/provisions, 49, 51, 104, 140
    mend guns/flints, axes, 65, 70, 101
    shoe horses, 56–57
    sickness, 49, 60, 76–77, 78, 92
    tools, 45
    See also Rachwistonis
Schohari(e)/ Sgochari/ Tgochari, ix, 102, 108, 114–15, 149, 221
Second Mountain, 17, 221
Seidel, Christian Gottfried, 137, 146, 160, 171, 177, 217
    See also Annutschi
Seneca, xix–xx, 112, 113, 200n6 (section 8)
    country, 129
    war with Catawba, 195n23
settlers, xxiv–xxv, 5, 6, 7–8, 15–16, 189, 196n24
Seven Years' War. *See* French and Indian War
Shamokin Island. *See* Packer Island
Shawnee, xix, xxiii, 5, 30, 52, 125, 128, 144
    business at blacksmith, 56, 72, 97, 135, 153
    familiar with Moravians, 50, 64–65
    John Shikellamy's wife, 121
    warriors, xxv, 102
Shawonogarati, 115, 217
Shekomeko, ix, 23, 30, 221
Shamokin, a preexisting Native settlement, 5
Shikellamy, Shikellemy (also Schikellimus), 69, 70, 71, 72, 88
    agreement with, 1, 3, 5, 13, 15, 36
    assistance from 40, 53
    blacksmith work for 51, 56–57, 61–63
    Brainerd and, 20
    burial of, 14, 92
    chief in Shamokin, xix, xxv–xxvi, 1, 5
    complaints about Moravians, 40 (*see also* Shikellamy, Shikellemy: request for a fence)
    conference with Moravians, 36, 46, 181–84
    council, 45
    daughter, 62, 93, 97, 111, 201n6 (section 12)
    Death of, 14, 92, 172
    death of grandchild, 58, 63
    family, 88, 97, 131, 152, 153
    gifts, 36, 48, 59, 60; meat, 55, 68, 73
    letter/words for, 35, 36, 46, 79, 81, 82, 87
    lodging with, 13, 32–33
    meals with, 67, 70, 73, 78, 81, 83, 85, 89
    Oneida, xxv, 3, 5
    request for fence, 68, 73, 80–83; completion thereof, 84–85, 86, 88
    son/s, 15, 59, 60, 72, 75, 95, 184 (*see also* James Logan, John Shikellamy, John Petty)
    Spangenberg/T'girhitondi and, 48, 50–51, 73–74, 79, 81, 82–83
    treaty, 13, 72
    visiting, 30, 80–81, 84, 86
    Weiser, Conrad and, 14, 34, 35, 46, 195n9
    wife, 39, 51
    Zinzendorf and, 8–9
    See also Swatane
shoemaker, 129, 139, 148, 155, 159, 162, 164
    See also Glück, Peter; Schäfer, Michael
Side hole/wound, 84, 86, 90, 96, 99, 104, 106, 116
Singstunde (Singing Hour), 19, 21, 25, 33, 122, 123, 190
Six Nations, 1, 3, 8, 15, 72, 138, 170, 193n2 (Introduction), 192n10 (section 3), 197–98n12, 199n2 (section 5)
skid, 40, 49, 52, 53, 124
skins, xxi, 16, 66, 68, 69, 71
    See also bear; hide
Smallpox, xxii, 130, 131, 198n1 (section 4)
Society for the Propagation of the Gospel (SPG), 4, 45, 197n6
Spangenberg, August Gottlieb, 3, 16, 185, 193n2 (Introduction), 198n20, 217
    See also Brother Josef; T'girhitondi
Spangenberg mountain, 33, 107, 221
    See also Königsberg
Spitzberg, 143, 221
squash, xx, 3, 5, 167
Sundays, understanding, 41, 48, 64, 67, 110
Susquehanna Country, 4
Susquehanna River, xv–xvi, 63, 74, 107, 133, 167, 175, 189
    across, 61, 98, 133, 136, 147, 149, 164, 173

communities on, 83, 103, 143, 145, 174
confluence, x, 4, 5, 13, 15, 16, 203n4 (section 15)
crossing, 37, 144, 145
ferry (*see* Harris's ferry)
forks, xv, 1, 4
help w provisions, 150–52
illegal settlements on, 200n6 (section 8)
Moravian travelon, 45, 49, 53, 79, 104, 140, 159, 160
Native travel on, 39, 52, 83, 84, 105
North Branch, ix, x, 15
risen, 51, 57, 140, 169
river stones from, 42
Zinzendorf and, 8–10
Susquehannock, xx–xxii, xxiii, xxv, 4, 5
Synod, 85, 90, 95–96, 134, 190
  in Bethlehem, 95, 96, 199n7
  in Warwick, 167–68, 203n3 (16)
Swatane, xxv, 90–93, 101, 102, 103, 111
  See also sachem; Shikellamy
Swatara Creek, 117

Tachnechdorus, xxvi, 83, 105, 105, 218
  See also John Shikellamy
Tachnechdorus's wife, 114
Tecarihontie, 112, 113, 120, 218
  See also Watteville, Johannes von
Teockhansoutehan, 70, 221
territory, xix, xxi, xxiv, 16, 196n25, 200n6 (section 8)
  See also land
T'girhitondi, 3, 61, 74, 85, 87–88, 101, 113
  John Shikellamy and, 106, 120
  Logan and, 93, 95, 112, 137–38
  Shikellamy and 36, 41, 46, 73, 78–79, 81–82, 83
  See also Spangenberg
Thürnstein mountain, 36, 100, 107, 141, 176, 221
Tianoge (Cayuga), 101, 102, 103, 218
Tioga, ix, 102, 111, 112, 149, 221
tobacco, 14, 36, 78, 92, 117
Trade, xxi, xxiii, 3, 16, 39, 191
Traders, 3, 43, 66, 73, 85, 97, 98, 109, 111, 116, 195n2, 199n9 (section 6)
  alcohol, 30, 39, 58, 73, 82, 97, 195n2
  bad behaviour, 68, 88
  Indian traders, 42, 213
  Native Americans and, xxiii, 45, 70, 75, 116
  work for blacksmith, 16, 61, 64, 97, 134
treaty, xxiv, 15
  of Albany, 1, 197n10
  of Fort Stanwix, 197n10
  of Lancaster, 195n9
  Philadelphia treaty, 13, 72, 194n22

Tulpehocken, 36, 102, 115, 116, 129, 154, 155, 221
  path, 16, 139, 214, 220
  provisions from, 27, 40, 105, 111, 112–13, 127, 153
  Shikellamy, 9, 43, 56, 57, 59, 78, 86, 92
  stop between Shamokin and Bethlehem, 73, 74, 164, 174, 176, 221
  Weiser, Conrad, 8, 50, 110, 129
turnips as gift, 56, 59, 60, 64
  See also horticulture
Tuscarora, xix, xxiii, xxvii, 102, 197n10
Tutelo, xix, xxiii, 13, 67, 98, 115, 172, 173, 196n24

Van der Merck, Jacobus, 120, 218
venison
  as gift, 38, 55, 68, 85–86, 88, 97
  as payment, 55

Wagner, Elizabeth, 34, 132, 141, 218
Wahochquage, ix, 102, 221
Walking Purchase, xxiv, xxvi
Wampum/Wampom/Wompun, 183, 191
  belt of 14, 170, 174
  fathom of, 103, 113, 181, 183, 185, 186
  string of, 36, 113, 184
war, xxv, 15, 24, 27, 39, 102, 110, 126, 172, 186
  against Catawba, 38, 68, 136, 172
  against Cherokee, 31
  declaration against the French, 170
  in Allegheny, 164
war cry, 109
warpath, 172
warriors, 5, 75–76, 109, 127, 131, 136, 186
  from Canada, 32
  to/from Catawba, 50, 79, 98
  from Oneida, 121–22, 123
  from Seneca, 128
Watchword, 54, 55, 191
Watteville, Johannes von, 50, 181, 189, 210n2 (section 10), 218
  See also Tecarihontie
weapons, 14, 76, 92, 121, 170, 173, 174
Wesa, Philip, xvi, 146, 148, 153–56, 157–58, 170, 172–76, 218
white people
  dressed as Indians, 170, 173
  quotes about, 13, 27, 31, 32, 57, 58, 61, 64, 67, 71
Whitefield, George, 7, 216
Wilder, Wilden, xxvii, 37–39, 40–42, 43, 44–46, 172, 195n22, 196n6
words (message), 36, 46, 79, 81–82, 87, 138
Wyoming, PA, 50, 52, 106, 137, 143–44, 172
  valley, 58, 83

Zeisberger, David, xxi, xxv–xxvi, 5, 10, 54, 95, 97, 98, 99, 100, 218
  alcohol, 103, 106, 110
  and John Petty, 117–18
  and John Shikellamy, 102, 115–16
  and James Logan, 93–94, 100–101, 103–4, 105
  and Native languages, 82, 84, 87, 101, 103, 111, 158, 161, 198n5 (section 4), 199n6 (section 6), 200n4 (section 7)
  in Nescopeck, 118
  and Shikellamy, 50–51, 82, 84, 86, 88–89
  and Shikellamy's daughter, 111
  on Shikellamy's death, 14, 90–92
  and Tianoge, 101
  See also Ganosseracheri
Zinzendorf, Nicholas Ludwig von, 1, 4, 6–7, 218
  in America, 7–10, 158
  letters to, 181, 185
  sermons by, 59, 64, 96, 97